Davide Lajolo

AN ABSURD VICE

A Biography of
Cesare Pavese

Cesare Pavese in July 1950

Davide Lajolo

AN ABSURD VICE

A Biography of Cesare Pavese

Translated and edited with an introduction by

Mario and Mark Pietralunga

A NEW DIRECTIONS BOOK

ACKNOWLEDGMENTS

All translations of Pavese's writings used here are by Mario and Mark Pietralunga. However, grateful acknowledgment is given for the use of the following: Excerpts from *The Moon and the Bonfires,* by Cesare Pavese, translated from the Italian by Marianne Ceconi. Copyright 1953 by Giulio Einaudi Editore. Used by permission of Farrar, Straus and Giroux, Inc. *Hard Labor* by Cesare Pavese, translated from the Italian by William Arrowsmith. Copyright © 1979 by The Johns Hopkins University Press. Used by permission. Thanks is also given to the University of Michigan Press, Walker & Company, and Howard Moorepark, Esq., for facilitating the use of Mario and Mark Pietralunga's translations of quotations from Pavese controlled by them.

Manufactured in the United States of America
First published clothbound and as New Directions Paperbook 545 in 1983
Published simultaneously in Canada by George J. McLeod, Ltd., Toronto

Library of Congress Cataloging in Publication Data

Lajolo, Davide.
    An absurd vice.
    (A New Directions Book)
    Includes index.
    1. Pavese, Cesare—Biography. 2. Authors,
Italian—20th century—Biography. I. Title.
PQ4835.A846Z7513 1983   853'.912 [B]   82–14482
ISBN 0–8112–0850–8
ISBN 0–8112–0851–6 (pbk.)

New Directions Books are published for James Laughlin
by New Directions Publishing Corporation
80 Eighth Avenue, New York 10011

To Ines and Matthew

Contents

Translators' Introduction

Four years have passed since we first began our translation of Pavese's biography. This seemingly long period involved a great deal more than we had initially anticipated. During the course of our work, we encountered many obstacles that could easily have undermined our labors had we not been motivated by our love for Pavese and by what Davide Lajolo had to say about him.

Our task would have been facilitated had we been able to fully rely on the many English versions of Pavese's works; however, upon scrupulous examination, we found ourselves in disagreement with some of them. Therefore, while feeling a great deal in common with all those who had the good taste to translate Pavese, we chose to do our own translations, proceeding in all cases from the Italian originals, not simply as they are quoted by Lajolo, but rather through a verification of the complete sources. While the entire Pavese diary and all the novels are already available in English, a large number of the letters, poems, and portions of short stories and essays presented in this biography are translated here for the first time.

In order to make the English version meet the scholarly standards we had established at the outset, we also took on the burden of editing the biography, making sure, however, to avoid any accusation of abridgement.

Lajolo's work remains, to this day, the most comprehensive study of Cesare Pavese. Born, like Pavese, in the Langhe region of Piedmont, Lajolo has always felt strong ties to his fellow "Langaroli" writers. His work on Pavese also includes a highly successful play also entitled *An Absurd Vice*, written in collaboration with the dramatist Diego Fabbri, and a comparative study of Pavese and Beppe Fenoglio, another writer from the Langhe. One of Italy's best-known biographers and memorialists, he has also written biographies of Fenoglio and the late syndicalist Di Vittorio, and *Poesia come Pane* (*Poetry as Bread*), a collection of literary profiles derived from personal encounters with writers including, along with Pavese and Fenoglio, such well-known figures as Quasimodo, Ungaretti, Vittorini, and Hemingway. His diary of the Resistance as well as four other autobiographical volumes have been published in Italy, and he has received a number of awards, including, in 1977, one of Italy's most prestigious literary prizes, the Premio Viareggio, for his novel *Veder l'Erba dalla Parte delle Radici* (*To See the Grass from the Side of the Roots*), drawn from his own experience of a near-fatal heart attack and courageous recovery.

Lajolo's multifarious and dynamic life serves as a source and background for his writings. He has been a commander in the Resistance, a congressman, the editor of one of Italy's largest newspapers and of a weekly magazine. Still active in journalism, he has also become a television personality.

An important dimension of Lajolo's production clearly lies in its social awareness, reflecting his involvement in one of the most tormented periods of Italian history, the same period he so effectively relates to Pavese's life. Lajolo firmly believes in the active participation of the writer in the social struggle, and in spite of literary limitations and some political errors, he has been able to respond to the call of an Italian critical tradition represented by Francesco De Sanctis, Benedetto Croce, and Antonio Gramsci who, although of different times and convictions, all taught, and not only in words, that a man of letters must be publicly involved. Social responsibility is, in our estimation, one of the main criteria by which Cesare Pavese is here observed and measured, with well-balanced affection, both for what he has accomplished as a writer and for what he has done, or not done, as a man.

The overriding distinction of Lajolo's biographic study inspired us all the more to rectify its shortcomings. In order to maintain its outstanding merits as a highly entertaining and accessible biography —a bestseller in Italy, translated into several languages—and to also make it a definitive reference for scholars, we set out to do a general housecleaning of the book with the same rigor used in examining the translations of Pavese's writings referred to. Quotations, names, dates, the chronological sequence of letters and episodes, had to be corrected, and the journalistic tone with which some facts were presented and some judgments passed needed to be made less simplistic, more subdued, and better adapted to a precise, controlled critical approach.

When we assumed the task of translating this biography, we saw as fundamental the importance of presenting Pavese in the complete picture provided by Lajolo—not only Pavese the writer but also the man who lived with extraordinary intensity many of the existential problems and vicissitudes his generation of intellectuals encountered under Fascism, during a bitter civil war, and later in an extremely difficult postwar era. Equally important to us was the necessity of offering our readers the portrait of a man whose life could not be extricated from his writings. With all his major works translated into English, the publication of his biography in America and England is long overdue.

Pavese's affinity for American letters, initiated with his brilliant and courageous translations during the Fascist era, shows its development in his excellent essays on American authors and in a narrative which indicates an awareness of the linguistic experiments, especially in connection with the use of slang, taking place in the United States. The Anglo-American world became curious about Pavese and, among the good effects accompanying the discovery of an important writer, one can see a special reciprocal understanding and a sort of cultural exchange between English-speaking readers and the Italian writer who translated Melville, Faulkner, and Joyce. As Lajolo wrote in 1960, in his "Conclusion" to the first edition of this biography, "Americans today read his works and through them, learn to understand contemporary Italy: a just reward for Pavese's efforts in making American culture known in his country."

Since 1960, Pavese has been the subject of interest in many sectors both in America and in England. He is highly regarded in universities even outside the specialization of Italian studies; articles on him have been published in the most varied periodicals, and his poems have consistently appeared in journals and magazines.

A leading British-American poet, Denise Levertov, has paid "Homage to Pavese" by publishing under this caption, at the very beginning of her book *Life in the Forest,* a series of fourteen poems that in her "Introductory Note" she recognizes as having "some humble affinity—however oblique—with what Pavese achieved in *Lavorare Stanca,*" namely a tendency "to rather long lines and a discursive structure." In the same introduction, Levertov, who found Pavese's poems of the 1930's in the Penguin edition translated by Margaret Crosland, writes that "Pavese's beautiful poems are about various persons other than himself; though he is a presence in them also, their focus is definitely not autobiographical and egocentric, and in his accompanying essays he speaks of his concept of suggesting a narrative through the depiction of a scene, a landscape, rather than through direct recounting of events as such."

This "Homage" is another illustration of the close ties that continue to exist between Pavese and the Anglo-American culture. Given his predilection for this culture and his meticulous interest in the English language and American slang, we feel confident that in realizing our wish, cultivated for so many years, to make Lajolo's excellent biography available to the American and English public, we have rendered our own homage to Pavese, divulging his life story in the language he loved perhaps as much as Italian and his native Piedmontese dialect.

Mario and Mark Pietralunga, 1982

Introduction

I loved Pavese, and precisely because of this I would never have
wanted to evoke the drama of his life.

But on August 27, 1950, ten years after his death, I decided to
write this biography, urged by two considerations. The first was that
too many people had written about Pavese without having known
him well. The second was a conversation I had with him in the now
distant 1945, a conversation which, at that time, seemed strange to
me.

We were crossing Piazza Statuto in Turin under the midday sun of
that scorching summer. Neither of us was perspiring. Suddenly
Pavese broke the silence: "Our not sweating indicates that you and I
are still worth something because we've remained peasants. The sun
finds a place on our skin and has no need to make it shine." I
answered, "You know, you're really a singular man because you
always take yourself back to the country. The critics who write
about you often misrepresent your attachment to the country.
In fact, on one hand, they don't understand how you became so
city-minded and, on the other hand, they don't know how strongly
rooted you are to Santo Stefano Belbo,[1] not only in your books,
but in each day of your life." I was joking when I added, "I'm
the only one who'd be able to write your biography, provided
our friendship does not prevent me from being impartial." And

Pavese: "I'm not a suitable subject for a biography. The only things I'll leave are a few books in which everything or almost everything about me is said. Certainly the best, because I'm now like a vineyard which has been overly fertilized, and I feel that even those parts within me I considered most healthy are rotting away. You, like me, come from the hills and know that too much fertilizer merely breeds worms and destroys the crop."

We had begun to slow down; Piazza Statuto stretched out ahead of us as if it were the road between Canelli and Santo Stefano Belbo. Pavese had raised his voice, as he did whenever words took hold of him. He continued to speak, allowing no interruptions. Abruptly, he stopped walking and said, "You talk about my biography. Even you would choose only the best part, that which is in my books. But I've something else inside. There is at least as much selfishness in me as generosity, and I always hesitate between betraying and remaining faithful. Perhaps only the sorcerer of Vesime[2] could reveal me completely. No one else can. I confess myself neither to priests nor to friends. As soon as I am aware that a friend is getting too close, I abandon him. I abandon women, those whom you call maternal, as soon as I deceive myself into thinking they love me. I am always desperately seeking the woman who has never loved me and never will. Suffering frightens me, but it is the same fear as that of a mother who must give birth. All this does not make me a complex man, as I have been called by those who have discussed my books. The vineyard is complex where the blending of fertilizer and seed, water and sun, will yield the best grapes. But I am made up of many parts that do not blend; in literature the suitable word is eclectic. It is precisely the word I hate the most in life and in books, but my aversion to it is not enough to eliminate it. Mine would be a biography to be written with a scalpel, mercilessly, and even you would be forced to refuse."

We resumed our walk in silence. Piazza Statuto was behind us. I caught a glimpse of Pavese when we had already started to walk under the arches of Corso Garibaldi: I noticed that his face was perspiring, especially his forehead and the part of his nose where his glasses rested. He was looking at the ground with an ironic smile and his pipe must have gone out because smoke no longer rose from it.

The conversation, one of the most revealing Pavese had ever had with me during the years of our friendship, ended there. With Pavese, certain discussions could not be concluded. Turning silently on Corso Valdocco, still under the sun, we entered the editorial office of the newspaper where I was working.

I wanted to recall that conversation here, before beginning to write about his life, as a pledge made to myself to remain Pavese's friend by confronting the truth. I shall look into his life and books without falling into the abstract or sensational, and without indulging in recrimination or sentimental regret.

Pavese the writer can without a doubt withstand genuine criticism; the man could come out defeated, but to better understand his defeat let's not forget the difficult times, politically and culturally, of his generation. If Pavese's life is to be seen realistically, it must be seen within that generation.

And so I gather the courage to write about Cesare Pavese. We shall accompany him step by step on the journey from his infancy in Santo Stefano Belbo to his boyhood in the schools and suburbs of Turin; from his political exile in Brancaleone Calabro to the editorial office of the Einaudi Publishing House. We shall try to understand and perhaps explain some of his contradictions: he challenged Fascism but he did not participate in the Resistance War[3]; he was a Communist in order to share with other men the political reality of his country, but at the same time he was searching for impossible myths. He was severe with himself, with his friends and adversaries, and strained in his exaltation of sex and in his anguish over women, between the light of his hills and the gloomy shadows of his sleepless city nights. We shall follow him from the Langhe[4] to Turin, Milan, and Rome, and examine his poems, his prose, his symbolic characters who are suffering and ruthless, until death comes—the death that will have *her* eyes.

I feel comforted in this difficult task by our common feeling for the land, by our peasant origin, and by our similar slow conquest of the city. Our friendship, born in the city, on Corso Valdocco in

Turin, was strengthened among the hills, books, talks, and the great silences. It was a friendship intensified by our contrasting characters: the one always aggressive and determined to live, the other always desperate and determined to die.

Davide Lajolo, 1960

1

Santo Stefano Belbo:
Birth and Childhood
in the Country

Pavese himself entrusted me with the most characteristic image of his childhood one day during the August holidays, when together we revisited the San Sebastiano farm in Santo Stefano Belbo where he was born. He said to me, "The people here remember me as a child who often stayed perched in the courtyard tree reading a magazine or a book."

We found the farm a few hundred meters from the town, facing the road that runs from Canelli to Santo Stefano Belbo. At the time of his birth, it had been a large farm with a hayloft and a barn on one side and the living quarters on the other. It was quite changed. The room with the balcony where he was born still remained, but the farmhouse had disappeared. The Giuseppini friars, who had acquired the house, had turned it into a boarding school and planted tall dark pines where there had been a garden. Now even the school has gone, and it has become a farmhouse again. Only the main facade has remained intact, surrounded by the three tall hills of Moncucco, Crevalcuore, and Bauda. On the top of the hill of Moncucco, a tiny church overlooks the valley. A little further, still along the road toward Canelli, is the Scaglione brothers' carpentry shop where Pavese often went as a boy and where he liked to return as a man. Pinolo Scaglione, Pavese's only true friend and confidant, still lives and works there. He is the Pinolo Scaglione who inspired the character of Nuto in *The Moon and the Bonfires.*

Cesare Pavese was born on this farm on September 9, 1908. He attributed his having been born in Santo Stefano Belbo to destiny, since his family had been living for some time in Turin, only returning to Santo Stefano for the summer. Pavese was born during the summer vacation, thus by chance amid those hills that had such an influence on his life. Cesare's family consisted of his father, Eugenio, mother, Consolina, and a sister, Maria, born six years earlier. His mother was from Casale Monferrato, of a wealthy family of merchants. His father came from the oldest of the many Pavese families of Santo Stefano. They moved to Turin where Cesare's father was employed at the Court of Justice.

It is essential that one become acquainted with the Langhe in order to fully understand Pavese as a child and as a man. Through the Langhe it is also possible to perceive his reasoning, to explain his contradictions, his brief joys, long torments, and torturing remorses. Besides understanding the man, we can judge the writer more completely: the moments of his poetry, the origins of his evasions, the stifled emotions, the loyalties and betrayals, the insistence upon the myths he strove to embody in those hills.

The air, the countryside, and the hills of the Langhe became a profound part of him, perhaps because the land in this area of Piedmont is different from all the others. Santo Stefano Belbo connects and grafts the Asti countryside to that of Cuneo like a bridge between the culture of the vineyards and that of the woods.

Every road has a very precise trait. Every hill has a human personality, not only in the fantastic visions of the Pavesean descriptions, but in the names given them by the peasants according to the physical characteristics visible in each: eyes in one, a nose in another, and in still another, hair rising toward the sky. Thus Santo Stefano Belbo, with its houses, vineyards, meadows, forests, fields, streets, paths, and the Belbo river, cannot be confused with Canelli, Calamandrana, Moncucco, Mango, Monesiglio, or Alba. Santo Stefano marks the boundaries of the two oldest farming provinces of Piedmont, Asti and Cuneo. Most of the farms scattered among the vineyards, as well as the center of town, have remained annexed to the province of Cuneo.

On the other side, the open, level road between the hills leads, after a few kilometers, to Canelli, in the heart of the province of Asti, and just next to Canelli is Calamandrana, and then Nizza, where the province of Asti goes on to border that of Alessandria. On this road toward Canelli, Pavese the boy—as he himself says in *The Moon and the Bonfires*—set out when he wanted to go toward the city, toward life, toward women. Canelli was for him the symbol of something he had to reach, a window open on the world of escapes, of adventures, of life. Beyond Canelli is Genoa, beyond Genoa is the sea, beyond the sea are America and "The South Seas" that we shall find in the poetry of *Work Wearies*.

Pavese's childhood is divided between sunshine and shadow, between winter and summer. At the end of autumn he returned to Turin, but it was in the long summer and autumn months in the country that he lived most intensely.

When he turned six, a family misfortune brought him unexpected luck. He was to return to Turin to start elementary school in the city, but his sister contracted an infectious illness which forced the entire family to remain in Santo Stefano. So that year Cesare did not abandon his playmates, and attended the first grade in Santo Stefano. Everything in the country had a charm for him different from that of the city. The strange shapes formed by the snow-covered hills and rows of trees fascinated Cesare. He stayed in Santo Stefano for only that year. Then his sister recovered and it was necessary to return to the city. Pavese continued his elementary education in Turin at the private institute "Trombetta" on via Garibaldi.

From that time he would anxiously await the end of the school year when he would return to Santo Stefano to spend his vacation in the hills. And every year his desire grew more acute throughout the many months of waiting, and the country became more and more important to him. From the first to the last day in Santo Stefano he felt as free as a bird, through the meadows and woods, along the paths, among the vineyards; and when he was tired of wandering about, there he was reading up in the courtyard tree or stretched out on the grass behind the house.

In 1914, when Pavese was only six, his father died. He felt a great sense of loss. He was already ashamed of his own tears and choked them back like a grown man. His father had been ill for many years, since Cesare was born. The illness, a brain tumor, was incurable. All the family responsibilities fell on his mother's shoulders. Cesare's mother was courageous, austere, and strong: a Piedmontese who had learned not to waste words but to work hard, be thrifty, and keep a tight rein on her children. The only way she could express her affection was by working for them. Behaving more like a harsh father than a gentle mother, she made her children feel the weight of authority rather than the warmth of tenderness. She was a mother who had long been tried by grief: before Maria and Cesare were born, she had lost three children. The first, a girl struck down by diphtheria at age six; the others, two boys, dead at a tender age. These blows cannot be forgotten, as they either destroy or strengthen a character.

Both the death of his father and the hardened character of his mother created the first emptiness in Cesare's heart. He became more and more withdrawn. Even at the dinner table he spoke very little, as did his mother and sister. When his mother placed the food on the table, she would not tolerate discussions; it was necessary to force oneself to eat everything, above all the squash soup that made Cesare nauseous.

Cesare felt humiliated by those sacrifices. They hurt him more than the beatings he earned every now and then. From that time on he felt an intolerance for his mother. It was difficult for him to confide in her. As the years passed, their relationship became increasingly cold.

In whom could he confide? With whom could he speak? With himself and with nature: the trees, the snakes, and the river when in Santo Stefano. His talk was always without response, an invocation of solitude and silence. Even as a child, Pavese placed himself in the middle of things, not being able to put himself in the middle of people, and he adapted these things to his emotions, to his way of feeling and of living. The landscape of Santo Stefano became a part of him. He not only saw it but felt it from childhood on. He penetrated it and discovered its people—the men, the women, the boys his age—because the construction of that landscape was not just the work of nature, but of innumerable generations of peasants. All had been tilled except the few roads necessary for the passage of carts and oxen. Entire families had to survive on that slip of land.

In the course of centuries the countryside has acquired an aspect of fatigue. It is not a natural landscape, one cannot grasp it at first glance. It is necessary to grow up there, to live there a long time, to feel it as it is—shaped with earth and men, with nature and human sweat.

In Santo Stefano, Pavese discovered a sense of tragedy among people afflicted with misery, because the land was scarce and the people were poor. When Cesare left for the city in the last days of autumn, he saw others leaving also—peasants who every year left for America or for Australia, more in search of bread than fortune. And he often became aware that many of his companions who played in the hills with him were bastards raised in Santo Stefano by peasant families who did so to receive a subsidy from the state. Certainly in an area so rich with good wine there were also festivals, hours of fun and joy, but Pavese was more inclined to feel the sad things. There grew in him, from childhood, the desire to escape from people, to go alone into the mystery of the woods, the instinct to look more intensely at the wretched and the desperate, in the same way that he was more attracted by the most desolate points of the landscape. Pavese himself testifies to these feelings in all his stories where he confesses that even as a boy he was more attracted by misfortunes than by celebrations, more curious about funerals than wedding banquets.

Few writers have left as many pages as Pavese about the countryside and childhood companions. Even if these pages only reflect his memories and interpretations of that time, they are nevertheless valuable in giving us the inner biography of his childhood. Leafing, for example, through *August Holiday*, the collection of stories in which characters and even plots of his later novels are anticipated, we discover the freshness of his early encounters. How does Pavese present that playmate of his, a boy called "Pale"? "Tall, real tall, with the mouth of a horse, protruding teeth and red hair." "Pale" is already physically different from other children. And what is his character? "He would run away from home and be missing for two or three days. His mother would call him, and his father, cursing, would wait in ambush with his belt to flay him. He was a methodical snake hunter, and when he would begin to hunt, the green juice of a blade of grass he had chewed trickled from his teeth."

From the description that Pavese gives, this playmate had a marked destiny: one of wandering and sadness. But there is more: "Pale, from the habit of running away from home, had become reserved like a man." With one stroke of the pen Pavese makes it clear that "Pale" already bears the sentence of the man. In the boy's growing solitude there is already a part of himself.

These were Pavese's friends and thoughts during his first years in the Langhe. The farm of San Sebastiano became again, at the end of every school year, his own true home. In his early adolescence, he had already formed a consciousness. He started to read novels, which he discovered in town and avidly devoured. Schoolbooks did not interest him. The city school was boring and Cesare participated unwillingly, but he completely immersed himself in novels, as in the woods. His childhood memories began to assume an order in his mind and became a plot of interwoven faces, houses, and sensations —as in the novels. His capacity to reflect, to build castles in the sky, developed precociously, more rapidly than his body. Those were the years when he reconstructed within himself the figure of his father in order to trace a part of his own character. Later, in a poem entitled "Ancestors," from *Work Wearies*, although speaking about an uncle, Pavese would refer to the image he had of his father.

In this poem Pavese's father appears as the proprietor of a store in the center of Santo Stefano. It is one of those stores commonly found in Piedmont, selling everything from groceries to the most varied household items, from stationery to novelties. Pavese's father was quite different from the usual merchants. He was absent-minded, disinterested, with an aversion to bookkeeping, and did not have the ambition to compete with the other store in town. He did not like to work and spent his time in contemplation.

When the little bell would ring with the opening of the door, he did not rush solicitously toward the customer. Instead, he remained seated, and only when the customer approached the counter did he raise his head to ask, without wasting any words, which item the customer wished to buy. If the request would have forced him to search the shelves, he merely responded that the desired item was out of stock. Then he returned to his chair to resume reading the novel from which he had been unwillingly separated.

Here is how Pavese expressed his admiration for "this man" in the poem "Ancestors":

> I'd discovered I'd always lived, before I was born,
> in men who were strong and self-reliant.
> . . . .
> Two brothers-in-law opened a store—the first luck
> for our family; the outsider was stuffy,
> calculating, ruthless, and mean, like a woman.
> The other, one of us, read novels in the store—
> something shocking in our town—and customers
> were briefly told that there was
> no more sugar, no sulphate,
> that he was out of everything.
> This man, it turned out,
> helped the bankrupt brother-in-law.
> When I think of these people, I feel stronger
> than when I stand, chest out,
> in front of the mirror, with a solemn smile.

In the father who read novels in the Santo Stefano store, Cesare saw himself and found a proud justification for his own tendency toward literature and solitude. The only reproach Pavese would have for his father was that he did not remain in Santo Stefano.

So like all children, Pavese inherited part of his character from his father and part from his mother: a father who was a dreamer and an avid reader of books, and a mother who was strong, hard, and practical in daily life. In these two family traits there already appeared the contrast that would constantly be with him until the end. A different role awaited his sister. In Pavese's life she remained a loving shadow. She did not make herself heard and Pavese almost never spoke of her, yet it was through her that family conflicts were diminished.

Especially as a boy, he felt, in Turin, the weight of living locked within the family, but during the vacations in Santo Stefano he reacquired his freedom. The older he grew, the more he felt the joy of this freedom, almost to the point of transforming it into happiness.

We find this need for escape confirmed in Pavese's writing, and particularly in the novel about Santo Stefano, *The Moon and the Bonfires*. Here we meet his dearest childhood friend, Pinolo Scaglione. Pinolo is "Nuto," the happy young man who plays the clarinet in the town band every holiday, who sings, who is always ready to participate in all the festivities, who takes Pavese by the hand to discover another aspect of the country—the people who dance, make love, have fun, know how to give a simple explanation to things, and have faith in life. Pinolo, eight years older than Pavese, had already seen Canelli, knew something about the well-dressed girls who lived there in the villas, and was aware that from Canelli one could go to Genoa and could take to the sea. Their friendship grew closer and Nuto became the model for the young student who returned from the city. In these pages from *The Moon and the Bonfires*, Pavese says of Nuto:

For me, listening to those conversations, being Nuto's friend and knowing him that way, had the same effect as drinking wine and hearing music. I was ashamed of being just a boy, a farmhand, not knowing how to talk like him, and it seemed to me that I would never amount to anything. But he treated me like an equal; he wanted to teach me to play the clarinet, take me to the fair in Canelli and to the shooting gallery. He told me that one does not recognize an ignorant person by the work he does but by the way he does it, and that on waking certain mornings even he had the desire to sit at a workbench and create a beautiful little table. "What are you afraid of?" he asked me. "You learn something by doing it; what's needed is the desire to do it. If I'm wrong, correct me." . . . It was Nuto who told me that one can go everywhere by train, and where the railways end the ports begin; that ships have schedules and the whole world is a tangle of roads and ports, a timetable for people who travel, who do and undo, and that everywhere there are those who can do things and those who remain poor devils. He told me the names of many countries and that it was only necessary to read the paper to learn about all sorts of things. And so, on certain days when I was hoeing under the sun in the vineyards above the road, I'd hear, through the peach trees, the train arriving and filling the valley with its noise, going to and from Canelli. In those moments I'd lean on my hoe, watch the smoke of the train and its cars, look at Gaminella, at the little villa called "The Nest," toward Canelli, Calamandrana, Calosso, and I'd feel as if I'd been drinking wine and had become someone else, someone like Nuto, and that some day I too would take the train to go who knows where. . . . .

From autumn to January, children play marbles, and adults cards. Nuto knew all the games, but preferred the one of hiding and trying to guess a card, having it come out of the deck by itself, or pulling it out of a rabbit's ear. When he came in the morning and found me in the sun between the house and the barn, he'd break a cigarette in half and we'd light it; then he'd say, "Let's go up on the roof." The roof meant the tower of the pigeon loft, an attic reached by a large staircase, with a ceiling so low we had to stoop. There was a trunk up there, and some broken springs, bedwarmers, and piles of horsehair. A small round window that looked out on Salto Hill reminded me of the window at Gaminella. Nuto would rummage through that trunk—it was filled with torn books, old rust-colored paper, ledgers, and broken pictures. He would leaf through those books and shake the dust off them, but touching them for awhile made our hands ice-cold. It was all stuff that had belonged to the grandfather, Mr. Matteo's father, who had studied in Alba. Some of the books were written in Latin, like missals, others had pictures of black men and wild animals. That's how I came to know the elephant, the lion, and the whale. Nuto took some of them home, hidden under his sweater. "Nobody's going to use them anyway," he said. "What are you going to do with them?" I asked. "Don't you already buy the paper?" "These are books," he said, "read them as much as you can. You'll always be a poor devil if you don't read books."

So through his friendship with Nuto, Cesare discovered another side of life and became familiar with a new aspect of Santo Stefano, the country, and the Langhe.

The child had become a young boy. Although he spent most of his time in the city, he really belonged to the country. His horizon, even in the city, remained that of Santo Stefano, the hills, and the vineyards. One need only look through his books to confirm this and learn directly how much love he felt for the town where he was born. Be it poetry or prose, his books tell the story of his childhood and adolescence. Let's choose the parts that seem most significant, beginning with *Work Wearies* and these lines from the poem "Displaced People":

> I see only hills and they fill my earth and sky
> with solid shapes, distant and near.
> But my hills are harsh, and streaked with vines
> grown with fatigue on the parched soil.

These verses are from "The Night":

> Through the empty window
> the child watched the night on the hills—
> the cool, dark hills—amazed to find them all massed together:
> vague and limpid immobility. Between the leaves
> that rustled in the dark, the hills appeared
> where all the daytime things, the slopes,
> the trees, the vines were clear and dead,
> and there was another life, made of wind, of sky,
> of leaves, of nothingness.

In a story from *August Holiday* entitled "The Vine," we read:

> A vine climbs on the back of a hill to etch itself into the sky; it is a familiar view, yet a magic door opens beyond the simple and deep rows of vines. Under the vines is the broken red soil, the leaves hide treasures, and on the other side of the leaves is the sky. In this sky, ever tender and ripe, the thick clouds of September—treasure and vines even these—are never missing. All this is familiar and remote, in short, childish, but it amazes every time, as if it were another world.

And "The Sea," which describes Pavese's attempt to arrive at the sea by crossing the Langhe, concludes:

When day came, I had been walking for some time around the bed of the bonfire; I could hear the singing of sparrows, and I was unable to sleep. The bushes became pink, then red, and finally the sun appeared behind the hill. I knew one thing: that the sun had lit the sea in the same way. The ashes of the bonfire were white, and, laughing. I thought that at that moment at home they were lighting the fire. But I was hungry, I was hungry and worn out.

In "The Langhe," we find this description of his birthplace:

My town consists of a few shacks and a great mire, but the main road, where I played as a child, cuts through it. . . . Haven't you ever heard of those shacks? Well, I come from there.

It has been indispensable to try to explain, through quotations from his writings, the influence of the country on Pavese's childhood and adolescence, not only in order to know him as a boy and later to accompany him through his schools and his city life, but also because those sentiments, those visions, that reality, and those dreams, characterize his life and his art. Even the myths, literary or not, that would later pursue him and carry him far from reality in the difficult search for truth, must be linked to the fables and myths of which he was deeply fond as a child. The people from our region hand them down from father to son: the one about the snake that sucks milk from the cow, the moon that influences the harvests and the birth of children, the serpent with three heads, the devil who roams the hills and knocks on the doors of certain houses, the dead who return to ask the living for Masses for their souls, the peasant who hides his money in the cupboard where it becomes food for mice, the hermit who lives in the cave and tells the future, and many other stories that have circulated from barn to barn and fascinated millions of people for centuries.

I often spoke with Pavese about our childhood in the country. We lived in neighboring towns full of vineyards. We spoke of it mostly one summer when we found ourselves together in our region and I brought him to see the places where I had been during the Resistance War with those Partisans about whom he wrote in *The Moon and the Bonfires*. Pavese wanted me to explain the details of every ambush and to take him along the paths we had beaten in retreat. He wanted to know what I would say to my men to encourage them in the winters when it had snowed and we were followed and hunted down night and day like hares, without the possibility of escaping or finding a hiding place. He also wanted to know from which towns these men had come to fight as Partisans.

The day I brought him to the barn of an isolated farmhouse on the top of the highest hill of Santo Stefano and told him that in that very place I had read the poems of Alfieri and those of Montale to my fellow Partisans, he stared at me and asked, "Didn't they tell you that you were crazy?" At my negative reply, Pavese moved a few steps away, absorbed in his thoughts and memories, until he mumbled: "Then those Partisans of yours were really country people."

When I would speak to him of how I loved my town, those streets and paths, Pavese became more and more effusive. He asked me if I knew this or that tree, this or that butterfly, if, as a child and as an adult, I liked to spend the afternoon stretched out in a meadow with my face in the grass, listening to the haunting chirp of the cicadas. Then he would become serene, with the wonder-filled eyes of a child.

2

The First Years in Turin: At School and in the Suburbs

Cesare began to know the city during his last years of elementary school. After the first year, he attended all his classes at the private school Trombetta, on via Garibaldi. Every year he brought home an average report card, without excelling in any subject. In the notebook where the teachers recorded their observations for his family, there was always written at the end of the school year: "Your son does passing work, but he could do much more. He is intelligent but too lazy."

Pavese first attended high school at the Jesuit institute Il Sociale. It was a school for the sons of the aristocracy and wealthy business-men, and Pavese felt uncomfortable because he was unable to fit in with those spoiled and snobbish boys. Instead of paying attention to his teachers, he let his mind wander while twisting a lock of his hair in a manner so intricate that even his comb could not loosen it. It was a habit he kept all his life, like that of folding and refolding the pages of his notebooks. The Jesuit teachers were not enthusiastic over the way he applied himself nor with his stubborn character. After three years he left Il Sociale and went to the Ginnasio Moderno, a public high school.

At home he continued to be silent with his mother and sister, ready to wear a long face for days when scolded. His relationship with his mother worsened. His family, however, recognized one good quality Pavese had even in those days, that of not lying lazily in bed. As soon as he was called in the morning, he rose and headed for school, sometimes without saying a word. If he left the house after returning from school, he never told anyone what the destination of his walks was or where he went to spend his free time. He often left the company of his friends, walked alone in the streets and stopped for hours at an intersection, counting the trams that passed and looking at the people inside. He would also stop at newsstands to read the headlines of newspapers he could not buy.

The apartment where he lived with his family was in a large building almost in the suburbs of the city. If he looked out the window, he could see, as in Santo Stefano, the green of the meadows that reconciled him with life. Along the street from home to school, his favorite encounters were with the trees, even if they were different from those of Santo Stefano. These trees were more barren and wilted; nevertheless, finding himself amid greenery again, Cesare felt in good company. His mother had brought Pinolo Scaglione's sister Vittoria to Turin, and Pinolo himself would live in Cesare's home during the entire period he attended elementary school. Thus Pavese still had a little of Santo Stefano in Turin.

He did not change in the way he dressed, walked, or behaved. He always wore short pants that came down to his knees and gave him an awkward air amid the other boys. On his head he wore a cap that was a bit crooked and pressed down firmly to contain the unruly hair that stuck out on the sides. A doctor had already prescribed glasses for him, and behind the lenses his stare became more sullen. He had long limbs, was too tall for his age, and walked with more and more of a slouch. When in the winter a cough would rack his chest, it seemed to those who heard it that his lungs would collapse. He was tall, but slender and frail. Yet, when he was born he had been considered an exceptional baby because he weighed eleven pounds. Instead of running out to play and make new friends, he threw himself with increasing eagerness into the reading of novels. At school his compositions were different from those of the other students. His teacher often said that Pavese "had strayed from the subject," but gave him good grades anyway, because he expressed thoughts clearly and did not plagiarize.

In Turin more than in the country, Pavese was not sociable, nor did he force himself to become so: his circle of friends was small and never changed. He chose them among those of an opposite nature, perhaps to get help and stimulation. When, unobserved, Cesare looked at the girls of his class, his eyes became timid, but one who had begun to know him might find in his gaze a tenderness that intimidated Cesare himself and forced him to be more aloof.

Of all the books that Pavese would write dealing with the city, there was not one in which he did not hasten to confess having lived there in sadness. Because of his nostalgia for the country, the city at first seemed far from the things he preferred. It would be his constant curiosity that would cause the city to slowly take him in its grasp, even against his will. In contrast to the country, the city seemed a great fair, a continuous holiday. During the day, it was full of life: the trams rattled incessantly; the many shops glittered with objects; the people walked hurriedly, whistled, spoke, and exchanged greetings. At night many lights were lit, much more numerous and closer than the bonfires on the Langhe. Crowds gathered in front of movie houses, theatres, and cafés. Everyone rushed to have fun; everyone knew how to spend an evening. It seemed that poverty and hardship remained entirely in the country, with the hoes, oxen, and plows. City people were always well dressed and lively. One heard music everywhere, in almost every house. During the day, the parks were filled with well-dressed children who ran shouting after one another.

The noise of the city, its tumultuous life, while fascinating Pavese, forced him to defend himself with all his might. Suspicious by nature, confronted with all that movement of people who were still unknown to him, he retreated deeper inside himself. He had to feel completely at ease before confiding in others. Even when the city became a daily habit, it did not make him lose the awkward demeanor of a stubborn and taciturn person.

As the years passed, the city revealed its most complex side to him. It was made up not only of lights, noises, and celebrations, but also of squalid and desolate sidewalks where one found drunkards trying to forget their problems, together with many lonely men and women.

Pavese discovered the factories—those thousands of workers who came out the huge front gates as if from school, who nervously got on their bicycles, greeted each other merely with a nod, and always had somber faces. Those on foot, either alone or in groups, with heads lowered, spoke only in spurts, walking most of the way in silence, even when they found themselves shoulder to shoulder with others. This to Pavese was work: oppressive as a nightmare. The workers' clothes were patched and torn, very similar to those of the peasants in Santo Stefano. The boy learned early that one also must sweat for one's bread in Turin; all those night lights and all that bustle during the day could not hide the fact that only a step from the buildings, poverty and hard work were stubborn and decisive protagonists. In its grayer and gloomier sections, among these silent people, he found his city. Being transplanted from the country, he fitted well with the inhabitants of the outskirts, and he tended to remain isolated from the livelier part of the city. As a solitary country boy, he felt more at home in the periphery, but at the same time he was curious about everything he could discover in the city.

Pavese would later write of this curiosity in *August Holiday*:

> "I've always been unlucky," I said. "But more than unlucky, I never grew up. Some nights I hate to go to sleep because it seems I am wasting time. I want to be awake, ready to breathe and to see. To see, to always see! I find a great excitement going out to look at the weather, the people, and to smell the odors. And then it's beautiful to dream of it. There are, of course, some humiliations, but never mind that."

We would not be able to put Pavese's life into its proper perspective if, after having attempted to define his attachment to Santo Stefano and to the country, we did not also understand his attachment to the city. Pavese, a solitary boy, was forced in the city to live in contact with everything. As he defended himself with silence, it was precisely through silence that he discovered the relations between things and people, between streets and men. In the country he lost himself in the infinite horizons; in the city he was able to take refuge in the indifference of others. He would learn quite early to use the city as a trench from which, without being seen, he could see and observe everything.

Again, he says it himself in the story appropriately entitled "The City," still from *August Holiday*:

> After the first year, in which we learned to observe the city in all its hours and in all its streets, we experienced an even livelier pleasure loafing around. Even the air of the streets had now become hospitable, and what I at last never ceased to enjoy were the everchanging faces of the people on the most familiar corners. Much more beautiful was knowing that at certain hours it would be enough to enter a café, stop at a main entrance, whistle into a lane, and one's old friends would come out, convene there, go and laugh. In company it would become beautiful to think I would be alone that night or the next day, if I wanted, and when alone, I had only to leave the house to find company.

It was the city that shaped Pavese's full, almost carefree years and that convinced him to seek friends. The country had left its marks on him, but the city showed him more each day that to live it was necessary to "leap to the other side of the hedge." He wrote: "We of the country are like this: we like to look at the other side of the hedge, but never jump over it."

But Pavese would make the leap. He confesses it to us in the story "The Houses," from *August Holiday*:

> There's always some street that's emptier than others. At times I stop to look at it closely, because at that hour, in that desert, I don't seem to know it. The sun, a little wind, and the color of the air have only to change and I no longer know where I am. These streets never end. It doesn't seem real that they all have their tenants and passers-by, and that they would be so silent and empty. More than walking along those tree-lined boulevards of the suburbs, where I could enjoy a breath of fresh air, I like to stroll around the piazzas and narrow streets of downtown. I feel they are even more my own because, although I can't understand why, everyone seems to have gone away.

As he grew, the city and the country provided a comparison. The first pages of the novel *The Harvesters* indicate this. On one side there is Pavese (the character Berto), a man from the city who goes into the country. On the other is the contrasting figure of the country Pavese in the person of Talino, the Monticello peasant, awkward, stupid, and at the same time, clever. Here Pavese describes the country boy in the city:

> "There is no one on these streets," I heard him say calmly, as if he were in his own house. He already seemed at ease and did not even realize that we were going along like oxen, without knowing where—he with his red handkerchief on his neck, his bundle, and his corduroy trousers. These country bumpkins do not understand a man who, no matter how much he's been around, when released from prison one fine morning, finds himself disoriented. He does not know what to do, because even if he expected to be freed, when he is actually freed he cannot at once feel a part of society and pounds the streets like one who has run away from home. Here Talino began laughing again, as if we were pals; he complained and laughed and took up the whole sidewalk. People began to pass by and bumped into him because Talino walked as if he were alone in the piazza.

When he arrives with Talino in Alba, which resembles more a large country town than a city, Pavese knows how to show us his nostalgia for the city and his taste for the country through this description:

> Talino brought me to the market that was spread out in front of the arcades; and he walked toward the sun to see the merchandise. I, without my bundle because I had left it at the station, remained in the background. Taking stock in secret, I discovered that I still had enough to smoke for two more days. But what beautiful red peppers the women were selling! Then we arrived in front of the watermelons and I got thirsty. They were shouting, especially the women, so that it seemed like a local market. "Look at them well, Berto," I said to myself without stopping, "it is in the hands of these people you have now placed yourself." From the arcades, looking at the market was like looking at a seashore. There were counters of shirts, sweaters, and berets that made one perspire only by walking in front of them, because in the country everything is thick, from the skin of one's feet to the corduroy of one's trousers. And Talino went along decisively, running into people, stretching out his legs to let the dogs pass under them, without even drying his neck with that red handkerchief that formed a triangle on his shoulders.

How many times in the long Turin evenings on Corso Valdocco do I remember speaking with Pavese about these pages! How wrong, I would tell him, are those critics born and bred in the city who find an American influence here. Here is everything that we of the country bring into the city; the image and tone are derived from the most accurate comparison which can be made only after having learned to look more closely at the people of the country and at those of the city. Pavese would look at me, invite me to sit down on one of the green benches under the trees, and would say to me: "You are referring to Talino's red handkerchief, to the thickness of his calloused feet and of the corduroy trousers, to the watermelons that one has only to look at to become thirsty. And you are right. They are things only we can understand. You see, even before the plot, I created this atmosphere of *The Harvesters* inside me back in my younger years. I created it every time I came from the country to live in Turin, every day I compared my country clothes and habits with those of my city schoolmates. The city is like a shoe that you have to try until you find the right size, and you have to put it on slowly."

Slowly Turin entered into Pavese and became as important as Santo Stefano. In the poem "A Generation," from *Work Wearies*, Pavese gives us a rare picture of his first years in the city:

> A boy used to come and play in these fields
> now crossed by the avenues. He found in the fields
> other boys, barefoot, as he was, and he jumped for joy.
> It was beautiful to go barefoot in the grass with them.
> One night from the distant lights of the city
> shots echoed, and with the wind arrived a fearful,
> intermittent clamor. Everyone was silent.
> The hills were unveiling points of light
> on their sides, animated by the wind.
> All was submerged in the darkening night
> and only cool breaths of wind lasted in the sleep.
>
> (Next morning the boys return to play
> and no one remembers the shots. In prison
> there are silent workers, and some are already dead.
> In the streets the bloodstains have been covered.

The distant city wakens in the sun
and people go out. They look each other in the face.)
The boys were thinking of the darkness in the fields
and were looking the women in the face. Even the women
were not saying anything and left them alone.
The boys were thinking of the darkness in the fields
where some little girls used to come. It was fun making
the girls cry in the dark. We were the boys.
We liked the city by day; and in the evening we liked to be silent,
watching the lights in the distance and listening to the clamor.

Boys still go to play in the fields
crossed by the avenues. And the night is the same.
As we walk by we can smell the grass.
In prison there are the same men. And there are still women
who bear children and say nothing.

No biographical description can give us the feeling of Pavese's childhood in Turin better than this poem. And no note can tell us better than these verses the drama of those days in the terrified eyes and already pensive mind of the boy.

In my copy of *Work Wearies*, right next to the poem "A Generation," I rediscovered, after many years, some annotations Pavese had written one night while he was waiting for me in my office at the newspaper *L'Unità*. When I arrived, the volume had already been put back in its place and I would not have been aware of anything if Raf Vallone, then literary editor of *L'Unità*, had not told me that to kill time, Pavese had written some notes in one of my books.

Pavese had made two annotations. The first said: "December 18, 1922. Remember: the Turin massacre (Brandimarte) at Barriera di Nizza." The second listed the names of the people killed there. They were written near the verse saying: "there are silent workers, and some are already dead."

I had no occasion to talk with Pavese about his notes, but they convinced me that the Turin massacre of eleven workers, and many other political events, had left profound impressions upon his adolescence in the city. The years of Pavese's early youth corresponded with the years of the Fascist punitive raids. Turin was a workers' stronghold that was difficult to conquer, and it was necessary to attack it at night, in a cowardly way.

The head of the Turin action squads, Piero Brandimarte, had led that expedition against unarmed people on that December date in 1922. The raid began with the burning of trade union headquarters and of two Socialist clubs. It continued with the devastation of *L'Ordine Nuovo*, the Communist newspaper whose editors, headed by Antonio Gramsci[5], were taken to the central park and threatened with execution before a firing squad. Then other leading Communists and trade unionists, completely unrelated to the events, were arrested and assassinated. They are the martyrs whose names Pavese had listed in his notes: the town councilman, Berruti; the secretary of railroad workers, Fanti; the secretary of the metallurgical workers federation, Ferrero, slaughtered in the most barbarous manner, his feet tied, dragged by a truck and disfigured; the tram conductor, Tarizzo, bludgeoned to death; the fireman, Andreoli; the factory worker, Becchio; the young Communist Chiotto; Mazzola, owner of a trattoria; another worker, Pachettino, the only one whose name Pavese did not mention; the bailiff Quintaglia; and Chiolero. Eleven dead and ten seriously wounded.

Reconstructing Pavese's life also has the purpose of linking him, from his earliest years, with the events of his times. As Pavese grew, so did Fascism, which exalted every characteristic he did not possess: arrogance, boldness, action at any cost, the rhetoric of "I don't give a damn," and the delusion of a fatherland that had no correspondence whatsoever with the real one. Irritated by all this and unable to accept the violent Fascist philosophy, he detached himself from Fascism and, almost frightened, retreated even more into himself and his studies.

In the city he had more opportunities to find books to read. Guido da Verona, author of erotic novels, was in fashion and became a favorite of Pavese who by then was awakening to sex. Another of his favorites was Gabriele D'Annunzio who, like Guido da Verona, wrote about passionate love, but had a more sophisticated following. It was especially through D'Annunzio that Pavese, as a young boy, learned to appreciate reading and, as a consequence, to enjoy school. He began to pay attention to his teachers, to study, and also to write his first verses.

He grew so absorbed in poetry writing that he began discussing it with his high school friends. His best friend was Mario Sturani, a thin boy, vivacious, always ready for fun, sure of himself in school and at play. He, like Pavese, had already read D'Annunzio and was interested in Edgar Allan Poe. He composed verses and enjoyed drawing and painting. His friendship with Pavese lasted a long time.

Pavese went from home to school on foot and spent his time, even along the way, reading. Sturani still remembers that one morning Cesare was almost struck by a streetcar while crossing the tracks with his eyes on a book. By then his taste for reading was accompanied by a passion for study. Since the school he attended did not teach Greek, but only Greek culture, he studied the language at home by himself until he learned to read the original texts.

He often went with Sturani to the public library and spent many hours there. He read everything; every subject fascinated him. Often his friends caught him doing English homework not yet assigned. The study of English particularly interested him because he wanted to be able to read certain books not yet translated into Italian. He rarely left his desk during the breaks between lessons. He took advantage of this time to scan the verses of the poems that were in his school anthology. His vocation as a poet began to reveal itself early.

During his high school years, Pavese developed, even physically, before his classmates. Lanky, bony, with the first fuzz on his chin, he felt awkward and his shyness increased. There were also girls at school, and he was already at the age when girls become important. It was at that time that his eyes often left his book to stare at the blonde girl in the second desk. Her name was Olga, and she was lively and carefree. She was not aware of the attention her classmate was showing her, and he suffered. It was his first crush. He had the feeling that his heart would stick in his throat every time Olga passed by. When she was near him, he wanted to tell her about his feelings, but the words froze on his lips. He became aware of the fact that many of his friends were different. They knew how to talk to their girlfriends and how to talk about their girlfriends with everyone. They knew how to arrange dates, while he did not have the courage to address an invitation to Olga. When he was with her, even the size of his big hands disturbed him and he felt like a country boy.

He tried to react. He felt inferior and understood that behaving in that manner he would never win the attention and heart of Olga. To free himself, he relied on long walks. Often, together with Sturani, he went to the Sangone. This river at the edge of the city reminded him of the Belbo and the swims with his friends of Santo Stefano. They crossed a long stretch of meadows to reach the Sangone, and those walks seemed to reassure him. Sturani's reckless joy momentarily distracted him from his romantic obsession. But one day, returning from the river and walking along the bank, he saw the name of a woman written on the side of a boat. Pavese stopped, widened his eyes at that name, turned white and fainted. The name was Olga.

This episode is significant in that it characterized early in his life the emotionalism Pavese always experienced before women. Was that sudden faint determined just by his mental obsession, or also by a peculiar physical state? In the rest of his life both are in evidence.

3

At the Lyceum Massimo D'Azeglio with Augusto Monti

His entrance into the lyceum (senior high school) in 1923 was one of the most important events in Pavese's life. His face was hollowed, and his eyes were deeper and more absorbed behind his glasses. He kept the peasant walk of the Langhe, drab gray suits, and a crooked beret. Yet when he returned to Santo Stefano during summer vacation, his friends noted that their playmate had become a young gentleman who preferred, instead of catching snakes, long walks to discover a suitable place to read undisturbed the novels he had brought with him from the city. In leaving Turin for the country, he placed in his suitcase only books and sheets of white paper to be filled.

During his first year of lyceum his favorite author became Vittorio Alfieri.[6] In this poet from Asti, Pavese discovered the pride of Piedmont, Pavese's own region and a more modern Italian with a tenacious will to become someone in life. For months and months he answered his school friends and playmates with quotations from his readings of Alfieri.

Alfieri became a passion into which Pavese, as always, hurled himself head first. He increased his energies in dedicating himself to study and was by that time considered by his friends to be a workhorse who took every lesson and every page of a book seriously. He wore himself out studying, and his health suffered. He had the first warning in the course of an outing in the Canavese hills during a vacation with the inseparable Sturani. After a short climb, Pavese was forced to stop. "It's asthma," he confided to Sturani, "I suffer from asthma."

But he did not abandon school for one day nor did he diminish the intensity of his studying. Pavese by then had the obstinacy of a man. The doctors later told him that his asthma was the result of nervous tension. His thoughts and preoccupations were in fact increasing and evolving, and even his friends at the lyceum assumed a different importance. One cannot stay alone when one is sixteen or seventeen years old. Not even a boy with a somber nature like Pavese could continue to guard his sentiments within him.

During those lyceum years Pavese met many girls in and outside school; his infatuations followed one another in rapid succession. But he often communicated with the girls he wanted only through surly glances that certainly could not always be understood as declarations of love. He then found it necessary to express his disappointments to Sturani and his other friends, whom he met even more frequently at the Sangone or the Po.

Sturani would become more of an advisor because he did not have complexes, not even those typical of his age. Unlike Pavese, he was confident in everything he did, always full of initiative, active and impudent with girls. When confronted with a conflict, he quickly resolved it. Among Pavese's lyceum schoolmates, Sturani was the one who exuded the most charm and he would continue, up until his university years, to be considered a child prodigy.

Sturani and some other friends, like Baraldi, Vaudagna, Monferini, and Barale, were able to shake Pavese out of his habitual indifference and tear him away from his solitude. They put him in touch with many environments, forcing him to occupy himself with other activities than studying and reading, bringing him to live a normal student's life. That collective life had a beneficial influence on him.

Entering the lyceum, Pavese also had the good fortune to meet a man of extraordinary character and culture who would have a great influence on his youth and the entire course of his life as a man and a writer. That man was Augusto Monti, teacher of Italian literature and Latin. Professor Monti's fame spread rapidly, not only among students and teachers of the Lyceum D'Azeglio, but in all the schools of Turin.

Severe and paternal, inflexible and frank, despite the terror he knew how to inspire in lazy students, he won the esteem and affection of all. Even on a political and moral level, his adamantine figure reflected the dignity and pride of an independent thinker.

Everyone in the schools of Turin knew that he was the teacher who did not carry a card of the Fascist Party. The Fascists courted and threatened him, but he always resisted. A friend of Piero Gobetti[7] and admirer of Antonio Gramsci, he would always know how to defend, in the solidarity of those two men, the important political significance of unity in the struggle against Fascism and in the vision of a modern society, where the proletariat ought to have hegemony.

With the articles that were published in *Rivoluzione Liberale, Baretti, Voce*, and *Corriere della Sera* about the problems of education and advocating progressive school reform, Monti added to his political and moral prestige the fame of acute and enlightened innovator.

Although known as an anti-Fascist, out of dignity and honesty Monti would never directly discuss current politics in school. He expressed his political views indirectly, through his interpretation of Dante's *De Monarchia*, Machiavelli's *The Prince*, and D'Azeglio's[8] *The Latest Cases of Romagna*. Monti taught, above all, to face life head-on without compromise or cowardice. His pupils were educated to despise tyrants, to distinguish the just from the unjust, and to see the causes of a political regime such as Fascism by witnessing its effects. Thus many of his students understood clearly the present problems of Italy and became active in the anti-Fascist movement to the extent that they preceded their teacher in being condemned and imprisoned. Even Pavese, who was the student most attentive to the explanation of the classics and the least attracted by any political appeal, would, not long after those school days, write to Monti from his political confinement.

But let us enter D'Azeglio, into classroom First B, where Pavese and Monti were. During the first few days the teacher's way of doing things bewildered his students. Pavese, seated in the first desk, got a disastrous impression. Having entered the lyceum without great preparation or a definite vocation, he found himself for the first time in front of a man who permitted neither distractions nor excuses.

Behind thick lenses that rendered his thin face, marked by deep wrinkles, more severe, Monti's eyes seemed to see into one's mind. When he pointed his finger at someone, there was no escape. It was essential to come to class always well-prepared. Heaven help anyone if he heard a whisper in the classroom! If that happened, Monti would suddenly stop speaking, look toward the part of the room where the whisper had come from, and strike his desk with small light taps of the nail of his index finger: the silence of the tomb was restored. When he asked questions no one ever knew which would be the exact answers to satisfy him. It was not enough just to know a lesson by heart, to directly quote paragraphs from the pages assigned. It was, in fact, the most dangerous thing. His sermon for those who memorized is still remembered by all his students: "They are not things to learn by memory. You must open your ears, not take notes, your ears and your brain if you have one. Reread the text and assimilate what it says. This, and nothing else, is called studying."

But the students quickly saw the other side of the teacher: when he did not ask questions, but when he lectured and explained. At that time the silence in the classroom was absolute. With a clear voice, Monti would read the texts. Pavese himself would later tell me that Dante, Boccaccio, Machiavelli, Ariosto, and Manzoni never had a better teacher. It was rare that even a single student was absent on the days Monti lectured.

Massimo Mila,[9] a friend of Pavese who was among Monti's students, reminisced about his teacher a few years ago in the magazine *Il Ponte*:

That discovery of the classics that one generally makes on one's own, ten, twenty, thirty years after school, Monti made it possible there, with a lecture that restored life to all those things that school tended to embalm. . . .

Italian literature, as taught by Monti, reflected to a great extent his vigorous civil conscience: implacable was his polemic against those men of letters who were pure aesthetes, curators of nothing other than the perfection of style and perhaps lacking human, social, and political interests.

Monti stressed to us, his students, the difference between the perfect and cold rhymes of Pietro Bembo[10] and the tormented and vivid ones of Michelangelo. The same difference we recognized between Ugo Foscolo,[11] always socially committed, even when he wrote the *Grazie*, and Vincenzo Monti,[12] always so desolately a man of letters, even when he eagerly struggled to versify the official bulletins on Louis XVI, the French Revolution, the Restoration, and the progress of science.

This is what Monti taught us with great simplicity long before the polemic on committed art was invented. While he taught us to value Michelangelo more than Bembo, Alfieri more than Metastasio,[13] and Foscolo more than Monti, he also taught us to give a fair opinion of Bembo, Metastasio, and Vincenzo Monti, and not to underestimate their importance.

Here is another report on Monti and the Lyceum D'Azeglio. It is a letter written many years later, in 1959, by Beppe Foà, an ex-student of Monti, who had to emigrate to the United States because of Fascism:

Professor Monti was a phenomenon, not only as a man, but also as the symbol of an academic freedom deeply-rooted throughout the centuries, so deeply-rooted that he could make use of it without hesitation, even under Fascism; a freedom that would seem inconceivable in America, even in the most independent universities. His influence was enormous, and the Lyceum D'Azeglio, during that period, in the modesty of that small, cold, and dark building, was certainly one of the greatest schools the world had ever known. It was a true center of learning in the most noble of all traditions, one of the few remaining, perhaps the last. The students didn't know it. I still have in front of my eyes Principal Lizier, who looked like Michelangelo's Moses, silent and inflexible, adored by all. He was the high priest, and the professors were other priests in that enchanted temple.

A few years after Pavese had graduated from D'Azeglio, another exceptional student, Giancarlo Pajetta, was in Monti's class. He was a quick-witted boy who came from an anti-Fascist family that lived in the suburb of San Paolo, the Communist district of Turin. Giancarlo Pajetta was co-editor of the school newspaper. In one of his columns, he satirized a classmate who had boasted of his Fascist beliefs. The infuriated student appealed to the principal (no longer Lizier) who made a serious political issue out of it and had the police intervene. All the Pajetta family ended up in jail, then the police reconsidered, freed the family, and sent Giancarlo back to school. But the case was not closed. The new principal of D'Azeglio wanted to make points with the regime and took advantage of certain affectionate letters written by Pajetta to a girl classmate to accuse him not only of anti-Fascism, but also of atheism. He was thus able to have him expelled from all the schools in Italy, against the vote of Monti and many other teachers at D'Azeglio.

In this school and this political climate, Pavese studied and grew up. These were essential experiences which would have a great influence on his life and on his works. The following episode, typical of those years, was related to me by Monti himself.

They were studying Boccaccio in his class, and one morning Pavese was called upon to give his comments on the tale of Friar Cipolla from *The Decameron*. He hesitated and then, as if he had not understood the story, left out the protagonist to occupy himself exclusively with a minor character, Guccio Balena, the friar's secretary. But his analysis of this character was so profound and he was able to explain Boccaccio's art in such an original way that Monti rewarded him with one of his rare words of praise.

In Boccaccio's tale, Guccio Balena, also called Guccio the Pig, is such a scoundrel that his employer describes him this way: "My servant has nine failings, any one of which, had it been found in Solomon or Aristotle or Seneca, would have sufficed to spoil all the virtues, all the wisdom, and all the saintliness they ever possessed. You can imagine what this fellow must be like, considering he has nine such failings and not a scrap of virtue, wisdom, or saintliness."

It is easy to understand why Guccio Balena attracted Pavese's attention. Are not the vagabond, the drunk, and the idle recurrent figures of his stories and poems? These Pavesean characters spend their lives in taverns amid wines and discussions, with some easy woman and some occasional friend, without a precise occupation, without love, addicted to drinking and smoking, satisfied to wander the streets with no fixed destination, and in the end they always experience a despairing melancholy.

When, in the classroom of his first years of lyceum, Pavese underlined the minor character of Guccio, he not only demonstrated that his sensitivity as a reader and critic was already awake, but also revealed his sympathies for a particular world around which he would construct many plots of his books.

In those lyceum years, besides school, there were women to occupy the minds of the young students. Pavese was not one of those ardent youths who forget everything at the sight of a skirt, but he did not want to be less than the others, and the love affairs of a timid person are often more serious than those of an impudent one. It was in those years that Pavese had his second crush. It no longer involved a schoolgirl because in frequenting the cafés and variety shows with his friends, he was attracted to girls less educated, who were simpler, even if more experienced in seducing men. The girl who mesmerized him was a performer who worked at the cabaret La Meridiana. One evening, after hearing her sing, Pavese broke through his timidity, gathered up his courage, and made a date with her. He had exchanged a few words with the girl on the preceding evenings and had had the impression that she was not indifferent to his attentions, which consisted mainly of persistent stares. The date was for six in the evening, in front of the main entrance to the cabaret.

Punctually at six o'clock, Pavese was waiting. But his waiting was prolonged: the girl arrived neither at six, nor at seven, nor at nine. Pavese kept waiting, and waited until midnight. The driving rain that fell on him from eleven o'clock on did not deflect him from his purpose, nor did he leave, even when he was certain the girl was not coming. Only when a clock beat the twelve strokes of midnight did he return home, sad and humiliated, soaking wet and freezing. He learned the next day that the dancer had left at six o'clock, but from the back door, where a less persistent but more fortunate admirer was waiting for her. That news, the rain, and the cold affected him morally and physically. After a fever, he grew worse and contracted pleurisy which forced him to abandon school for three months. The friends who went to see him during his illness were struck by his thinness which made his face seem transparent. If he responded to their greetings, it was only to say that together with his physical strength, he had lost every bit of faith he had in himself.

Fortunately, when he returned to school after three months of illness, he would find Professor Monti waiting for him, and would thus be helped to shake off part of his depression and catch up with his classes. The days of lively gatherings returned. Every day, from then on, as soon as winter was over, he found himself on the banks of the Po or the Sangone with Vaudagna, Baraldi, Monferini, and Predella. The long swims restored his health and his morale recovered along with his body.

4

The Lyceum Poems and
the "Absurd Vice"

At the home of Mario Sturani, I found a rich correspondence from Pavese that goes back to the lyceum period. In these letters Cesare revealed his thoughts, emotions, attempts at poetry, and his early opinions about writers and painters.

During the second year of lyceum, Sturani, to follow his vocation, left Turin and moved to Monza to attend its school of decorative art. Pavese thus lost the company of the friend who knew how to encourage him most firmly, but their conversations were substituted by letters. Through this correspondence we learn from Pavese himself the most interesting part of his inner biography.

The letters need no commentary. Some were left undated, like the following that begins in verse:

Dear Mario,

> My thanks to you, good friend! Your fervor
> pulls me along, even against my will.
> From you I learn that joy blossoms
> along the path and that here is our sole aim.
> The creative flame of the moment
> dispels your thoughts
> on what has been created, do you not see the universe
> as one perpetual creation
> only for the greater glory of its own God?

I've always thought that all one needs to do is to mount the creative muse like a horse and control it by the reins, but my cross is that I'm convinced my muse is like one of those bony, impotent hackneys in the public square. With this conviction, how can I have the nerve and the enthusiasm to seize the reins? The more I think about it, the more I reject the insipid verses quoted above.

But in writing to you, I shall follow the impulse of the moment. Since this strophe by Tagore is burning within me now, here it is for you:

Melancholy weighs on your heart and slumber is always in your eyes.
Haven't you observed how the flower reigns splendid amid the thorns?
Wake, oh awake! Let not time pass in vain.
At the end of the rocky path, in the country of virgin solitude
my friend sits all alone. Deceive him not. Wake, oh awake!
What if the sky rumbles and shakes in the heat of the midday sun?
What if the burning sand spreads its mantle of thirst?
Would joy not be in the depths of your heart? Would the street
not resound with harmony at your every step, as a harp made sweet by
    grief?

Doesn't that describe me completely? I shall make it my law. Tell me, don't you agree that *no joy surpasses the joy of suffering*?

Don't laugh. I beg you to always tell me honestly what you think. Remember that I told you that some of your poems "weren't worth much"? Now do the same for me. It would be the greatest proof of friendship you could give me. I hope I'll have plenty of work to keep you busy. Would you like a word of advice when considering my poems? Force yourself to forget they're mine.

One of these days, I'm counting on finding fresh inspiration and rekindling my poetic fire (a flash in the pan) by taking another look at the *Vita Nova*, trying not to let my own thoughts intrude.

I notice, and I'm not too pleased about it, that you are getting to be a real highbrow: quotations from here, quotations from there. I assure you that in this field you are far ahead of me.

Some day I'll manage to write you about something I don't know if you'll understand. It will be an outpouring of my entire youth. Oh, the memories of my early studies of the *Vita Nova*! You certainly don't understand, not even now. I'm talking about the innermost depths of my soul.

Meanwhile, moving on to philosophy, you say: *Poetry is the feeling for beauty.* It is more than that. It is the feeling for everything—beauty and ugliness, truth and falsehood, good and evil, *that clash of good and evil that is life itself.*

From my reflections you have drawn exactly what I wanted you to; there can be poetry even in a painting. Poetry is everywhere. Any emotion is *poetry.* And this divine gift is the only thing that is truly ours, since *science,* from a certain aspect, is a reality outside of ourselves, belonging to everyone and to no one.

And then, after all, even he who turns to science does so because of an emotion that draws him to it.

The fact that you enjoy life stems from an emotion. Poetry is queen of the world. You could call it God (always speaking from the point of view of man).

Your verses seem to me too detailed. Aside from that, you have a surprising propriety of words, a freshness of phrasing that is all your own, and a keen power of observation.

C. PAVESE

(The more a man is dissatisfied with himself, the larger his signature becomes.)

February 21, 1925

I'm writing you because it's been a while since I've written, but I still don't have anything new to tell you.

I've read your poem in free verse, a real triumph for you. You were right in saying, "As you see, it is in free verse, because that is how I feel them." I too am no longer able to confine a feeling within the prison of rhyme. The most I can do is hammer out blank verse. As always, the liveliness, or should I say the sharpness of description in those poems of yours is admirable. One actually feels the spring morning! As to your cleverly worked-out allegory, well, it's not bad, but the subtlety of all those hidden meanings tends, in my view, to detract from the effectiveness of your poetry. Take, for example, the lines "Flock after flock go the little grey lambs," then "And the wind delights in ruffling their fleece." Let me enjoy them for their own sake, as I feel them immediately, and don't make me notice so many other things!

All things considered, you had a good hand in revealing your intentions: the spring morning was well-chosen. Now, precisely when this season begins again, I feel myself being reborn little by little.

My spirit glows with fresh inspiration. I'm happy, I laugh at misfortune, trying to remedy as much of it as possible, and enjoy all that is good. *Good* in the vast meaning I give to it and that you certainly perceive without any other explanation. More and more, I realize how much I hate science and love every kind of art.

I shall enjoy the spring, rambling in the country with Baraldi and Barale, revisiting, of course, those rocks by the Sangone. All I need is the baptism of love (as others would say the baptism of fire). Then I shall be content. All the lovely faces and beautiful bodies I see make me feel that I'm missing something. Write me in detail sometime about your feelings on the subject.

I can't tell you the happiness your criticism of those few poems to Luty[14] gave me. For one whole day I did nothing but laugh, fantasize, and look people up and down, feeling superior or embracing them fraternally. You gave me a greater pride than Dante ever knew. Not that I feel superior to Dante: I see now, much more clearly than in the past, his greatness. Certainly you too, as an artist, understand better every day the greatness of Leonardo.

Speaking of painting: I have at last succeeded in understanding a painting by Botticelli. The Madonna and Child with the pomegranate is sublime. The canvas is discolored, with a technique somewhat unsure, many imperfections in the figures, and an insignificant background; but if you gaze at it long enough, you will see what depth of expression there is in the face of the Madonna, so childlike, so thin and pale, so reddened by her tears. What seems to me a distinctive feature of Botticelli's art is—I don't know how to say it better—that free application of harsh lines and of colors, the original slight distortion that makes his figures so interesting. You know about such things. Tell me if I'm right. Here it is: I know very little about the painters of that period, but it seems to me that the one who comes closest to Botticelli, at least in technique, is Fra Filippo Lippi.

So much for the artistic-literary section. Back to us, I want to say that you, in your descriptions, resemble Botticelli.

My mind is stagnating. Once you reach materialism you can go no further with art: everything is ruined, nothing remains but to seek pleasure for pleasure's sake. I can't bring myself to do this. I struggle to pull myself up; but more and more I'm convinced there's nothing I can do about it.

I hope you'll catch the fever (that of creation).

PAVESE

Dear Sturani,

At this moment as I write to you, I'm fairly satisfied with myself. But there are times when I feel my life isn't worth two cents.

I've made a lot of progress this year. Although I still go on convincing myself that I am worth very little, I do, in some rare moments of complete happiness, catch a glimpse of my future strength.

My ideas are becoming clearer and broader. I'm discovering my own personality. Many vague intuitions of years ago now appear more precise and fit into the broad scheme of who I am. I'm always in ferment, more than ever when I'm in despair. I convince myself that I've done some good work and that I shall do more.

Now that you've been subjected to a study of me (with what boredom I can imagine—since there is nothing more tedious than listening to others talk about themselves), what would you like to hear? I've nothing else to tell you.

I hope you wouldn't expect me to describe the rebirth of spring to you. At any rate, long live, now more than ever, the beautiful nature of the paintings by Fra Lippi and Botticelli!

During Easter vacation, from March 28 to April 7, I'll be traveling through Tuscany and Umbria. Try to stay in Turin so that I can see you when I return.

C. PAVESE

Dear Sturani,

Each of us is fully intent on himself, and that's quite natural. I write to you with clenched teeth because I am more and more convinced that your genius is a strong conscious unity, wholly devoted to its ideal, while I'm only a little poet, a little poet who is afraid to open his eyes wide in bright sunshine lest the light should hurt him. Yet I hope that you, and all those who do something out of the ordinary, may to some extent share my endless uncertainty. But, I assure you, my sickness is no longer the usual depression I used to feel in the past (remember?): it is a battle I have to fight every day, every hour, against inertia, dejection, and fear; it is a conflict that sharpens and tempers my spirit as metal is smelted and hardened by fire.

This struggle, this pain that I find so harrowing yet so very sweet, keeps me on my toes, always ready, and is, in short, what draws my works from my soul. It seems to me I have already done a good deal and shall, I hope, do much more.

Well, now you can claim to be the main cause of my transformation from the usual depression to constructive pain. If I ever complete a great work, I shall not forget that your strength has been a great stimulus.

"It has been a pleasure," you'll say, "give my best to your great work," but bear in mind that however wretched I may feel, I am a proud man and glad to be so; remember that nothing thrills me more than thinking of the splendid isolation men of genius know. Notwithstanding my love of working alone, I bow my head before you and acknowledge you have been my master. I should shout for joy if you were to write the same about me. . . .

And now let's come to the point. Here is a poem written last summer, amid free nature, in a morning full of life:

> I am terrified by the thought that I too
> must, one day, leave this earth
> where even the pains are dear to me
> for I try to render them in art.
> And I tremble even more, thinking of the agony,
> the long terrible agony
> that will perhaps precede my death.
> What is life to the moribund
> who are still aware and feel themselves slowly,
> slowly die in a dismal room,
> alone inside themselves? Oh, if I knew a God,

I would offer him this prayer: "When my chest
swells, filled with a wave
of burning poetry, and from my lips
escape broken words that I anxiously
strive to connect in a shape of art,
when I most burn and I'm most delirious,
I wish a vein could burst near my heart
and I could suffocate this way, without regret."

I await your pages with great interest. I know, to my disgrace, that even here you maintain a very broad synthesizing vision and that you are always in accord with your own ideas. Please add your opinion of my verses.

C. PAVESE

December 10, 1925

Dear Mario,

It's extraordinary. Each of us feels inferior to the other and takes a kind of bitter pleasure in declaring himself small and insignificant. But note that we both feel our individuality above all, and I believe that you would not want to change into me for anything in the world, just as I would never like to change into you. We're both dissatisfied with ourselves, that's all. And this is the best possible sign, because if it weren't for the fear of falling behind that stimulates us, we would never do anything.

Cheer up: it is a sign (and here you should play the national anthem) that we are both destined for great things.

Meanwhile, the comparison you made between your smile and that of Leonardo gives me something to think about. You call it a "smile of resignation" but there is not only a resigned smile on the lips of Leonardo's figures, there is a whole world under them and you bear on your face, in my opinion, precisely the mark of all that world.

Leaving aside now the consideration of our respective talents, which serves no useful purpose—whoever will be alive thirty years from now will see for himself—I want to tell you that your letter gave me a whole day of complete happiness, abundant and productive (let's hope this continues). Listen, I want to unburden myself of a thought that continuously torments me and upon which my entire inner life is hinged.

In life, in our every action, even in our sacrifices, we try to please ourselves; our satisfaction is either on the material or spiritual level.

Which raises this point: "Why should I despise and condemn, as certain futuristic thinkers do, all that has passed?" I say: the past is past. Customs, institutions, languages, and history, all have fallen and are dead forever, but the feelings that have moved men in the past and that live eternally in the art they created—why must they be considered by me as something dead? A feeling, when you experience it, is a living thing. And what is art but a means by which a feeling, a conception, lives forever and can be relived by other men?

Why should I deny myself the pleasure, the exaltation, of reliving (understand: *reliving*) a life which, idealized in its own art-form, uplifts me, and *fills my breast with a surge of burning poetry*? If I compose something, it is with the hope (!!!) that it will last forever, with the hope that those who will call our time the past will still be moved and exalted by it. To enjoy this pleasure, this satisfaction of finding exaltation in the work of others, you must experience it as any other pleasure, and find satisfaction in its inherent life. But then, in your own work of art, don't begin to say: "Such and such a great poet did this, therefore I must do the same, otherwise I shall fail as an artist." Such stagnation is absurd, since each moment has, above all, its own character, it is nothing but itself. I find enjoyment and stimulation in all that I can, even in understanding works of the past, but then, when it is I who creates, I only try to express as clearly and effectively as I can my own exaltation, my own feeling. It seems to me that this is not worship of the past since my exaltation and my feelings are modern, expressing my own spirit. All this I have written to you in rambling fashion, for this is the first time I have tried to explain my theory of art fully. Try to make some sense of it if it interests you; if not, go on to my review.

Critical Review

I must tell you that the first of your two poetic compositions is, as you say yourself, not worth much. Ideas are set forth starkly and crudely, and the feelings that accompanied them in your mind are not expressed in such a way as to convey those ideas and feelings to the mind of the reader. But this judgment is not absolute: there are a few verses, especially at the beginning (and don't think I'm saying this to sweeten the dose) that move the soul. The thought behind them is good and says things I think myself.

Don't imagine that by saying this I am contradicting those poems of mine you praised so highly. In those verses I was simply giving vent to the terror and the anxiety that seize me at the thought of a very slow, conscious death agony, and I long instead for a quick death "with no regret," a death that takes me in a moment of exaltation, therefore of joy.

Your second composition is better poetically because it conveys more clearly the sentiment you wished to express. . . .

I've told you everything I felt, nothing more. It is not flattery, believe me. I would have been pleased to find you inferior, but no. Listen closely: it seems that you surpass me even in poetry.

Now I ask you whether this shouldn't bother me tremendously: since poetry is not exactly your art, you deal with it solely as an amateur, and you succeed so well at it. What then am I to do, I who have made poetry the ideal of my whole life?

Finally, here is a bomb I dropped a couple of months ago, one evening returning from the movies:

> My soul is hopelessly consumed
> by the desire for a living woman;
> soul and flesh, to be able to squeeze her
> without restraint and excite her, pressing
> her trembling body close to mine;
> but then, on more serene days,
> to stay sweetly beside her, with no
> carnal thought, to gaze upon
> her sweet, childlike face,
> unaware, as if absorbed in grief,
> and listen as her soft voice
> speaks to me, slowly, as in a dream.

(The adjectives in line ten describe the "face," not "me.")

And here's another bomb, written the day the professor praised one of my compositions (as you see, in the school of Dante, I become more modest):

> Wasted, deluded, and despairing
> of ever being able to stir up in the souls
> of men a flame of passion
> with an art all my own, I live
> sadly throughout the long days . . . yet, at moments,
> I overflow with a life
> burning and powerful, which, if
> I ever could express it, would fulfill
> all my existence!

Naturally, besides the manuscript, I'm waiting for your reply and opinions, thoughts, works, something by you, so that I can feel you talk. I don't want praise (or, at least, not just praise), but reasoned opinions and you can give them.

Don't plan to tell me that you don't give opinions because you feel inferior to me: this is only an excuse for your laziness.

C. PAVESE

January 13, 1926

Dear Sturani,

I'm sending you only this poem:

> To wander through the lonely streets
> continuously tormented by the terror
> of seeing the long-desired creations
> vanish before my very eyes,
> to feel passion, hope . . . everything . . . everything
> grow weaker within my soul
> and so remain with neither love
> nor greatness, small and vulgar,
> condemned to daily sadness
> and with the incessant thought
> that countless men already suffered

what I'm suffering now
and died in obscurity, without rising
to a light of glory, desperate.
In my grief nothing is left to me,
not even the pride of feeling alone!

C. PAVESE

Turin, February 4, 1926

Dear Sturani,

It's not I, but my sister who's writing you, because I'm in bed. Let's hope it lasts. I won't write you about anything important because I don't like to reveal myself to strangers, and in this case my sister is a stranger.

I don't know how to judge your poems because there's something too modern in them which I—perhaps it's a question of temperament—am unable to feel, or better yet, am afraid to feel. Besides, this is a compliment.

That famous work I told you about two years ago is coming along, with great difficulty, but coming along nevertheless. For now that's all I'm going to say about it, but if I finish it, you'll be the first to read it (you'll be the first one to have the misfortune of reading it). I've exhausted all my poetic resources and have nothing more to send you. And then, here in bed, I feel more like sleeping than thinking. You can work, so get on with it. As for me, my will to work gets feebler every day, but if I lose it altogether, I shall kill myself. You'll deliver my eulogy, and I assure you that's nothing to laugh about.

Greetings,
C. PAVESE

May 10, 1926

Cheer up! You're not the only one who's grown lazy. Now that it's exam time, I, being the way I am, must study, or at least appear to be studying desperately hard, and I don't have a minute of that freedom which is the only thing that induces enjoyable study. I can say that my entire inner life is turning into a very eager, mechanical, and very stupid effort to memorize. But this summer I'd like to get my revenge.

As soon as exams are over I'll be able to tell you when and how you can come to Reaglie.

I've heard nothing more, so far, from the *Ricerca di Poesia*.[15] I feel somewhat consoled by your words about my little poems. The only thing in the world that sustains me is the hope that now or later, I can do something worthwhile with my pen. That too seems an empty dream when I really start to think about it. But let's drop the subject, since it's not good to pass intentionally to others our own syphilis. . . .

Now that we have reached the end, here is my final thrust, by treachery, under the guise of four verses written down in a moment of desperate exaltation:

Without a woman to clasp to my heart!
Never have I had one, never shall I have one. Alone, exhausted
by immense passionate desires
and incessant thoughts, without aim . . .

CESARE PAVESE

January 9, 1927

With the two strophes you sent me to begin the new year well, it appears you are trying to reproduce a state of mind by describing a series of phenomena, or, more simply, of small events that had inspired this state of mind in you or at least accompanied it. Now then, I'll tell you, you don't succeed at all in the first strophe.

The facts you chose are too disparate, without an underlying link, namely the feeling or feelings you wanted to express.

The conclusion then, is banal and springs up like a mushroom, without having been prepared by the preceding images. Moreover, it lacks that harmony of free verse which is the first condition in tying together the different parts, since it is the music of the sentiment only that must pervade the piece from beginning to end.

In short, it seems that throughout your journey, while the most different things passed through your mind, you had, from time to time, written down whatever struck your eyes and ears (*written*

down for memory's sake and not for poetic representation). It
seems that you then added to those notes, only to have a proper
conclusion, a thought (you yourself say *I thought*), an incidental
thought expressed in a verse I would have expected from
Vaudagna, not from you.

But *to my misfortune,* your lack of strength is never absolute.

The second strophe, although it is not one of your masterpieces,
seems to have quite a different value. In fact, in this work your
notes are no longer chaotic. And so, even one who judges the
words alone would perceive in them a feeling that is carried
throughout the strophe and pervades all the scattered descriptions.
This feeling is a desire for solitude: "barred doors," "deserted
streets," "being alone," etc.

Then there is silence and the desire for things *subdued*, "light" and
"humble," as you say: "dim light," a "dairy bar," "the sound of the
pendulum," "the water dripping from a tap," "the color and smell
of milk," "to slice bread," and "to drink from a bowl." (This work
of infinite detail makes me shiver, and to think that this will be my
life's work!)

Then there is order and what one would call a small successful
drama, the passage from the deserted winter street to the warmth of
the dairy bar and the accompanying sensations.

Naturally, all this is aided by the rhythm. For example, the
aforementioned passage is marked in its rapid and sudden
movement by that "*to enter,*" single and incisive after the long
preceding verse, a final hesitation of someone walking and searching
outside. And then as soon as he enters, he is immediately in that
environment: the dripping of water and the smell of milk. It's very
beautiful.

In conclusion, perhaps your problem is that you write poetry too
often. Those first verses reflect a desperate effort to *write*.

It might be that I lack that poetic soul I'd like to have, but I say
to you that a poem of mine costs me, before I begin to write it,
entire months of life and suffering.

See if I'm not by now, the perfect professor!

But listen here to the antidote. I wrote these verses on January 4
at three in the morning, after an evening of wandering and three
hours of meditative crisis in my room.

Listen to how well I began the year. (It will seem to you like a
search for the tragic, but it's not so: it's *all* true.)

I went, one evening in December,
along an all deserted little country road
with turmoil in my heart.
I had a gun with me.
When I was sure to be well distant
from every dwelling, I pointed it to the ground
and pressed the trigger. It jolted at the blast
with a rapid jump, so that I felt
as if I were shaking it alive in that silence.
It truly shook between my fingers
at the sudden light that burst
from the barrel. It was like the spasm,
the last atrocious fit of one who dies
a violent death. I replaced it
then, still warm, inside my pocket
and I resumed my way. Thus, walking
among the naked trees, I imagined
the tremendous jolt it will give
on the night when the last illusion
and the fears will have abandoned me
and I will place it against my temple
to shatter my brain.

Greetings,
PAVESE

P.S.: Write often, be thrifty, and take care of your health.

Dear Mario,

The moment I received you letter I dashed off a reply. That was three weeks ago, and after continuous postponements I have finally decided to make a fresh copy. I'm feeling rather lazy, and can't be bothered to make all the necessary changes on the rough copy.

Here is the document. At one time I was inclined to indulge in an affectation of melancholy, and you lectured me against it for the sake of dignity, strength and idealism. It seems it's now my turn to assist a wavering friend. But cheer up, I don't know how to *persuade,* so I shall not even write to you with that purpose in mind.

I have felt the way you are feeling now, on countless occasions, yet I'm still alive, as you see, and I've written things that you've told me were not too bad.

Remind yourself that your field is painting and related arts, and you can give to poetry only your spare moments. I, on the other hand, am compelled to give my whole life to poetry.

But then, of course, to each of us our own things seem poor and pretentious, while the work of others strikes us as highly original, simply because it is easier to be impressed by what someone else has said. . . .

Incidentally, I must say that my own situation is very odd. I'm trying to cheer up someone who is depressed, and at the same time I'm writing verses as joyful as those of the gun. But it is a fact that since the night I put my state of mind in those verses, my mind has stopped tyrannizing me. If one had the will and the time, there will be material to write a treatise on *Art as the liberation from the egotistic immanence of life and as the assumption to superior forms of mysticism, of ascetic and objective contemplation, etc.*

Keep cheerful, and when you least expect it you will give life to a beautiful verse, like your usual ones so wonderfully decorative and intense: "Archangels in the darkness of my sleep," etc.

But who knows? While I'm rambling on like this, you may already have prepared for me some triumphant act of faith! I would be envious, very envious. Nevertheless, I would accept it with bowed head, *resignedly,* as you say that life must be accepted. But I would like to throw kicks and punches instead.

CESARE P.

April 8, 1927

I haven't written to you lately because I had nothing to send you, and so much to tell you that I didn't know where to begin.

Finally tonight, when I'm moved by spring, I'll manage to put down on paper some account of my "*true self.*"

First I must tell you I shall not write anymore. I shall not write anymore, I'm almost certain of it. I no longer have the strength, and besides, I have nothing to say. After having arrived at the verses of the gun, I can only put down the pen and go on to the action.

For the past three months I've lived in an agony of uncertainty: shall I do it or shall I not.

What is terrifying is that bloody shattering of the brain and skull.

In my latest passion, the one with the ballerina, I thought I had definitely reached the point, but I hadn't the courage.

Now I'm carrying on passively, amusing myself, forgetting myself, studying *for the exams*; not for myself anymore, since my longing for higher things is dead.

Recent events have definitely taught me a lot about myself: I am incompetent, timid, lazy, uncertain, weak, and half mad. Never, never shall I be able to settle into a permanent job and make what is called a success in life. Never, never.

I no longer have the energy required for this achievement, for I know it would be useless: I would not succeed. Even if I did, would it be worth the trouble?

From now on, I mean to make the least possible effort in life. But it won't go on like this, it can't go on. Too many ferments torment me.

Since, as I said, I shall never manage to control these fermenting impulses, see what state I'm in!

I am not able to drink and to brutalize myself. I would like to, but I can't. I'm just a fool. As for cocaine or morphine, heaven knows what they cost! That way I should at least have the exaltation of a grandiose end! But no! I haven't the courage. I am a child, a cretin, and a "poseur"!

More probably I shall masturbate myself to death.

Although I behave like a desperate man, think how lucky I am that no woman has ever accepted me: with the fine personality I have now, we would both be in trouble.

Pavese is dead.

Write and tell me what you've done and what you'll be doing: I still enjoy talking about such things.

Don't worry about sending me a consoling letter; I know how annoying that can be. Don't even try to cheer me up. Let me enjoy my depression in peace.

CESARE PAVESE

Reaglie, July 14, 1927

Dear Mario,

Here is an unusual, imaginative composition in free verse. It is a
true novelty for me:

Gardens

Often I stop before the windows
of the perfumeries. And all those
colors arranged inside clear little bottles
trimmed with beautiful ribbons,
amid the powders, the puffs, the mirrors,
and the little, fragile items
shiny, shiny
that will pass through frail feminine hands
and, while waiting, they seem to have already assumed
    their fragility and dreamy shape.
or delightful oval soaps,
the little atomizers, the hairnets;
but above all the perfumes, the beautiful perfumes scattered
in strange order
on the crystal shelves
where the most beautiful colors mix in a diaphanous shade:
above all the perfumes capture my soul
and force my eyes,
the inept eyes of a coarse stranger,
to remain suspended
in the prodigy made of a thousand tiny wonders,
and then my mind is filled by one thought:
the thought that no earthly scattering of flowers
living under the vibrant sun, shaken by the wind
or damp under the sky,
with its own odor strong and wild,
nor the most beautiful mixtures of flowers
arranged by light hands
breathing stupors of perfume,
nothing, nothing that's called nature,
seasons, gifts man pulls out of the earth,
nothing to me is worth the frozen garden,
clear, immobile under the crystals,

where the most marvelous offerings of the seasons,
the colors and the smells
are gathered divinely in small glass bottles
and have the shape of the feminine dream:
a transparent frailty,
almost crystal purity,
that at times sings a note of its own which is light,
        ineffably serene,
but other times, pervaded
by an intense green soul,
or dark, desperate,
breathes all around
in labyrinths of depravation,
in fatigue of decadence,
in stenches of death.
And near me pass females
with scanty clothes
revealing each shape,
some of them all permeated,
tormented and consumed
terribly, with no more escape,
by the small objects of dream,
immobile, behind the great crystal;
others are all freshness,
as if their body, their life
were nothing but a full, uninterrupted, inebriating song,
and all of them, with this shape and others,
and infinite ones never known,
create another wonderful garden
as vast as the earth,
of which this crystal one is nothing but the proud image
gathered in a small space, perfume in a little bottle.
And with the stars in the sky,
the highest garden woven with darkness and light,
so simple as to make children clap their hands,
so awesome as to make saints shudder,
they form my great garden of life,
where I suffer and rejoice continuously
and, grieving to give some song to my flowers,
I await death, the last song, the most beautiful.

And this is why I happen to stop
before the fantastic windows of the perfumeries.

I demand a prompt reply and a critique. Thank you.

C. PAVESE

This collection of lyceum letters is not important so much for the value of the poems Pavese enclosed in them, as for its testimony to the moods that were already at that time clashing within him. The letters show, first of all, how Pavese passed from pride to self-destruction, and how he went on, even in Tagore, to discover those similar to himself. They also show how melancholy weighed on his heart when he was still a boy, and how for him, "no joy surpassed the joy of suffering." If this is not masochism, it is certainly the worst and most dramatic "Pavesism," which would lead him, in life, to beat his head even against imaginary obstacles.

An attentive reader of Dante's *Vita Nova,* he wanted to aim at great things, to have a great destiny, and to write "something that would last forever." At that age he already knew how to present serious theories on art; but right next to them he wrote that the only hope left for him in the world was to be worth "something at the pen."

The arc from his youth to the end of his life was brief. In those young years he committed suicide imaginatively, in the poem of the gun. And he analyzed himself, as we have read in one of his letters to Sturani, as being "incompetent, timid, lazy, uncertain, weak, and half mad," with no ability "to settle into a permanent job and make what is called a success in life." The terrible thing is that this would not just be a declaration made in a moment of depression, but would remain the web in which his life would be entangled. At eighteen he had already written: *Pavese is dead.* And if, immediately afterward, he announced that he had to return to the struggle, it was only to devote his entire life to poetry.

His struggle, as he explained it, consisted exclusively in persevering in the search for the "isolation men of genius know." He could not achieve resignation and, for this reason, in the final poems of the revealing collection of his lyceum letters, death is still the protagonist. It is the same death to which he would sacrifice himself, invoking it again in the final desolate verses:

> Death will come and it will have your eyes—
> this death which accompanies us
> from morning to night, sleepless,
> deaf, like an old remorse
> or an absurd vice.

This was the same "absurd vice" that tormented his lyceum years and entered into his blood like a disease. It was his "syphilis," as he wrote, a kind of suicidal fever that, as soon as it had gone, quickly returned, incurable.

To soothe this fever, only poetry and women were of use. The rest did not exist. The life around him, the events of the world, of his town, of Turin, had no importance for him. Yet in those years Fascism was present all over. In the schools as in the factories, and above all in Turin, the city that remained hostile and closed, every method was tried by the Fascists. People spoke of it everywhere, they discussed it in cafés, in the streets, and in school.

Pavese seemed deaf to all this. But it was not so. Even in his letters to Sturani, the events that struck him most directly were not revealed except in the hints of his poetry. For example, he did not write to Sturani about an episode that he would never forget. It was a suicide, that of his schoolmate and friend, Baraldi. The enterprising Baraldi, the one who had already found himself a girlfriend. More decisive than Pavese, he knew how to be liked by women and to win them. The news of his friend's suicide chilled him. How could this have happened? Baraldi of all people, so sure of himself, so fortunate, and so happy?

The manner in which the suicide was committed shook him up even more tragically. Baraldi and his girlfriend had gone to Bardonecchia, a town in the mountains where Baraldi's family had a home, determined to kill themselves with two gunshots. The boy kept his promise while the girl managed to save herself.

Baraldi's suicide crushed Pavese and drove him to a rash action.

Three days later, when Professor Monti told him of having encountered Baraldi's father returning from the cemetery, destroyed by grief, Pavese decided to go to Bardonecchia and kill himself. He took a revolver with him. He did not have a girlfriend and could not die for love like his friend, but he had to carry out the same act, although for different reasons. Above all, he had to prove to himself that he was as decisive and courageous as his friend. In front of the same tree against which Baraldi had fallen dead, Pavese pulled out his gun. But he did not have the heart to shoot; his desire to live was still too strong, and he fired the shots against the tree. He returned home, ashamed of his cowardice, more dejected, and more desperate. From that day on the spectre of suicide would return ever more insistently.

Baraldi's suicide was not the only one during those years. The son of Professor Predella, who was the same age as Pavese, also took his own life. At this time a chain of suicides spread through Turin. They were perhaps a consequence of that tormented postwar period, a collective madness that pushed men and women to escape their anxieties by poisoning or shooting themselves. The shots of war were followed by other shots, the dead by other dead. Italy had not found its order or its peace. War continued within its consciences.

5

The University

The last year of lyceum was at an end. Strained by study yet sure of himself, Pavese passed the very hard university entrance exam. The time had come for him to bid farewell to the D'Azeglio lyceum's gray building, to his professors and his schoolmates, but someone made it possible for the circle of the best students not to break up. That someone was Augusto Monti. The severe teacher became an industrious friend. His frown was replaced by a smile and paternal advice. He put Pavese and his classmates in contact with other university students who had also attended D'Azeglio.

Under the auspices of Monti, the fraternity of ex-students of D'Azeglio was born. Of all its members, Pavese was the one Monti wished to follow most attentively. He was sure of Cesare's talent and seriousness in study, but he was also aware of his complexity and knew he had no one in his family to rely on as a guide. Monti too was Piedmontese. Like Pavese, he came from the Langhe, from Monastero Bormida, not far from Santo Stefano. He was afraid that the boy would lose himself. He remembered the sadness that would take hold of him even at his school desk, and his answers which often went far beyond the questions. Pavese, in turn, had always understood the teacher's concern for him. And it was to his former teacher that he wrote his first letter after his final exam.

I spoke with Augusto Monti. He still remembered that letter, sentence by sentence, and repeated it to me himself. In the first part,

Pavese dealt with classical writers, with frequent quotations, to show Monti that he had assimilated his teachings and thereby to express his gratitude. Because of his natural reserve and innate aversion to flattery, he thanked the teacher very briefly for helping him learn the classics so effectively. Then, suddenly, the letter changed its tone and Pavese was confessing things which until then he had jealously kept to himself. The tough teacher had thus conquered the heart and not just the intelligence of the student.

Pavese expressed to Monti his desire to be, with women, a man as strong and virile as all the others, referring to an episode from Horace: "I read, in an unexpurgated edition, a story that suits me, which tells of a well-known personality who, coming out of a brothel, gives a young man Cato's excellent advice to descend, when driven by necessity, into a place such as that. 'For similar releases,' he said, 'one comes here, instead of going into the streets to bother the girls.'" Then Pavese told his teacher that he behaved as the Horatian youth did.

If we reflect upon the timidity, secrecy, and sullenness we already had occasion to notice in Pavese's character, this need to have his professor know his private life assumes a very strange significance. At the same time, it is the indication of a complex that would become aggravated in Pavese with the passing years.

Another episode that again linked Monti to Pavese reveals a virtue that Cesare always obstinately kept hidden: his gentleness of heart. It was he, in fact, who took the initiative of sending, as a memento to his ex-teacher, the class picture of the third Lyceum B with students and teachers posing together. The only one missing from the group is Augusto Monti, who did not care to be photographed. Under the picture Pavese wrote: "No quotations and no long phrases, since you taught us to consider men of letters as the last thing in life. We will show you our gratitude through our work."

Besides being a demonstration of affection, these few words indicated that Pavese, upon entering the university, wanted to make a choice and a pledge to his teacher. Never having made a mystery to himself or others of his desire to become a writer, he declared, out of loyalty to Monti, that he did not want to be merely "a man of letters," but to force himself to produce works worthy of a new Italian, of a "hater of tyrants."

Those were times which imposed political and cultural choices on everyone, particularly on young people. On one side was Fascism, on the other were active anti-Fascist movements. Culturally, it was a matter of choosing to yield to the Fascist rhetoric, to avoid it without taking an adversary position, or to work for something new, for an out-and-out liberal renewal.

While Italy was at that time full of conformists, servile journalists, hermetics for convenience's sake, and Catholics herded with Fascists, Turin remained the city of political and cultural resistance. Out of Turin came the most important political and cultural movements of Antonio Gramsci and Piero Gobetti. Even after these two anti-Fascist thinkers had been imprisoned and could no longer be with the masses and with other intellectuals, their ideas would inspire the revival that gave Turin an unmistakable pre-eminence.

During Pavese's university years, these two voices had already been silenced and their comrades were forced to work clandestinely. Pavese showed no interest in politics. To whoever asked him why, he repeated his political indifference with the words: "Only I know."

In the meantime, Monti, pulling strings from his summer retreat in Cavour, or from his "self-exile" in Giaveno, had put Pavese in contact with young people committed on both cultural and political levels. It is enough to name a few: Ginzburg, Vittorio Foà, Tullio Pinelli, Norberto Bobbio, Enzo Giacchero, and Massimo Mila. All these youths had taken a road very different from the more or less conformist movements then dominant. They were neither in the movement of "Strapaese" nor in that of "Stracittà." "Strapaese" defined itself as the only cultural movement in which one breathed Italian air and thought in the Italian manner; in fact, in an "arch-Italian" manner. Its supporters repeatedly affirmed their will to remain faithful to the Italian tradition until they revived it and made its greatness felt again. Their tradition was, in reality, nothing more than the grafting of Roman-Fascist rhetoric, and their purpose, to encourage men of culture to become "patriots" and "perfect Fascists." Behind this movement were landowners and reactionaries who used "Strapaese" to give a cultural justification to Fascism, exploiting a confused idealism capable of encouraging reckless and violent action. Not all the writers who joined "Strapaese" fully understood this political undertone, and perhaps did not even want it, but they accepted it in practice.

Even the followers of "Stracittà" were forced to cover themselves with the Fascist shield. They wanted to put an end to the remains of the nineteenth century, to naturalism, aestheticism, sentimentalism, and the petty values of the middle class, committing themselves to writing that would become an act of energy rather than an uninspired chronicle. They sought to rediscover a sense of mystery, groped for a balance between heaven and earth, without, however, having the courage to deal with the reality that surrounded and imprisoned them.

In their noisy encounters, the ex-students of D'Azeglio found the time to discuss these issues. When they did not meet at one another's homes or at Sturani's studio, they gathered at the inns in the outskirts of Turin. To distinguish themselves from "Strapaese" and "Stracittà," they chose a name that referred to the city limits: "Strabarriera." Pavese took pleasure in the discussions with the other members of "Strabarriera" and felt at ease in the inns, together with the workers and the street vendors. Many of these people would become characters in his novels. Even Monti would join them, almost every Saturday. When he retreated to the country, his ex-students went to visit him. In one of those encounters at Giaveno, Pavese brought his first short stories to read to the teacher.

Those stories did not please Monti, for two principal reasons— not so much matters of style, but of content. His first objection was that they were imitations of D'Annunzio; the second, more serious, regarded the endings of the stories themselves, namely the suicide Pavese imposed on the various characters.

Pavese was annoyed and disturbed by the accusation that he was imitating D'Annunzio, but after much discussion, he recognized it as just. He replied to the second accusation more fiercely and obstinately. He felt that those desperate endings suited the characters, and were indispensable. Did they not follow the reality of daily life, in which there were so many suicides? The discussion with Monti became a dispute. Monti did not give in and Pavese rebelled. Then the old teacher got the upper hand. Pavese was more frightened than convinced, because he saw himself in the characters. In recounting their suicides he not only recalled the cases of Baraldi, Predella, and others, but he ended up repeating the thoughts jotted down in his lyceum letters to Sturani.

The university created new friendships and Pavese's circle of friends grew larger. At the center of the fraternity was Leone Ginzburg, who would soon become the political brain of the group. Leone was able to win everyone's respect and friendship without effort. He was already well-read and had many interests: social, cultural, and political. Ginzburg knew how to discuss each issue and everyone listened attentively to him. He was the only one who constantly brought politics into the discussion, and even Pavese, who persisted in his aversion to it, was so fond of him that he would listen to his political arguments. Leone knew how to insist, fight, convince, and make one think. When Monti did not meet with the group, it was Ginzburg who took his place, leading, with the teacher's stubbornness and assurance, the debates on fundamental issues.

Together with Ginzburg, Norberto Bobbio entered the group. He came from a family different from the ones of Pavese's other friends. His house was the best furnished and the most hospitable. Norberto's father was a celebrated surgeon and his brother a fine connoisseur of music. In the Bobbio home the group found new friends in the Giacchero brothers, one of whom knew how to play the piano and sing, talents that rendered him indispensable at the gatherings for lively parties. Argan, Laguzzi, Martelli, Chabod, Giulio Einaudi, Giua, and Geymonat often joined them. Geymonat was the one who introduced the most advanced political ideas and who was nicknamed "the moralizer" for his habitual austerity.

Caught up in the vivacious circle of that collective life, Pavese seemed tranformed. He had conquered solitude and sulkiness; it was finally a period, perhaps his only one, of serenity. His favorite pastime was going to the movies. He became a fan of American films and a good judge of the actors, actresses, and directors. That interest in cinema would leave traces in many of his works.

It was also the time of his intense readings and discussions of Benedetto Croce's works. Pavese grasped his philosophy and his aesthetics. In the light of his Crocean studies, he revised many of his beliefs and scrutinized all his theories, but he would later modify many positions he had acquired from Croce.

Perhaps it was only in those years that Pavese felt young, and found life appealing in all its aspects. He even felt at ease when he collaborated with his friends in writing the verses of a "Pornoteca," in which each one demonstrated his poetic qualities and pornographic inspiration. And when, in the Bobbio home, Giacchero would sing the popular songs of the time, Pavese would follow each song with a parody in the aesthetic style of Benedetto Croce.

In the summer, he often returned to Santo Stefano, sometimes in the company of his old and new friends. His mother had sold their farm in 1918 and since then, when Pavese went to Santo Stefano, he stayed with relatives, most frequently with his cousin Battista.

He spent his longer vacations in Reaglie, where his mother had purchased a small home. In the hills of Reaglie, Pavese often brought the entire gang of his friends to carouse. His mother and sister were kept busy in turning out pans and pans of "bugie," a Piedmontese specialty, which the young men fully enjoyed with an abundance of good wine, while taking turns in reading aloud their poems and short stories. The poems, often satiric, were immediately set to music, and sometimes Pavese would read and act out his stories in Piedmontese dialect.

However, the site for Pavese's favorite pastimes was, particularly in those years, the great Po River. More than Santo Stefano or Reaglie, the river became for him a true refuge from the city. The Po soothed his nerves and allowed him a rest from studying and writing because it put him more rapidly in touch with the trees, water, grass, and greenery of the woods. Pavese was always ready to go to the river. All his friends knew that it was his only hobby. He did not care for the mountains, for sports, or for playing cards; he only loved to swim and row in the river. Almost every day Pavese, with a group of friends, took the Number 7 tram to the outskirts of the city. Then they continued on foot along a downhill road, which suddenly opened onto the country. In no time they were at the river.

It was Pavese who shouted the ferryman's name so that he would come and transport them to the other side. It was a strange name: Tofò. Soon after the first crossings, Tofò and Pavese became good friends. He was the type of man Pavese liked: honest, witty, always ready with sayings in dialect, one who knew all the Piedmontese proverbs.

At Pavese's call, Tofò arrived calmly, on his flatboat. He was distinguishable from a distance because of the old waistcoat, fastened at its only remaining button, with his Buddha stomach shining in the sun, and he was always smiling. His house was on the river. His work was to ferry whoever wished to cross from one bank to the other. He lived the kind of life that Pavese would later make many characters of his stories live.

This was the time when Pavese translated *Moby-Dick*, his favorite novel. On the river he imagined the atmosphere of Melville's novel and he saw Captain Ahab in himself or in Tofò.

The dock at which they arrived seemed a part of nature and was as simple as the trees: no signs, cabanas, or varnished boats. Only the barges of fishermen were moored there. As soon as they were in the boat, headed up the river toward Moncalieri, Pavese took over as helmsman. Standing in the center of the boat, he directed the slow navigation with the assurance of an old sailor. The physical strain elated him and the contact with the river and with nature transformed him. Baked by the sun, he had none of the anxieties that seized him on evenings in the city. His asthma and headaches disappeared. He dominated his companions with his physical strength.

Pavese knew the riverbed by heart, as Ahab knew the whims of the sea. He knew when to exert pressure on the oar and when to let the boat go along with the current, and was proud of his skill, which increased with every trip. On the way back to the dock, when the boat moved along the river almost by itself, Pavese would lie down, with his eyes half-closed, watching the clouds, the forests, and the hills on the horizon.

He also observed ever more attentively the inns with the arbors visible through the trees on the shore, the bocce lawns from which came voices and applause, and the gasoline pumps, shiny under the sun. This was the Po Pavese loved, the Po which began where the city ended, linking the people of the city with the people of the country. In his encounters along the riverbanks, he found the relaxed wisdom of the peasants, rich in maxims and proverbs, as well as the quick sense of humor and joking attitude of the city workers.

Pavese returned restored from those adventures on the Po. Then he would even join in the discussions in which he usually did not take part. The D'Azeglio fraternity frequently debated the issue of industrialization in their city. They wanted Turin to become a bold and modern capital, a true industrial metropolis. When they held these discussions in the trattorias, they found that the workers agreed with them. And every anti-conformist action in the cultural area found solidarity in the D'Azeglio group; every artist who tried to interpret current social issues became a symbolic figure for them to defend. One example: the painter Casorati, who had been a friend of Gobetti and had remained an anti-Fascist. His studio was visited with respect by Pavese and the rest of the fraternity. In the wooden figures of men and women that Casorati painted at the time, they saw more, perhaps, than he wanted to communicate. For them, those huge feet, large hands, and weary figures represented workers deformed by labor, by exploitation, by Fascism. They saw in them a denunciation of the offenses against man in a mistaken society.

This experience and many others of the same significance enriched Pavese's university years. The warmth of those human contacts, of those discussions, the passion that he put into his studies, all this seemed to save him from dejection and disenchantment.

In the meantime he had been writing his graduation thesis. This work, which would cause a sensation in the university and forecast Pavese's cultural developments as well as his literary and artistic predilections, analyzed the poetry of Walt Whitman.

Pavese had worked on it with his usual dedication, and when he read it to his friends, some were perplexed and amazed. They discovered in those pages and interpretations, a new Pavese, more logical, more critical, able to reveal, through documentation and original analysis, a poet at that time almost unknown in Italy. But there was more. The Crocean aesthetic, viewed with hostility by the Fascists, had been completely assimilated by Pavese.

That courageous work caused him his first bitter difficulties. The thesis was rejected. The professor attributed a political interpretation to the Crocean influence and Pavese was given the alternative of revising his dissertation or changing the topic. He did not give in and peremptorily refused to do either. He was saved by Leone Ginzburg, a student already on familiar terms with the most influential professors, who cleverly used his connections to win Pavese the right to defend his original thesis with Professor Ferdinando Neri. Pavese graduated with the highest marks.

6

The Woman with
the Hoarse Voice

During his final university years, Pavese had an encounter that would affect his entire existence. He met the only woman he would ever really love. Until then his relations with women, although followed by acts of desperation and fainting fits, were manifestations of his exaggerated emotion, not of love. It was with this woman that Pavese experienced the fullness of his feelings. He was captivated by her from the day they met.

We shall give no other name to this woman than the one used by Pavese in the poems of *Work Wearies*: "the woman with the hoarse voice." The harmony of Pavese's life was broken by his involvement with her; it was a crucial turning point. In losing her, he would lose his hope, his tenderness toward women, his sense of masculinity, his hope for fatherhood and family. He would even see his childhood in a different light, and all his works would reflect this love, betrayal, and disenchantment.

The woman with the hoarse voice was not very beautiful, but she had a firm, cool, and strong-willed personality. She was as good as a man in sports, and her chosen field at the university, mathematics, was the opposite of Pavese's choice in the humanities.

It was not difficult to recognize when Pavese was in love. But this time he kept the name of his loved one secret and remained impenetrably silent at his friends' curiosity. He confided in Sturani only when he thought that she returned his love, but as soon as his friend advised him to be cautious, he brusquely refused to listen to him anymore.

For Pavese, this woman was different from the others. Her fascination came from her strength, masculine attitudes, hard features, and decisive, self-assured character. The timid Pavese felt he had a companion and a protector who encouraged and defended him. His weak character and the constant doubts that tormented him found a solution and strength in her. With her he felt that he could hope, that he could live and think without fears for the future.

Here we must refer back to the letter written to Professor Monti after the lyceum final exam in which Pavese tried to show, through the episode of the Horatian student, that he was a man as able and virile as others. Evidently the love he felt for the woman with the hoarse voice gave him the assurance that he could behave like the man described in that letter. Perhaps only at this time did he believe himself able to learn the "business of living" not only in books, work, and self-doubt.

Throughout the time he felt that he had this woman beside him, Pavese appeared more human, natural, and happy than in any other moment of his life. His timidity became tenderness; his discomfort in front of women turned into confidence. His tragedy would begin as soon as he realized that this woman would reject and leave him without pity.

After that betrayal, Pavese would present every woman in his short stories and novels as only a creature of flesh, or as the embodiment of indifference and infidelity. The shadow that would weigh heavily upon women would always be that of pain and desperate contempt. Some of the most intense themes of *Work Wearies* derive from Pavese's relationship with the hoarse-voiced woman. Here is a poem that was part of the first edition of *Work Wearies*, but excluded from the second Einaudi edition. Under its dramatic title, it evokes images of Pavese in a boat on the Sangone River, with his woman.

Betrayal

This morning I am no longer alone. A new woman
lies here and burdens the prow
of my boat which moves slowly in the water now tranquil
after an icy and turbulent night.
I came from the Po that roared in the sun
with echoes of rapid waves and workers,
I made, teetering, the difficult turn
into the Sangone. "What a dream!" she observed
without moving her supine body, her eyes at the sky.
There is not a soul around and the banks are high
and narrower upstream, crowded by poplars.

How awkward the boat is in this tranquil water!
Standing at the stern to keep it in balance,
I see that the boat advances slowly: the prow is sinking
under the weight of a woman's body, wrapped in white.
She told me that she is lazy, and she has not yet stirred.
She remains reclining and gazes, alone, at the tops of the trees
as if she were in bed, and she burdens my boat.
Now that she has put a hand in the water and lets it skim,
she is also crowding my river. I cannot look at her—
on the prow where she stretches her body—as she turns her head
and curiously stares at me from below, moving her shoulders.
When I asked her to come in the center, leaving the prow,
she answered me with an impish smile: "You want me near you?"

Other times, drenched from a violent plunge among the trunks
        and the stones,
I continued to push toward the sun, until I was drunk,
and landing here in this spot, I hurled myself to the ground
blinded by the water and the rays, the pole thrown away,
to calm my fatigue at the breath
of the plants and in the embrace of the grass.

Now the shade is oppressive
on the sweat which burdens the blood, and on the tired limbs;
and the vault of the trees filters the light
of an alcove. I sit on the grass, not knowing what to say,
and I hug my knees. She has disappeared

into the forest of poplars, she is laughing and I must pursue her.
My skin is darkened by the sun and uncovered.
My companion, who is blonde, in placing her hands
into mine to land on the bank, has made me perceive,
with her delicate fingers, the perfume
of her hidden body. Other times the perfume
was the water dried on wood and the sweat in the sun.
My companion calls me with impatience. Dressed in white
she wanders among the tree trunks and I must pursue her.

The obsession with an adverse destiny, the fear of tiring her, the
terror of losing her, heightened the poem and gave it more warmth.
That woman brought back to him the enchantment of his childhood
in the hills of the Langhe. Let us read "Encounter," a poem from
Work Wearies, dated 1932:

These hard hills that have made my body
and stir it with so many memories, opened to me the wonder
of this woman, who does not know I live her and cannot
        understand her.
I met her one evening: a lighter speck
under the ambiguous stars, in the haze of summer.
Around there was the smell of these hills,
deeper than shadow, and suddenly rang out,
as if it had come out of these hills, a voice both clear
and harsh, a voice of lost times.

Sometimes I see her, and she comes before me
defined, immutable like a memory.
I have never been able to grasp her: her reality
eludes me every time and takes me far away.
I don't know if she is beautiful. Among women she is very young:
so young that I am caught, thinking of her, by a distant memory
of childhood spent in these hills.
She is like the morning. Her eyes suggest
all the distant skies of those faraway mornings.
And she has in her eyes a firm purpose: a light clearer
than the dawn has ever had on these hills.

I created her from the depths of all things
that are most dear to me, and I cannot understand her.

Pavese thus gathered his entire world in the hands of his woman: the hills, his childhood, the sky, and the mornings, limpid and remote, because "she is like the morning." Her harsh voice was the voice of the hills, of nature. With her, even the landscape acquired a human aspect.

Pavese remained attached to the woman with the hoarse voice even when he became afraid of losing her. She returned in his dreams, memories, and hallucinations. We see her again in "A Memory":

There is no man who can leave a trace
on her. What has been dissolves like a dream
in the morning, and only she lasts.
If, for a moment, a light shadow did not touch her brow,
she would always seem startled. Each time there is a smile
on her face.

Not even the days amass on her face
to alter the light smile
that radiates around her. She is firm
in all that she does, and each time seems the first;
yet she lives every moment.
Her hard body and her reticent eyes
unfold in a voice that is low and a little hoarse: the voice
of a tired man. And no tiredness can touch her.

If one stares at her lips, she cautiously offers
a waiting glance: no one dares a bold act.
Many men know her ambiguous smile,
the sudden shadow on her brow. If there is a man
who knew her moaning, humbled by passion,
now he suffers for it day after day, not knowing for whom
she is living today.

She smiles to herself
the most ambiguous smile, as she walks.

Suffering, disappointments, and betrayals would injure both the man and the poet. But if there were something for which he could hope, only that woman could awaken it. If he was still living, it was because she was still the life: "she lives every moment." And she alone was the family, when he burned with loneliness, longing for a child. Here are some verses from "Fatherhood":

> A man alone facing the useless sea,
> waiting for the evening, waiting for the morning.
> There are children playing, but this man would like
> to have a child of his own, to watch him play.
> . . . .
> . . . From the dark window
> comes a hoarse gasping, and no one hears it
> but the man, who knows all the tedium of the sea.

Again the hoarse voice. And it was again to this woman that Pavese returned in the poem "Work Wearies":

> . . . .
> Is it worth being alone to be always more lonely?
> When you just wander through the squares and streets,
> they're empty. You must stop a woman,
> talk to her and persuade her to live with you.
> . . . .
> . . . If they were two,
> even when he walked down the street, his home would be
> where the woman was and it would be worth it.

Perhaps no other writing by Pavese expresses his awareness of hopeless loneliness as much as this writing. It was still the hoarse-voiced woman who provided him with that awareness.

Other women had relationships with Pavese, and some appeared able to make him believe he was once again in love. However, these women, and those from his books, would be linked to that first unforgettable love. Often they served as outlets for his rancor. They became a pretext for his contempt and represented the weak beings on which he released his wrath, his disappointments, and his defeats. After the woman with the hoarse voice, at the center of Pavese's life would be only Pavese himself: his torment, and his poetry.

One cannot understand Pavese's expressions of anger without trying to penetrate his most secret side and grasp the consequences of his failure with the hoarse-voiced woman. Pavese wanted to succeed both in literature and with women. There is no short story, novel, or page in which the memory, the face, or the desire for a woman does not arise. His continuous anxiety was undoubtedly also due to his obstinate will to scourge himself and to curse his solitude, but its primary cause was always the woman.

Each new encounter was a painful effort to rediscover love and to reconcile sex and emotion, life and abandonment. It was a cruel drama that slowly affected his body, until he became convinced that he was sexually impotent. I remember the occasions when he would confide in me with shame on this subject. It was always at night, while we strolled in the darkness of the Turin boulevards. It was hard for me to free him from that concern, to find words of reassurance, or to recommend that he see a doctor. In his diary he wrote similar confessions with obstinate cruelty and perhaps he did so just because his fear of being impotent was unfounded. In fact, Pavese had the habit of assuming a role with others and with himself. He enjoyed performing this role in order to more painfully degrade himself.

Of the women who entered Pavese's life, at least five, after the woman with the hoarse voice, were able to give him some strength. The beautiful woman he encountered shortly before his death came from America and brought with her all the fascination Pavese felt for that country. During this period he wrote me that he received "an unexpected lark from America." Immediately he added, almost as if to diminish the happiness of his announcement: "She stopped near my sheaf of grain, only because she feels lost and wants me to help her fly in the skies of our country. But she will soon leave, I feel it. I will hear her wings flapping, and I will lack the strength to attempt a cry to call her back."

Pavese seemed transformed once again by that last love. He was able to abandon his increasingly modest and severe habits. Leaving his work behind, he ran to Rome with the American woman. He once again wandered through the streets, proud to know he still could walk hand in hand with a woman. From the city he went to the sea and to the mountains, always with her. In her, even if only briefly, he found trust and, perhaps, the illusion he could finally overcome the memory of the other woman.

I remember that in a photograph Pavese showed me in July 1950, during his last trip to Milan, his eyes were blissful as he stood next to her in front of the mountains. However, it was a brief time, just the space of a season. Like the woman with the hoarse voice, the lark from America had grown tired of the little warmth he could offer her, and she flew away.

I have never forgotten what he told me late one night in Milan: "She fled at night from my bed at the hotel in Rome and she went to bed with another, with that actor you know. Like the other woman, even worse. Do you remember the one from Turin? She is the one who ended it between me and women."

If a woman was not the sole cause of Pavese's suicide, she was the most immediate and constant inspirer of his suicidal thoughts. This was apparent from his youth on, from his letters to Sturani, through the last part of his life, when he wrote in his diary: "One does not kill oneself for the love of *a* woman. One kills oneself because a love, any love, reveals us in our nakedness, our misery, our impotence, our nothingness."

His persistent search for a woman, even after all the torments of betrayal and the desertion, must also be considered in measuring his struggle to learn "the business of living" and to resist his fascination with suicide. Undoubtedly, he realized more each day, while he felt more involved in the business of writing, that literature would not be sufficient to save him. Nor could he be rescued by political involvement or by those people to whom he attempted to attach himself at times, through sacrifices and difficult compromises.

He might possibly have been saved by the tenderness of a woman he could call his own, and by the warmth of a home life. Pavese, who regarded himself and wanted to be regarded only as a suffering man, rather than a complex man, probably needed the simplicity of a vital experience so common to others. His inability to realize this experience turned his feelings toward women from yearning to anger. This attitude is already apparent in some poems of *Work Wearies*. In "Ancestors" the women of the family are defined in the following way:

> And women do not count in our family,
> I mean, our women stay home
> and bring us into this world and say nothing,
> they just do not count and we forget them.
> Each woman puts in our blood something new,
> but they efface themselves in the process. . . .

In "Landscape I," the peasants of the village,

> sneer at the groups of women
> and ask when, dressed in goatskin,
> they will loaf in those hills and get black in the sun.

In the poem "He-goat God," women are represented as animals, and Pavese, between myth and reality, sees himself as the he-goat god "who sought the she-goat and butted his head against the tree trunks."

Pavese's schoolmates at the lyceum remembered that he behaved in a similar manner when, closed in his house, "tormented" by love, he beat his head against the walls.

The woman is identified with his solitude: bitter, both present and distant, untouchable and necessary. In "Landscape VII," he wrote:

> Everything in the sun ripples at the thought
> that the street is empty except for her.

And when the woman, here the hoarse-voiced woman, seems to withdraw from him, he identifies her with the disappearing moon, as in "Passionate Women":

> That unknown woman, who swam at night
> alone and naked, in the darkness when the moon changes,
> disappeared one night and has never returned.
> She was tall and she must have been dazzling white
> for those eyes to reach her from the bottom of the sea.

In "Burnt Lands" we encounter those women of the city who "know how to enjoy love":

> One arrives in Turin at night
> and sees at once along the streets
> the flirtatious women, dressed for the eyes, walking alone.
>
> . . . .
>
> . . . These women, who wait
> and feel they're alone, know life in depth.

And again, in "Tolerance":

> . . . The shutters
> on the house are closed, but inside there is a bed
> and on the bed a blonde earns her living.
> The whole town rests at night,
> everyone but the blonde
> who washes in the morning.

In "Deola Thinking":

> At the house she had to sleep at this hour
> to regain her strength: the mat by her bed
> was always soiled by the dirty shoes of workers and soldiers,
> the clients who wore out her back.

It was the time when Pavese desired and needed even casual encounters to somehow reassure his manhood. In "Adventures" he described a boy spying on the furtive love of cats:

> . . . At the first light of dawn
> also closed are the eyes of those cats in love
> whom the boy used to spy on. The female cat wails
> for she is without her mate.
> Nothing is worthwhile—
> neither the treetops nor the red clouds—
> she wails at the bright sky, as if it were still night.

But the love bought on the street, although better for Pavese than the total absence of love, begins to draw his contempt, as in these verses from "Portrait of the Author":

> I don't smell because I'm not hairy. The stone freezes
> my bare back that women like
> because it's smooth: is there anything women don't like?

And again in "Ballet":

> . . . The woman does not count,
> each night she is different, but she is always the small girl
> who laughs, and her little bottom dances when she walks.

It is the same motif in "Instinct":

> . . . She too,
> like all bitches, did not want to hear of it,
> but she had the instinct. The old man—
> not yet toothless—sniffed it and when night came
> they went to bed. It was beautiful, the instinct.

It is always the woman: bitch, she-goat, cat, lust, but always present and indispensable in his mind. She is present even in the noise of a cart rumbling along the road, in "The Wagoner":

> With the wagon moves a warmth
> that smells of taverns,
> of pressed breasts and clear nights

When the woman leaves, all becomes useless: nature, the trees, the sea, and the lights. From "Sad Supper":

> . . . It's cold at dawn,
> and the embrace of a body would be life.

In spite of the contempt, as soon as the face of a woman appears, a faint hope returns and with it a sense of attachment to life. The following are verses taken from "Nocturnal Pleasures":

> We all have a home that awaits in the dark
> and we return there: a woman waits for us in the dark
> lying alseep: the room is warm with smells.
>
> . . . .
>
> We will return tonight to the woman who sleeps,
> to search her body with ice-cold fingers

> and a warmth will stir our blood, a warmth
> of dark wet earth: a breath of life.

There is no poem in *Work Wearies* that does not carry the mark of a woman—and it is almost always that of the woman with the hoarse voice.

A large part of Pavese's life was a pursuit, happy and painful at the same time, of the woman. He anxiously tried to affirm his masculinity and suffered for the betrayals and for what he felt to be the irremediable bitch instinct of woman. He was continuously torn between his need for tenderness, for giving affection to the woman he loved, and the urge to transform himself into the he-goat god, to hurt her and himself, butting "his head against the tree trunks."

In the short stories written by Pavese from 1936 to 1939 and published posthumously by Einaudi, first under the title of *Festival Night* and then as part of *Short Stories*, women are the dominant theme.

Resentment often yields to pity, and on many occasions the apparent contempt is still affection. However, it would be futile to try to find, even among these many female characters, a happy and fortunate woman. Each woman is destined to adversity. One of them, disillusioned in love, kills herself.

In the short story "Honeymoon," Pavese endeavored to describe the kind of life he would have inflicted on his wife, had he married. He had already suffered the disappointment with the hoarse-voiced woman and wanted to convince himself that even if he had been able to realize the dream of having a wife, he would have treated her as an enemy. In this short story, it is the character Cilia who endures his misery and his temper. While she is happy with her husband, that happiness indisposes the man:

I would turn my head against her in our warm bed and lie close beside her as she slept, or was pretending to, my breath ruffling her hair. Then Cilia, with a drowsy smile, would put her arms around me. How different from the days when I woke alone, cold and disheartened, to stare at the first gleam of dawn! Cilia loved me. Once on her feet, another joy began for her: moving about, dressing, opening windows, looking at me stealthily. If I sat at my desk, she would move cautiously around me, so as not to disturb me; if I were about to leave the house, she would follow me with her eyes until I disappeared from sight. On my return, she would leap on her feet, ready.

However, Pavese, as the husband, reacts this way: "I felt a shadow of resentment at that sign of a joy I did not always share. 'She married me and she is enjoying it,' I thought."

So it happens that the man grows increasingly tired of her. The honeymoon ends with the husband's escape from the bedroom; if they return together to the city, it is only to waste away more years in their absurd union and mutual incomprehension.

In the short story "Land of Exile," a man in prison relates the story of his wife who has betrayed him, concluding: "Women are bitches. I am here leading a monk's life, and she gets herself laid."

In the short story "The Three Girls," the themes of contempt and of the misfortune a woman carries with her, are combined. Here one of the three girls talks about her friend:

That is Lucetta, who on rainy days calls men wicked. Lucetta is carefree and lives each moment, whether it be joyous or sad, the same way. She despairs only when her sardonic lover clearly tells her he has no intention of marrying her. She is anything but stupid, only a little crazy: she expects too much from life. She appears so indifferent as she strolls down the street laughing at men, but nothing is easier than to surprise her and catch her eyes full of desire. At times it seems to me that she is going around naked and does not know it. One evening while we were walking, we were approached by an obnoxious fellow. I pulled her away and kept silent. A few minutes later, Lucetta, somewhat upset, remarked, "Too bad there were not two of them."

And later on in the story, an old woman reproaches one of the girls, saying:

"Ah, Lidia, you're joking. You make my blood run cold at times. I know what you girls are like. You think it's enough to look men straight in the eyes like dogs and dominate them. You don't realize that the lowest, meanest, most stupid man can bend a woman, humble her, and crush her existence. So nature wanted it."

In another short story, "Suicides," there is again, together with his obsession with death, the haunting memory of the hoarse-voiced woman:

When I met Carlotta, I was just recovering from a bitter blow that almost cost me my life, and I experienced a grim amusement in walking through the deserted streets, fleeing from Carlotta who loved me. Before then, it had been my turn to spend nights and days humiliated and exasperated by the whim of a woman.

The revenge against women, already brooding in his mind, reaches its extreme when the man, besides making Carlotta suffer by neglecting her, even describes in detail the suicide of a friend to indirectly tell her what she should do. The story ends with Carlotta's suicide.

In the short novel *The Political Prisoner*, published in 1938 but conceived during the months of Pavese's political confinement in 1935–36, women are present in the solitude of the exile. All alone in his small room "before the useless sea," far from home, Turin and the Langhe, Pavese felt true loneliness and detested it. He remained unsociable with men, fearing to say or reveal too much; however, he sought the company of women. The memory of the hoarse-voiced woman tormented his nights, and he confessed that his heart, "lost in the hazy fragments of a dream," "suffered a carnal anguish."

Then suddenly Elena appeared, the female protagonist of this first short novel. "She had a plump and pale face: she used to dress in a tranquil black." It is she who sought him and who arrived one night at the door of his small room:

Elena appeared at the door, shut it behind her, and, as she closed the shutters, she leaned against them, black as mourning. She allowed herself to be embraced and kissed, whispering that he must be gentle. On her frightened face her eyes were moist with tears. Stefano understood it would not be necessary to speak and drew her toward him. The closed and lamp lit room was stifling.

The description of this first encounter with Elena tells us the nature of the contrast between Pavese's desire and his reaction as soon as a woman gave herself to him. Every woman, not only Elena, became suffocating. Since Elena was one of the many women who grew fond of him, Pavese rejected her. He could not love a woman who loved him; instead, he had to pursue the one by whom he was not loved. This is a fate common to many, but Pavese attributed it to his own inferiority. Elena is described, precisely, as one of those women who are completely devoted to men: "While she cried in Stefano's arms, she would whisper with excitment, 'Talk, I like it when you talk. Hug me. I am a woman. Yes, I am a woman. I am your little mother.'"

Pavese did not care for maternal or for submissive women. He wanted them strong, with minds of their own, even if they were perverse and unfaithful. The other women gave him only the pleasure of their bodies. At one point, in fact, Elena asks Stefano with trepidation: "Do you only want my body? . . ."

And a few pages later:

Elena did not talk much, but she would look at Stefano, trying to smile at him, with a yearning rendered maternal by her age. Stefano would have liked her to come in the morning, enter his bed like a wife and then leave like a dream that requires neither word nor compromise. Elena's slight hesitations, her timid way of speaking, her mere presence in fact, caused him a guilty uneasiness. . . .

All at once Stefano felt in his ear that somewhat awkward yet warm voice: "Do you really want me to stay for a few moments? Wouldn't you like to spend a whole night with me?"

"I'm a loner, you know that," said Stefano immediately, "there is beauty even in acting like this. Don't come at night. I love you this way."

This woman who asks for words of tenderness, entrusting herself completely to him, bores him. But there is more. The plot of the novel *The Political Prisoner* develops with the arrival of another woman, Concia, in Stefano's life. She is the woman he desires because he can never have her. His destiny becomes clear, and he makes this confession: "Here was the pain he had in his heart: his woman was Concia, the lover of a filthy old man and the lust of young boys. But would he have wanted her different?"

Why is it that Stefano, while having Elena, desires Concia? "She has an animalistic beauty. She is something between a statue and a goat. . . . She came from the mountains and was a real mountain goat, ready for all the he-goats."

Stefano, like Pavese, while desirous of every woman's embrace, became sad and bored the moment the embrace occurred, and dreamed of being in the arms of another woman: "If he only had had Concia in the room with him instead of Elena. . . . Stefano thought a lot about Concia, and he saw her as wild, he saw her as unattainable, willing to give herself once and then flee."

In Concia, goat and statue, mistress of a filthy old man, Pavese vented the embittered love he felt for the hoarse-voiced woman who no longer wrote to him and who would marry someone else the same day Pavese returned from exile.

Stefano would never have Concia, and his affair with Elena would end:

If one day Elena had dared a gesture, a word of true possessiveness, Stefano would have torn her from him. And even that pleasure renewed between them in the morning, which Elena affected to keep futile while enjoying it as something owed her, exhausted him and chained him too much to his prison.

Stefano returns, therefore, to his solitude; at this point another woman enters the story. She is Annetta, a young prostitute brought to the village where he is confined. Stefano visits the house where Annetta works, but when he enters her room and finds her ready, he decides, without fully understanding why, not to make love to her. The explanation will come later:

Stefano began to understand how much strength he derived from that poor Annetta he had casually left untouched. Yet this strength did not come from her, but from his own body that found a balance in itself and contributed an energetic peace even to his mind. He told himself how foolish it was for him to try to proudly isolate his thoughts and allow his body to exhaust itself in Elena. To be truly alone took only a trifle: to abstain.

We are, therefore, at the renunciation. With it, Pavese had the illusion of finding the solitude of mind and body necessary to attain that balance which, unfortunately, he would never realize.

7

The Other Women as Revenge

After a few years came the women of *The Harvesters*, the novel written in 1939. Pavese, disguised as Berto, the main character, departs from Turin, leaving behind the whores of Madame Angela, and Michela who slept with him while her lover was in prison. Away from the city, he now encounters the country girls of the Langhe. They are girls with rough skin, convulsive laughter, and inviting eyes, who are always exhausted from labor. There is Miliota who, "At twenty, had the skin of a man of forty, as coarse as the crockery she was eating from." And there are Miliota's three sisters, Gisella, Adele, and Pina, all with faces which "in the sun became burned and fuller."

The introduction of these women, who bring life to the novel, is completed when their father ". . . took off his belt and struck Gisella as if she were made of shoe-leather. But Gisella did not run away; she buried her face against Adele's side and, twisting like a snake, she whined."

Here Pavese's contempt for women is mixed with both pity and condemnation. Berto, representing Pavese the city man who returns to the country, courts Gisella, "the only one in that house who knew how to blush."

Here is a description of their first date:

Then I stopped. I heard her laugh as she rolled in the grass. I fell on her and we wrestled. It seemed as though she were still running, even lying there, and she babbled like a lunatic. As soon as I left her she covered herself, crossing her legs. She was streaming with sweat, as wet as a tongue. . . . Then with my head on her breasts we rested, and I heard her heart beating. . . . She let me caress her, exhausted as we were, and she said things softly, with her eyes closed. And the sun, slowly advancing along the grass, came to fall on her legs up to her waist.

Besides scorn and desire, Berto almost feels compassion for the woman who rests at his side even when he discovers scars from an abortion on her abdomen. Gisella, with the tenderness she is capable of, will return at other times with Berto to make love in the valley between the hills, but Berto's reflections become more bitter:

I always feel sorry for women at such a moment. I don't know why, but they fill me with pity. Gisella less than some, because I understood that if I said, "Forget it!", she would be ready to laugh in my face and answer me back. But even she seemed afraid that I might not want her.

Then the tragedy explodes and the women are at its center. It is Gisella, the least vulgar of the sisters, who is the victim. Talino, Gisella's brother, is jealous and spies on her. He knows she is having an affair with Berto, and, at harvest time, under the scorching sun, he commits the insane crime:

Talino, with eyes of a raving animal, had leapt back to steady himself and had driven the pitchfork into her throat. I heard a loud gasp from everyone, then Miliota's voice calling across the farmyard: "Wait for me!" Gisella let the bucket fall and the water soaked my shoes. I thought it was her blood and I jumped. Talino sprang away too, and we heard Gisella gurgling "Holy Mother!" Then she coughed and the pitchfork fell from her neck.

I remember my cold perspiration and that I too was holding my hand to my neck. Ernesto had already grabbed Gisella at the waist as she, all soaked with blood, became limp; and Talino had disappeared.

Blood, death, and women. The entire book, in the heat of the countryside, is full of sex that bursts like the blaze of a burning sun.

The Harvesters ends with this tragic vendetta against women; but there is also a great deal of self-punishment, as if the pitchfork had been driven into Pavese's neck.

His narratives dealing with women of the city pass on them a judgment no less harsh than that passed on the women of the country. In the short novel *The Beautiful Summer*, written in 1940, women are the sole protagonists. The author speaks directly through them, and men only appear in the background. The four women protagonists are Tina the cripple, Ginia the virgin, Amelia the model, and Rosa the factory worker. Amelia is already experienced with men. Her profession, which forces her to pose nude in front of men, had made her shameless. And Pavese feels the need, as he did with previous women, to compare her to an animal: "Amelia looked rather heavy round the hips in her bathing suit, and her features likened her to a horse."

Ginia, the virgin, knows only how to fall in love with one man, Guido, the artist for whom Amelia poses. Before she becomes intimate with Guido, her thoughts are still fresh as early morning:

> "How strange life is," she thought. "Guido, whom I barely know, would take me by the arm, we would stop at the street corners, he would tell me that I am a real woman, and we would look at each other. He calls me Ginetta. We don't need to know each other to be in love."

After these words one has the impression that Pavese wants to save at least one of the women, but soon even for Ginia there is an unfortunate love affair:

> Then Ginia leapt to her feet, pushing away Guido's hands, put down her cigarette, and walked across the studio without speaking. She moved the curtain aside and stood still in the darkness. The conversation behind her sounded like a distant buzzing. "Guido," she whispered without turning, and she threw herself face down on that bed.

And later:

> When Ginia saw Guido the evening before he left, she suddenly felt that the kind of love Guido liked was something deadly, and she remained dazed, to such an extent that Guido drew back the curtain to see her face,

but Ginia held his hands, stopping him. . . . Stunned, she went downstairs, this time convinced that she was no longer herself and that everyone would notice it. "This is why," she thought, "making love is forbidden; this is the reason."

Meanwhile Amelia has arrived at the ultimate degradation. She has contracted syphilis from a woman, and she says, "The woman who gave me this gift is worse off than I am. She doesn't know it yet, and I am not going to tell her, so she will go blind."

This is Pavese's cruelest statement. Even he must have been aware of having gone too far in his revenge against women, and at the end of the story he seems to be trying to soften his position by granting one of the women, Ginia, the redemption of tears:

> Then she realized that Guido was sleeping, and she felt it was impossible to sleep embraced like that; she moved quietly away and found a cool spot, then she became uncomfortable, because she felt naked and alone. Again she was seized by the same disgust and sadness she experienced when she was bathing as a young girl. She wondered why Guido made love to her and she thought of the next day and all the days she had waited for. Her eyes filled with tears and she wept quietly so that no one could hear.

In 1942 his short novel *The Beach* was published. The atmosphere was new, difficult for Pavese, because without the countryside and the city he was alone with the sea, the "useless sea" he had known during the months of his confinement. But women are always present. Pavese wrote this book thinking about the marriage of a companion from his Turin days. It was a double vendetta: against women and against marriage. In *The Beach* Pavese spies on the happiness or unhappiness of two newlyweds, Doro and Clelia. He observes them carefully, probing the secrets of their relation, which remains constant, although without passion. He is certain he will discover something that will destroy their love and their marriage, but the secret he wants to find, the wife's infidelity, does not exist. The desolation of not having a wife led Pavese to his attempts to deride marital happiness, but he ended up more desolate and more convinced of his inferiority.

From 1941 to 1944 came the women of *August Holiday*, a collection of short stories based on memories of his childhood. In "The End of August" he wrote, "I detest people who are sure of themselves, and for the first time I detested Clara." Later in the same story:

> But a man presupposes a woman, *the* woman; a man knows a woman's body, a man must embrace, caress, and crush a woman—one of those women who danced, deeply suntanned, under the lights of the café in front of the sea. . . .
>
> Clara, poor girl, loved me that night as always. Perhaps even more, for she too has her little tricks. We sometimes play at re-establishing the mystery between us as if we were strangers to each other, and thus avoid the monotony. But by then I could no longer forgive her for being a woman, one who can transform the faraway scent of the wind into the smell of flesh.

In *Dialogues with Leucò*, written in 1946, in which Pavese wanted to transfigure everything into myth, the same accusations against women return through the faces of the goddesses, the human sacrifices, the blood, and the incests. Women continue to be burdened with unhappiness and contempt.

The dialogue between Endymion and the Stranger, entitled "The Lady of Beasts," contains these words referring to the goddess Artemis:

> Endymion: "Oh wanderer god, her sweetness is like dawn, it is earth and heaven revealed. And it is divine. But for others, for things and beasts alike, she, the wild one, has a brief laugh, a command that destroys. And no one has ever touched her knee."
>
> Stranger: "Endymion, resign yourself to your mortal heart. Neither god nor man has touched her. Her voice which is hoarse and maternal, is all the wild one can give you."

That hoarse voice, that woman whose "command destroys," reflects Pavese's relentless longing for the same woman, even when he pretended to search among the secrets of Artemis.

In "Sea Foam," the dialogue between Sappho and Britomart, Sappho says, "I have never been happy, Britomart. Desire is not a song. Desire crushes and burns, like the serpent, like the wind." And when Britomart asks Sappho if there was ever a happy woman, she answers:

". . . Helen, the daughter of Leda . . . She needed no one. She did not question her fate. He who had the will, and enough strength, took her with him. When she was ten, she followed a hero. They took her away from him and married her to another man. He too, lost her. Countless men fought for her across the seas. Then the second man took her back and she lived with him in peace. She was buried, and in Hades she knew still more men. She lied to no one, she smiled at no one. Perhaps she was happy."

Even in the myth, the comparison between woman and beast returns, as in the dialogue entitled "Mankind," when Bia speaks to Kratos: "Women or animals, it's all the same. What do you think you are saying? They're the choicest fruit of mortal life."

At the same time as he was writing the *Dialogues with Leucò*, in 1946, Pavese teamed up with a woman, Bianca Garufi, to write his strangest novel, *A Great Fire*. This book, published after Pavese's death, is about Giovanni, a man in love, and Silvia, his fiancée who has had a previous sexual experience she does not have the courage to confess to Giovanni. The story, intended to end with Silvia's suicide, was left unfinished at chapter eleven.

Once again it is the drama of a woman. Silvia's misfortunes began during her childhood: her father dies and she becomes the mistress of her stepfather who leaves her pregnant when she is thirteen. The story develops slowly, amid lust, suspicions, and anxieties which Giovanni, wanting to see Silvia only as a sweet, sincere creature, would prefer not to understand.

When Silvia returns with Giovanni to her mother's house, she is overwhelmed by another tragedy, the death of her brother. This very night of her painful return also becomes a night of absurd love:

. . . "Turn off that light," I said. She hesitated, leaning over me. After a while she did as I asked and we were in the dark.

She had looked at me with intensity while she lay on me, her body pressing against mine. In the stillness, I felt a jolt within me, a foam of bitterness, a futile rage. I understood that with Silvia I could do nothing else but love her this way—without a kiss which, anyway, was useless, without talking to her, without a gesture of love. I remembered my clothes on the floor and thought it was like being at the whorehouse. We would take off our clothes, put them back on, and leave. It would not even last the whole night.

Then I took her violently. She said my name, I kept silent and at last I blindly bit her throat. Perhaps I wanted to hear her scream. She uttered a cry. I fell exhausted. . . . "You're a monster," her wet voice said close to my face. "You're a monster." A secret voice of blood. "You're a monster," she repeated, as another woman would have said, "You are my love."

The drama of Silvia and Giovanni deepens. She confesses to him the suicidal desire she had felt since she was a child:

"This is the place from which I wanted to throw myself when I was truly desperate. I desired it so intensely that it seemed unnatural to me not to be able to run up here and then leap head first from the cliff, so that afterwards there would no longer be my room, nor my mother, nor the night wind."

In 1946 Pavese wrote *The Comrade*. Although it is a novel of political commitment, women are present and they bring gloom to everything: to the sound of the guitar, the outings in the hills, the dances, the drinking parties, the vaudeville shows. And in the background there is remorse.

The female protagonist of this novel is a strange woman, Linda, who has the tastes of a lady and a somewhat mysterious life. Pavese defines her this way:

Who knows if Linda likes milk? Then I thought that Linda, like all women, had to have milk inside her. It came to mind that a baby sucks the milk of a mother who has made love. And how he cries if he does not get it. . . .

"Listen," he told me with a businesslike air, "there are no exceptions. I make women undress in order to know who they are. All of them undress without thinking it over. A woman who knows her worth undresses. But do not be confused by this. Women want other things. They're all ambitious. There are some who want a special friend. There are some who are mad. Have you ever seen a woman drunk? Some of them change boyfriends merely out of spite. They spit on money."

For Pavese, women are always the same and he continues to write about them in the same way, obstinate in his contempt or anguish:

I . . . thought of how women are . . . Even Linda. If for them every man is truly the same, they might just as well give themselves only to one man and follow him like a dog with its master. Instead, no, they want always to have their pick, and they choose by putting them all together, playing with all of them and seeking some benefit from them all. Thus everyone is unhappy, and even they, in the end, do not have a friend.

Later, Pablo relates a dream that ends with the murder of a woman:

"We arrived at the seashore. We were running. She fled on a bicycle on the sand. I picked up a stone and threw it, aiming at her head. The stone struck her head and bounced into the water. Lilli fell dead."
"It is he who loves who kills," Linda remarked.

Women, blood, murder, suicide: these are the thoughts that continued to besiege Pavese.

Another of his works, *Among Women Only*, begins with the unsuccessful suicide attempt of a girl in a city hotel, and ends when the same girl repeats the same act which this time is fatal.

In this suicide climate is the story of certain women who live in one of Turin's strangest environments, but who, for Pavese, represent all women. Almost as if to increase his morbid sensitivity, he impersonates a female character to describe, moment by moment, all her feelings. The name chosen is Clelia; however, the identification of Clelia with Pavese is at once expressed in this squalid presentation:

"You hate other people's pleasures, Clelia, and that's a fact. You're wrong, Clelia. You hate yourself. And to think you were gifted. Make people around you happy, forget your grudge. The pleasures of others are also yours."

In *Among Women Only* there are loveless adventures, based solely on sex and pleasure, encounters that last only an hour or a night. There is also the love of a woman for another woman. A sense of "absurd vice" correlates this passion with the principal theme of the story, suicide. Suicide is no longer hinted at, it is slowly and coldly described:

> Rosetta, stunned, told me that she had no idea herself why she had entered the hotel that morning. In fact she had gone in happy. After the all-night ball, she felt in good spirits. For a long time, nights had made her shudder: the idea of having finished another day, of being alone with her disgust, of waiting for morning, stretched out in bed, all became unbearable. At least that night had already passed. But then, precisely because she hadn't slept but paced around the room thinking of all the foolish things that had happened to her during the night, she was again alone, unable to do anything. Slowly she became desperate, and finding the barbiturates in her purse . . .

What follows is the justification of the suicide:

> Rosetta Mola was naïve, but she had taken things seriously. After all it was true she had no motive for killing herself, certainly it was not because of that stupid story of her first love for Momina or some other predicament. She wanted to be alone, to isolate herself from the uproar; and in her world you can't be alone or do anything alone unless you take yourself out of it completely.

Pavese grew more cruel toward women as the almost masochistic torment he inflicted on himself became more acute. And when he wrote *Among Women Only* he was still closer to his own suicide. He too had to take himself "out of it completely," not only because of his disappointment in love, but in order to remove himself from the "uproar." Still, he would do it stepping on the memory of all women, attempting to destroy them all. "I am afraid nothing matters. We are all whores," declares one of the solitary characters from *Among Women Only*.

The novel's chilling conclusion anticipates, even in its details, Pavese's suicide.

In 1949 Pavese wrote *The Moon and the Bonfires*, a return to his village before his final departure. It seems that his native air and the close memories of his childhood had the power to rouse him. Even the women are again creatures to look at and to love, like the vineyards, the hills, and the trees. When he re-entered the heart of his land, Pavese wrote: "The women, I thought, possess something similar." This is, however, a fleeting tenderness that fades away after a few pages, and the women of his childhood become like the others, like all of them:

> The thing I could not understand in those days was that all women are made the same way: they are all looking for a man. That's the way it must be, I said, thinking it over; but it amazed me that all women, even the most beautiful, even the most sophisticated, liked such a thing. I was already wise then; I had heard so much and I saw how even Irene and Silvia chased after this one and that one. Still, it amazed me. It was Nuto who told me: "What do you think? The moon is there for everyone, so is the rain, so is sickness. Whether they live in a hole or a palace, their blood is red everywhere."

Such were the girls Pavese knew as a child in Santo Stefano. And the women whom the protagonist of *The Moon and the Bonfires* meets during his emigration to the United States are the same as those encountered in Pavese's life.

> In the months Rosanne was my girlfriend, I understood that she was really a bastard, that the legs she stretched out on the bed were her only strength. . . . She was even ready to be photographed naked with her legs spread on a fireman's ladder, anything to make herself known. How she got the idea I could be of any use to her, I don't know. When I asked her why she went to bed with me she laughed and said that, after all, I was a man.

His curse against all women continued; on both sides of the ocean they had a common stigma. Pavese, who felt that he would never be able to become a father, took revenge on women by writing:

> Rosanne would have been willing to give me a son if I had consented to go to the coast. But I held back, I didn't want to. With that mother and with me he would have been another bastard, an American kid.

Here, in his last novel, is Pavese's vendetta against all women. Irene and Silvia, the girls from his native village, end up like the other women of Pavese's stories: Irene marries a vulgar man who beats her every night, and Silvia dies from an abortion.

Still to come is the destiny of their youngest sister, Santina, who is like a child in need of affection. Perhaps remorseful in having to condemn also Santina, Pavese attempts to redeem her by having her run from the Fascists to the Partisans, bringing them news and warning them. But it is too late. Who can trust her? The law of civil war is inexorable and the Partisans execute her.

Santina is more than a woman who is shot in a war. In the final lines of Pavese's last novel, she assumes the symbolic value of a human sacrifice:

> One could not cover a woman like her with earth and just leave her that way. She could still tempt too many men. Baracca took care of it. He had a lot of dry vine branches cut, and we piled them on her until there were enough. Then we poured gasoline on the pile and set fire to it. By noon it was all ashes. Last year the mark was still there, like the bed of a bonfire.

This is all Pavese could concede to a woman: the honor of fire, of becoming ashes like the bed of one of those bonfires that illuminated the nights of his childhood.

Pavese left a diary, *This Business of Living*, in which he revived all the images of the women in his life and the torments he had suffered by them. This is what he wrote in 1936 about the woman with the hoarse voice:

> How did she hurt me? There was the day she raised her arm to wave at someone across the street. The day no one came to open the door for me and then she appeared with her hair disheveled. The day she was whispering to him on the embankment. The thousands of times she made me hurry here and there. But this has nothing to do with aesthetics; this is grief. I wanted to count my memories of happy moments and all I can remember is the pangs I suffered.
>
> Never mind, they serve the same purpose. My story of her, therefore, is not made up of dramatic scenes but of moments filled with the subtlest perceptions. So should a poem be. But it is agony.

In 1937, already behaving in the manner of the later books we have quoted from, he felt compelled to record his contempt for women in order to conceal or defend himself from the suffering:

A woman, unless she is a fool, sooner or later meets a piece of human wreckage and tries to rescue him. She sometimes succeeds. But a woman, unless she is a fool, sooner or later finds a sane, healthy man and makes a wreck of him. She always succeeds.

And again, still in 1937:

The reason why women have always been "bitter as death," sinks of iniquity, perfidious Delilahs, is fundamentally this: a man, unless he is a eunuch, can always achieve ejaculation with any woman. But women rarely experience this joyous liberation, and then not with just any man, often not with the man they love, precisely because they love him. Once they achieve an orgasm, they dream of nothing else, and because of their legitimate longing for this pleasure they are ready to commit any wickedness. *They are compelled* to commit it. It is life's fundamental tragedy, and a man who ejaculates prematurely should never have been born. It is a defect that makes suicide worthwhile.

This remains Pavese's most explicit confession. It is the harshest and most painful presentation of himself and of his partly real, partly imaginary sickness. Along with this self-indictment, he started to consider suicide more intensely. In the same year he wrote:

The only women worth the trouble of marrying are those a man cannot trust enough to marry.

But this is the most terrible thing: the art of living consists in concealing from the persons dearest to us our pleasure in being with them, otherwise they leave us.

The real failure is not the man who does not achieve great things—who ever has?—but he who does not succeed in little things, making a home, keeping a friend, satisfying a woman . . . He is the most miserable failure.

And above all remember that writing poetry is like making love: one never knows if one's own pleasure is shared.

It is incredible that the woman you adore tells you that her days are empty and unbearable, yet she wants no part of you.

In return for having suffered so much, you end up dying like a dog.

Pavese's feelings toward women and love became more conflicting and he recorded them almost in a state of confusion. On November 28, 1937 he wrote, "In love, all that counts is having a woman in one's home, in one's bed. All the rest is nonsense." Two days later he noted, "A love thought: I love you so much that I wish I had been born your brother, or had brought you into the world myself." But in December he returned to denounce what he called his "mutilation." The sense of being inferior to other men in his relationships with women frustrated all his energies. On December 23 he wrote:

> The child who passed his days and nights among men and women, knowing vaguely, not believing in that reality, troubled, in fact, that sex should exist at all, did he not foreshadow the man who spends his time among men and women, knowing, believing that this is the only reality, suffering atrociously from his own mutilation? . . .
>
> I was allowed (like a mouse, my boy!) to let that wound heal over, and then (with a whisper, a caress, a sigh) it was torn open again and tortured, adding a new pain.
>
> Neither disappointment nor jealousy has ever given me this *vertigo of the blood*. It took impotence, the conviction that no woman finds pleasure with me, or ever would (we are what we are); hence this anguish. If nothing else, I can suffer without feeling ashamed: my sufferings are no longer of love. But this is truly the pain that kills every energy: if one is not really a man, if one must be among women without being able to think of possessing them, how can one find the strength to carry on? Could a suicide be better justified?

From time to time there were days of hope, moments of affection during which Pavese discovered his own goodness and generosity. A glance, a gesture from the woman who returned to him, was enough to revitalize him, as when he wrote on Christmas Day, 1937:

> Now, truly, I wish I believed in God, to be able to pray that she won't die, that nothing will happen to her, that all this is a dream, that there will still be a tomorrow, and that I would die instead of her.

This is a prayer not to be found very often in Pavese. With women, he feared more his unselfishness than his egoism: a fear of appearing weak, because in reality he was. He would offer a frown to avoid bursting into tears, and perhaps he would attempt to joke or tease. On December 31: "To love someone is like saying: 'From now on she will think more of my happiness than of her own.'" On the same day: "A man who is not jealous even of his girlfriend's underpants is not in love."

Pavese thought he had discovered the fundamental reason for his inadequacy with women, love, and perhaps with other feelings. He started the new year, 1938, with these words:

And she would always be more sensible than you, because you lean only in one direction; because you live on thoughts, she on reality, and reality is never unbalanced, never at fault. . . . Harm always comes from the person who is unbalanced, not from the one who is realistic. . . .

This much is certain: you can have anything in life except a woman who calls you *her man*. And until now all your life was based on that hope.

To love without mental reservations is a luxury for which one pays and pays and pays.

If you only think of your own interest, you can only be called an egotist. Look at women! You could strangle them, but never will they forget where their interest lies. And would you call them virtuous?

A woman is proud to be able to arouse a man's desire, but she is scandalized if this ability of hers is recognized.

Who would ever have thought that after having aimed in all possible ways at sexual isolation—"self-sufficiency"—I should have discovered in myself the wish to marry, essentially as proof of a woman's confidence in me? And for sexual serenity?

If you were to be born a second time, you should be careful not to attach yourself even to your own mother. You can only lose by it.

It's clear, isn't it, that without her you no longer find life worth living? Clear, too, that she will never come back to you? And even if she did, we have hurt each other too deeply for us ever to live together again? Then what?

It is easy to be good when one is not in love.

The thing we secretly dread the most always happens. When I was a little boy, I *shuddered* at the thought of what it would be like to love someone and see her married to another. I *was trying to get used* to that thought. And, voilà.

I have become a fool. I repeatedly ask myself: what wrong did I do to her? Be brave, Pavese, be brave. Think of your merit if you kill only yourself. You will deserve credit for it.

The idea of suicide stemmed from there, from the hoarse-voiced woman.

Toward the end of the 1930's and at the beginning of the 1940's, Pavese tried to liberate himself from his negative preoccupation with women. But by December 1945 the turmoil would return:

You still feel in your blood the low blow she dealt you. You did everything possible to withstand it, you even forgot it, but it's pointless to run away. Do you know you are all alone? Do you know you are nothing? Do you know that this is the reason she leaves you? Does talking about it resolve anything? You saw it resolves nothing.

And in March 1946: "The women you love feel about you just as you feel for one of those women you don't want." In September of the same year: "Women are a hostile people. Like the Germans."

Only toward the end of the diary, in March 1950, would some tenderness return. Pavese loved and possessed a new woman, a woman from America. For awhile he seemed happy with her, but then, inevitably, he saw in her the hoarse-voiced woman. His life was very close to its conclusion. On March 25, 1950 he wrote his testament: "One does not kill oneself for the love of *a* woman. One kills oneself because love, any love, reveals us in our nakedness, misery, vulnerability, nothingness."

In only a month, from March to April 1950, Pavese wrote his last poems, published in the book *Death Will Come and It Will Have Your Eyes*. These poems were written, in reality, for that same woman with the hoarse voice who had inspired *Work Wearies*. The first poems of his last collection blossomed in spring; as if with Constance, the American woman, hope and joy of life had returned. Pavese wrote them effortlessly, day after day, in his small study on via Lamarmora, in Turin. There is a flow of memories, her "glowing laughter," her "dappled smile." These words are from the first poem, "To C. from C." (To Constance from Cesare), written in English, so that she would understand immediately. However, the American woman would soon lose her identity and become *the* woman, as the hills of *Work Wearies* reappear:

> Grey light of your eyes,
> sweet drops of dawn
> over the dark hills.

As in *Work Wearies*, the woman returns to be ". . . the light and the morning."

As in other poems of the past, she brings to mind "gathered clouds," and she is identified with the earth:

> . . . but you, you are earth.
> You are fierce roots.
> You are the waiting earth.

And she is death:

> Death will come and it will have your eyes—
> this death which accompanies us
> from morning to night, sleepless,
> deaf, like an old remorse
> or an absurd vice.

. . . .

> Death will come and it will have your eyes.
> It will be like quitting a vice,
> like seeing a dead face
> emerge from the mirror,
> like listening to closed lips.
> We shall go down the maelstrom in silence.

The woman of *Work Wearies* and the woman of *Death Will Come and It Will Have Your Eyes* combine to form one single image. It was not by chance that Pavese himself placed, among those verses he left to be published after his death, a poem written in 1940 for the hoarse-voiced woman:

> The man alone listens to the calm voice
> ' with half-closed eyes, as if a breath
> would reach his face, a friendly breath
> that goes back, incredibly, to past time.

. . . .

>A woman's voice that sounds secret
>on the threshold of the house, at nightfall.

The return of the hoarse-voiced woman was explicitly told by Pavese in a poem to the American woman:

>Your light step
>has reopened the wound. . . .

The light step of the woman had become the step of death:

>The breeze and the dawn will still
>blossom lightly
>as though beneath your step,
>when you enter again.
>Between flowers and windowsills
>the cats will know.

His last love, Pavese wrote in his final poem, "was only a flirt." What never healed was the pain he suffered in his youth for the first woman, whom he could not forget:

>. . . someone was hurt
>long time ago.

. . . .

>Someone has died
>long time ago—
>someone who tried
>but didn't know.

To trace the history of women in the life of Cesare Pavese, chronological order has been interrupted and his final moments have been presented in advance. But this was necessary in order to carefully illustrate one of the most important events in his life and a decisive factor in his suicide.

8

The Period of the Translations

A few months after receiving his degree, Pavese was dealt a severe blow by the death of his mother. Life with his mother had been one of numerous clashes, disputes, silences, and harsh words. Yet she had given him the protection he wanted. She represented his roots and she had had that sense of security Pavese needed. Although a rebel in words, he had been, in fact, submissive to her.

This woman had left the country to follow her husband to the city and had bravely assisted him during the long, painful years of his illness. After the death of her husband and with two young children to care for, she had become the pillar of the family. She represented a constant support to her son. Never having shown her his admiration and tenderness, Pavese also felt a bitter remorse after her death. He never spoke of her. Among his papers, I found photographs of the funeral. Cesare is behind the coffin, his face hard and sad, with a dark overcoat thrown over his shoulders.

After the death of his mother he did not want to live alone, and he decided to stay in the old house at 35 via Lamarmora with his sister Maria. He would remain there for the rest of his life, in a room he jealously reserved all to himself, using it as bedroom, study, and parlor.

However, without his mother, the house was not the same. His sister had her own family: a husband and two daughters, Cesarina and Maria Luisa. Cesare withdrew to his room to work, to write, and to translate. He had an urgent need to seek a livelihood. Although he had not had the opportunity to become fully aware of the necessities of life, he realized that he could not aggravate the already difficult financial situation of his sister's family.

Since his university years, he had translated with enthusiasm. In 1931, his first translation was published in Florence. It was the novel *Our Mr. Wrenn* by Sinclair Lewis. The publisher, Bemporad, accepted it after reading Pavese's articles on Lewis and on other American writers in the magazine founded by De Lollis, *La Cultura*.

Pavese's translations opened the way to a new period in Italian fiction. They were a contribution not only literary but also political. Through his translations Pavese showed his longing for freedom and his need to break the scheme of nationalistic rhetoric, to discover new cultural and social horizons.

This peaceful revolution, consisting of translations, essays, and articles, originated in Turin. The working class of Turin, which remained silent but was nevertheless hostile to Fascism, instilled in Pavese's heart the certainty that the rhetoric then afflicting Italian culture was only temporary. Having already realized that all the adversities suffered by the peasants of the Langhe had not weakened their stubbornness and common sense, he became aware that the city too withstood the political storms and knew how to resist.

Gramsci, in prison, wrote prodigiously, filling one notebook after the other. Turin's workers and intellectuals were able to assimilate his message through a clandestine network organized by the Communists. The memory of Gobetti, buried in the cemetery of Père Lachaise, in France, continued to inspire the battle for freedom. Augusto Monti had formulated the commitment to this battle when, at his home in Turin, he commemorated Gobetti in 1926. Several other Turin intellectuals were also involved in the underground work, and they were connected with anti-Fascist intellectuals throughout Italy.

Pavese was aware of these resistance activities which took place at the university and among the workers of Turin. Without being a man of action and without engaging in political commitments, he allied himself, through his studies and literary works, with those who wanted to quash the Fascist rhetoric of extreme nationalism. In order to comprehend Pavese's enthusiasm and also his doubts in the whole course of his public life, one must understand his role as a translator.

At that time the Fascists were striving to regiment intellectuals into a uniform program which left them only free to be nationalists. All newspapers were the same and all books were supposed to be regimented as well. Many writers and poets acquiesced. In Turin probably more than in any other place, many were able to resist. Benedetto Croce, under the pretext of visiting relatives of his wife, who was from Turin, often came to this city. He loved to meet there with men who understood him and with whom he could safely speak. Around him gathered Ruffini, Solocri, Egidi, Falco, Monti, Ambrosini, Debenedetti. There were also the young ones: Bertini, Alberti, Garosci, Mila, Ginzburg, Antonicelli, and Carlo Levi.

In that climate, Pavese too joined the battle on the terrain that was most congenial to him. His translations were not only perfect in style and accuracy, but they also carried a political significance, considering the countries of the authors he translated.

It was then that his life acquired one of its most important characteristics. The direction chosen by Pavese, and also by Vittorini, although in a different manner, corresponded to the turning point of all Italian literature. Many of the essays Pavese wrote in those years on American authors remain valid today in their basic judgments. Pavese wanted to offer as a discovery the cultural horizon of North America, rich with vital content, in order to compare it with the void of contemporary Italian culture. More important, he intended to define the rapports between literature and society, between social and political commitment. In opposition to the aesthetics of the times, he proposed, in substance, new structures of inquiry and vaster comparisons. In translating American novels, he consciously presented "the gigantic theatre where, with greater frankness than anywhere else, everyone's drama was performed."

Analyzing those years now, it is much easier to link that cultural battle to social themes. While the Fascists stopped and condemned strikes, denying every initiative to the masses, American novels showed the eruption of impulses and popular movements capable of creating new social relations. Against the asphyxiation of Italy's literary language, Pavese also demonstrated how the contact of these novels with the American masses brought the vivifying contribution of popular idioms to the language, making it more congenial to the new social content. Thus Pavese expressed Gramsci's ideas even without directly knowing them. In fact it was Gramsci who from prison wrote that Italian literature under Fascism was "neither national nor popular."

Here is how Pavese later explained his commitment during those years, in an article titled "Yesterday and Today":

Around 1930, when Fascism was beginning to be "the hope of the world," it happened that a group of young Italians discovered America through its books, an America pensive and barbaric, happy and truculent, dissolute, fertile, heavy with all the past of the world, and at the same time young, innocent. For some years these young people read, translated, and wrote with a joy of discovery and revolt which outraged the official culture; but the success was so great that the regime was compelled to be tolerant in order to save face. Was it a joke? We were the country of the resurrected Roman world, where even land surveyors studied Latin, the country of warriors and saints, the country of God-given genius; yet these new boors, these colonial merchants, these vulgar multimillionaires, dared give us a lesson in good taste, getting themselves read, discussed, and admired. The regime endured it with clenched teeth, and meanwhile kept alert, always ready to profit from a false step, a page more crude, a more direct blasphemy, to catch us in the act and strike the blow. It struck a few blows, but without result. The smell of scandal and easy heresy that surrounded the new books and their content, as well as the passion for revolt and truth that even the most thoughtless readers felt pulsating in those translated pages, were irresistible to a public not yet entirely stupefied by conformism and rhetoric. One can frankly say that at least in the fields of fashion and taste, the new trend helped a good deal to rouse and nourish the political opposition, however vague and futile, of the Italian reading public. For many people, the encounter with Caldwell, Steinbeck, Saroyan, and even with their forerunner Lewis, provided the first light of freedom, the first suspicion that not everything in the world's culture led to Fascism.

I remember quite well that Pavese turned this article in to me for *L'Unità* on August 2, 1947. At that time, he said, he saw things with more clarity than he had when he had started to translate; however, his present commitment was substantially the same he had felt when he was translating. The place Pavese had taken from which to attack Fascism was indeed more comfortable than the jails from where other writers continued their resistance, but in his extreme sincerity, he never hid the doubts that assailed him in those years. He described some of them in the article "Fascism and Culture" written in 1945:

> . . . And yet one can claim that the best of us, suspicious and desperate as we were, often found ourselves imagining that only one thing could have saved us: a dive into the crowd, a sudden fever of proletarian experiences and interests through which the subtle malady inoculated by Fascism would finally resolve itself into the humble and practical general health. Something like going toward the people, we thought every so often. But of course "to go toward the people"[16] was part of the catastrophe. And then weren't we too the people? Isn't it the most neurotic thing, to feel the need to move away from ourselves? Do the true common people have these whims?

Obviously Pavese found the true common people among the workers, but in the Fascist climate a dialogue with them was not possible. So he turned to the true people in American literature and introduced them to the Italians.

In 1930, writing of Sinclair Lewis and his characters, he said: "Basically, the thirst of these characters is for one thing only: freedom, freedom of the individual from the irrational chains of society." And he also wrote: "They are not supermen, but rather poor creatures, even when they possess genius."

Pavese would revive these characters in his stories. In Lewis he saw himself, as when he wrote that:

> . . . he himself is the described rebel and his characters are only the innumerable faces of his own personality. . . .
>
> The little man who suffocates and yearns and doesn't even know what he wants or where he is going, or rather, continually discovers new avenues but suffers torments and struggles, perpetually in flight, is of course the figure of himself we can glimpse between the lines.

While translating the American novels and fighting his cultural battles, Pavese studied and observed the people around him with a new interest. Country and city were seen in the light of his American experience. His essay on Anderson in 1931 illustrates this discovery:

In order to understand the modern American novelists—I refer to the group, more famous than read, of three innovators: Theodore Dreiser, Sinclair Lewis, and Sherwood Anderson—it is not only necessary to know the common historical need their works met, but it is indispensable to find an historical parallel between familiar situations at home and those aspects of an overseas life most often regarded as very exotic. And the parallel exists, clear and exact.

Let's look at the significance for Italian literature, of the discovery of regions which went hand in hand with the quest for national unity, toward the end of the eighteenth and through the entire nineteenth century. From Alfieri on, all the Italian writers try, often unconsciously, to achieve a more profound national unity by penetrating always further the character of their own regions, their *true* nature; thus they arrive at the creation of a human awareness and a language rich with all the blood of the province and with all the dignity of a renewed life. My countrymen from Piedmont especially should remember these things, for it is in Piedmont that the ferment of this aspiration is still felt most powerfully and is farthest from realization, lost as we now are behind too much specialization of dialect. Let us from Piedmont think of it, for it was in our name, with Alfieri, that this renaissance historically began; yet, from Alfieri himself, and then through D'Azeglio, Abba, to Calandra and even later, we have never had that man and that work which, besides being very dear to us, would truly achieve that universality and originality which would make them understood by all men. This is our still unsatisfied need. Meanwhile, the American novelists of whom I speak have in fact met the corresponding need of their nation and region. We must, therefore, learn from them.

With these words Pavese answered those who, in that Fascist era, accused him of betraying his country because he translated the Americans. And he did something even more advanced by perceiving, in the regional experience, the signs of a more authentic social democracy.

As to the importance of the economic and ideological social structure in the frame of an artistic work, Pavese specified his ideas in an article on Anderson's book *A Storyteller's Story*:

Having read this book, you will have learned something about the profound dignity and the human value of every honest experiment by the writer who wants to renew himself, who wants to be himself; you will have acquired the habit of not considering a work of literature only as an amusement or a banality. But you will also have understood that the little words, the sentences, the literary modes are never accidental, that they are never, like bread and wine, simple data of unchangeable common sense; in them is reflected a whole economic, ideological, and social situation. Anyone who has a class consciousness realizes this. But he must also realize that it is inconsistent to strive to renew the structure and ideologies of a given society if he then continues to be happy with a style of painting, a way of making music, or of writing, clearly determined by an environment which, in our opinion, is already condemned.

There is no doubt that in the essays published in the 1930's in *La Cultura*, Pavese demonstrated, besides the clarity of his critical method, a cultural and political courage. At the same time he engaged in another and no less important battle: that involving the search for a language. About Sinclair Lewis, Pavese wrote:

The true, provincial nature of Sinclair Lewis is shown in his use of slang and the vernacular. This kind of jargon and dialect, a national expression of America, is understood by him, loved, and ultimately turned into poetry, resulting in the true creation of a language—the American vernacular: a thing that has its precedent only back in the time when the neo-Latin peoples crystallized their virgin idioms in works of art and life.

And about Anderson:

Anderson's style! Not a crude dialect still too local . . . but a new texture of English entirely constructed of American idioms, a style no longer *dialect*, but *language*, reworked in the mind, recreated, *poetry*.

Of Mark Twain:

Mark Twain . . . undeniably touched the chords of real poetry—and created a language of his own, of great originality in the stylistic tradition of America, nourished by many dialects from the river valley. . . .

Of O. Henry:

Finally, this literature that culminates in the "prince" O. Henry has a new characteristic: it is a dialect literature. It is a curious kind of literature, because we Italians imagine dialects to be local . . . But in America, dialect is the colloquial speech spoken by everyone in contrast to the cultured and lofty English taught in the schools.

Pavese was publishing these first directions for a linguistic renovation of Italian prose at almost the same time that Antonio Gramsci, with a much broader scope, wrote: "Each time the question of the language reappears, it signifies that we are confronted by a series of other problems: the formation and broadening of the leading class, the need to establish more intimate and secure relations between the leading groups and the nation's masses."

Thus Gramsci and Pavese, although so different, were fighting for the same cultural and political renewal. It is said that the true writer is also a prophet. Examining that period of Pavese's life and his writings of those years, we can understand how, in defending Edgar Lee Masters' characters from the accusation of representing only clinical cases, Pavese was also defending himself from the same accusation that would be directed toward him after his death:

A book that begins with an elegy on the cemetery, and continues with unhappy husbands, adulterous wives, cantankerous bachelors, stillborn babies, and where practically everyone laments a wasted life, might well seem, in a casual reading, a survey of clinical cases. The difference lies only in the eye of the poet who observes his dead not with morbid or polemical satisfaction, nor with the pseudoscientific indifference which is now, unfortunately, so popular in the States, but rather with an austere and yet fraternal awareness of everyone's suffering, of everyone's vanity; from all he elicits a confession, from all he extracts a definitive answer, not to derive a scientific or social document, but only out of passion for human truth.

When in 1932 Pavese wrote, again for *La Cultura*, of his favorite author, Herman Melville, he not only pronounced a serious judgment on the writer, but he also indicated his own aspirations:

Melville is truly a Greek. Read the European attempts to get away from literature and you feel more literary than ever, you feel small, cerebral, effeminate; read Melville, who was not ashamed to begin *Moby-Dick*— that epic poem of savage life—with eight pages of citations, and who goes on discussing, quoting still more, acting as a man of letters, and your lungs expand, your brain exults, you feel more alive and more a man. As with the Greeks, no matter how dark the tragedy (Moby Dick) is, so great are the tranquillity and purity of its chorus (Ishmael), that you always leave the theatre exalted in your own capacity for life.

Pavese's great admiration for Melville was also a form of opposition to the Fascist rhetoric of the "Roman tradition." He wrote: "To have a tradition is less than nothing, only by seeking it can one live it."

In continuing to praise Melville, Pavese took another opportunity to attack Fascism and its opposition to men of letters: "I think it takes less courage to face a whale or a typhoon that to risk passing for a pedant or a man of letters."

Through his translations and essays on American and English authors, Pavese approached what would be his themes as a writer. We find the nostalgia for childhood, his sense of the tragic, the roles of destiny and myth, his polemics against art for art's sake, the fight against positivism which he interpreted as the fight against Fascist nationalism, and, in contrast, his admiration for Sherwood Anderson, precisely because he wanted to "bring order and structure where there is chaos."

Pavese was able to develop a prose which is one of the most exemplary in Italian contemporary writing, and its origin is to be traced back to his studies as a translator. Among his papers I found many notebooks containing his annotations of all the meanings of English words and American idioms. He wrote hundreds of letters to America in order to know certain derivations, certain slang expressions, and he worked long hours at the translation of a book, even one not as complex as *Moby-Dick*.

The list of his translations is impressive, both for the number and the importance of the works. They are: Sinclair Lewis's *Our Mr. Wrenn* published in 1931; Herman Melville's *Moby-Dick* and Sherwood Anderson's *Dark Laughter* in 1932; James Joyce's *Portrait of the Artist as a Young Man* in 1934; John Dos Passos's *42nd Parallel* and *The Big Money* in 1935 and 1937 respectively; John Steinbeck's *Of Mice and Men* in 1937; Gertrude Stein's *The Autobiography of Alice B. Toklas* and Daniel Defoe's *Moll Flanders* in 1938; Charles Dickens's *David Copperfield* and Christopher Dawson's *The Making of Europe* in 1939; Gertrude Stein's *Three Lives* and Herman Melville's *Benito Cereno* in 1940; George Macaulay Trevelyan's *The English Revolution of 1688–89* and Christopher Morley's *The Trojan Horse* in 1941; William Faulkner's *The Hamlet* in 1942; Robert Henriques's *Captain Smith* in 1947; and finally, in 1950, Arnold Toynbee's *A Study of History*, done in collaboration with Charis de Bosis. The publication dates indicate that Pavese continued to translate year after year for a good part of his life, with the purpose of broadening the horizons of Italian readers.

If Melville was for him the paragon of all the writers Pavese translated and studied, it was the American critic F. O. Matthiessen who became the conscience of his destiny as well as his presage. Pavese and Matthiessen had in common a conscientious search for language, the need for an organic unity between art and society, the sense of mystery and of tragedy, and finally, the notion that life becomes futile after the achievement of maturity. Matthiessen's influence remained with Pavese until *The Moon and the Bonfires*, when he attempted to find the right balance between symbol and reality. Pavese and Matthiessen would also have in common the gesture with which their lives would end—the American critic killed himself in April 1950; Pavese spoke to his friends of that suicide as a gesture which was inevitable not only for Matthiessen. And in August of the same year, he too killed himself.

There is a thread which leads us to understand the particular influence on Pavese of the two American writers, Melville and Matthiessen, together with Shakespeare. We find it at the end of his essay on Matthiessen, entitled "American Maturity" where, concluding a discussion of tragic greatness, he cites the definition of maturity which had been underlined by Melville in his copy of Shakespeare's *King Lear*: "ripeness is all." It is the same verse we find as the epigraph to Pavese's last novel, *The Moon and the Bonfires*.

There can be no better conclusion to this part of Pavese's literary life than what Pavese himself wrote in 1948 in answer to a question asked him by the magazine *Aretusa*:

. . . The period between 1930 and 1940, which will go down in the history of our culture as a decade of translations, was not a product of my idleness, nor of the idleness of Vittorini, Cecchi, and others. It was a fateful moment, and precisely in its apparent exoticism and rebelliousness one can find the only vital vein of our recent poetic culture. Italy was estranged, barbarized, and calcified—it had to be shaken, decongested, and re-exposed to all the spring winds of Europe and the world. There is nothing strange in the fact that this conquest of texts could not be pursued by bureaucrats or literary handymen, but required instead, youthful enthusiasm and choices. We discovered Italy—this is the point— seeking the men and the words in America, Russia, France, and Spain. This love for foreigners did not result in a betrayal of our supposed social and national reality. Some of us, in fact, continued to develop and arrived at an unexpected phase—authentic and unmistakable even to the most malevolent critics—without any break in continuity and without the feeling of being a turncoat. At least in my case, I don't think I was one.

9

Politics in Turin
and the Einaudi
Publishing House

Around Pavese, the fraternity of the D'Azeglio Lyceum former students became each year more politically interested and more active in the clandestine struggle against Fascism.

Monti had, for a long time, been under the surveillance of the Fascist police. Ginzburg had broadened his field of action, and his political network was not limited to Italy. When the fraternity met, Ginzburg often had private talks with Mila or with others and when they rejoined the group, those he had consulted always carried mysterious pamphlets with them. One day, Pavese took one from Mila's hand and he realized that it dealt with ways to organize a resistance to the regime. Along with Ginzburg, the most active were Mila, Vittorio Foà, Renzo Giua, Bobbio, Sturani, Antonicelli, Castallera, Chessa, and Olivetti.

While pretending not to understand what took place and feigning a lack of interest in his friends' political discussions, Pavese was well aware that Mila's prolonged absence from Turin meant he had gone to France to visit the anti-Fascist refugees. Even the woman with the hoarse voice served as a "missionary" for the resistance. With Pavese she spoke very little of politics and even less of her underground work, but he understood.

It was no mystery to anyone that Fascism had multiplied its enemies. As a result of the continuous abuses of Fascism, political passion arose even in those who would have preferred to devote their time to other things. Whoever was not a member of the Fascist Party could not find work. The students who did not belong to the university's Fascist organization were labeled "panciafichisti" (useless pacifists) and considered potential traitors. In 1929 an event occurred that seriously disrupted the university and stirred great interest throughout Turin because of the well-known men involved in it. Some professors and students had been arrested simply for having signed a letter of solidarity with Croce. Among them was Professor Cosmo and with him were Antonicelli, Bertini, Treves, De Bernardi, Geymonat, Umberto Segre, and Mila, all Pavese's friends. It was in fact Pavese who, sent by the woman with the hoarse voice, ran to warn Mila that the police were looking for him.

Pavese disapproved of the gesture of signing that letter, considering it a "useless bravado," but a little later he personally experienced what not being registered in the Fascist Party meant. After obtaining his degree, he was not allowed to take the examinations for teaching in public schools because he was not a member of the party. Thus began for him, as well as for all his friends, the race for temporary positions which forced him to leave Turin in order to teach Latin, Italian literature, or philosophy in Bra, Saluzzo, and Vercelli. Eventually he was given a temporary assignment in Turin where he taught for a few months as a substitute at his D'Azeglio Lyceum. However, in order to have a more regular income, he had to be content with private schools and some evening classes.

Pavese was teaching one evening at a school in Turin when his fraternity friends accompanied Monti to listen at the door and peek through the window of his classroom. They wanted to show Monti how Pavese imitated him in his tone of voice, his gestures, and, above all, the manner in which he too, kept a finger raised while he asked questions or explained the lessons.

In that period, Pavese began an assiduous collaboration with the publisher Frassinelli, who would later publish some of his best translations.

Thanks to Monti, he found employment during the summer as a tutor. His friends still remember today the letters he wrote them from Bibbiana, where he was teaching in the house of an ex-high official of state, married to a woman of nobility. Italy's crown prince was also a guest in that house. In an amusing letter Pavese gave an account of one reception where his shoes full of holes had become the center of attention, forcing him to remain still to avoid showing the holes until the "illustrious guest" had left.

In those years Pavese began to work with the magazine *La Cultura*, then edited by Arrigo Cajumi. He also wrote the first poems of *Work Wearies* which he had Monti and his other friends read. By then Pavese met with Monti almost daily. The teacher was completing his trilogy entitled *The Story of Father*.

Monti read Pavese his novels which he defined as family chronicles, and which had a great influence on Pavese's writings. Monti's novels were Piedmontese stories, based on memories of his family who lived in Ponti, in the Langhe, not far from Santo Stefano. Monti's books, besides nourishing more and more Pavese's roots in the Piedmontese land, were of great interest to the younger writer because they insisted on the search for a language derived from popular speech. Other reasons for Pavese's attachment to Monti were described by Massimo Mila in an article published in the magazine *Dante*:

. . . [Through Monti's books] I relive that joyous amazement with which I discovered, as a student, the other side of that teacher who, during the three years at the lyceum, appeared to me as the symbol of austerity. Once we had received our diplomas, he descended from his podium, came toward us with a broad smile, took each of us by the hand, and initiated us into the marvelous fraternity of his former students: the university, the café, the study of a painter friend, the small restaurants in the suburbs, the billiard hall, the Turin girls, life. A life to be lived fully, without believing that literature and study could ever become its surrogate; and in the middle was Monti himself, serene, humorous, easygoing, invisible moderator. . . . In his books one discovers a civic sense that urges individual interests and experiences to find fulfillment in the social function, linking the man indissolubly to the citizen and making him fully alive only in the frame of his country and of his society. . . . His principal characters were not cheerful people, they were overburdened with concerns, their own and those of others; as a result of the strain, they had acquired a severe face and could no longer afford so much as a smile. . . . In Monti's novels, which would appear to be merely descriptions of private situations only to superficial readers, public history is continuously a part of domestic history, the present enlightens the past and vice versa. . . . This seems to me to be the secret of Monti's work, the reason for its vitality and value. . . .

Pavese would not make any decision without first discussing it with Monti, or publish a book that would not create a discussion between him and the professor. When Pavese seemed to vacillate or to stray from the path of high responsibilities on which Monti had tried to lead all his pupils, his former teacher bluntly criticized him, while continuing to be his mentor with his example, advice, and writings. Monti's books, written and published during the height of Fascism, represented a salutary reminder to those like Pavese, who could understand their real significance.

In 1933 an enterprise began in Turin that would have a great influence not only on Italy's cultural and political life, but also on Pavese's future: the Einaudi Publishing House.

Even this venture had its roots in the D'Azeglio Lyceum. Its founder was Giulio Einaudi, a former student of Monti. Being a refined young man from a well-known family, he had difficulty during the gymnasium years in holding his own against the band of his schoolmates whom Monti called "diligent and intelligent rogues" and who were always ready to take advantage of another's shyness. But at the lyceum he had acquired the respect of his classmates and was noted for his literary compositions.

After his second year at the lyceum, since he was weak in Latin, Monti suggested that he take lessons from Massimo Mila, who was then at the university. In Dogliani, at the splendid home of the Einaudi family, Mila and Giulio, besides working on the Latin, started a close friendship. Back in Turin, Mila introduced Giulio to the fraternity of ex-students, beginning with Leone Ginzburg and Cesare Pavese: the first called "Tass Agency" because he was born in the Soviet Union; the second called "Ces" or "Paves" and considered the outstanding student in Italian literature. After the lyceum, Giulio had enrolled in the school of medicine. However, living at his family's home amid the books and journals of his father, the famous economist, he was more attracted to the printed page than to medicine. For some time he had been fervently interested in the editorial success of his father's periodical *La Riforma Sociale* and in De Lollis' *La Cultura*, but in 1933, encouraged by a growing public interest in those magazines, he felt it was time to organize a publishing house around them. The idea might have seemed presumptuous, but in his initiatives Giulio Einaudi was as headstrong as his friend Pavese. The fraternity of D'Azeglio warmly supported the project which was realized on November 15, 1933 when the new organization, named "Giulio Einaudi, Publisher," registered officially with the Turin Chamber of Commerce.

The new publishing house, launched without much concern about future funding, established its first offices in two rooms on the third floor of 7 via Arcivescovado, in the same building with the headquarters of Antonio Gramsci's *L'Ordine Nuovo*. Einaudi began publishing in 1934, and from the title of the first collection, "Contemporary Problems," one can already see the intentions of the new firm.

The first volume of the series, entitled *What Does America Want?*, was by an American author, Henry A. Wallace, the associate of Franklin Delano Roosevelt. Considering Wallace's country and the subject, it is not difficult to notice the influence of Pavese's essays and translations. It is also apparent that the publisher's father, Luigi Einaudi, who wrote an introduction to the book, was definitely behind his son's enterprise.

Already in its first year, Einaudi's company had as many as nine books to its credit, all on economics, demonstrating the same interests as Laterza, the publishing house associated with the name of Croce, which had its center in Bari. The alliance between the anti-Fascist intellectuals of the two cities, Turin and Bari, was strengthened and continued for a long time to undermine Fascism in the cultural field. Einaudi's objective was to open new political avenues. Its editorial emblem consisted of an ostrich swallowing a nail, with the Latin motto "Spiritus durissima coquit," to indicate a will that is capable of digesting even nails.

The first books of American origin on economics were followed by texts from England and the Soviet Union and, a few years later, by explicit treatises on revolution and Socialism. The boundaries established by Fascism were openly crossed. At the same time, urged by the collaborators of *La Cultura*, Giulio Einaudi was considering the possibilities of broadening his editorial work to other fields.

Leone Ginzburg, a member of the original team that organized the Einaudi House, selected, as collaborators, Monti, Pavese, Geymonat, Mila, Antonicelli, Balbo, Cajumi, and Carlo Levi. Therefore, together with the publishing house, a group was formed composed of writers and critics who were open to all discussions, all problems of culture, and whose opposition to the dictatorship became increasingly apparent.

Pavese continued to teach in private schools, but he was very interested in the new publishing firm that would soon be at the center of his work and life. It was the collaboration with Einaudi that enabled him to meet new writers, from Eugenio Montale to Pietro Pancrazi, from Luigi Salvatorelli to the scientist Enrico Fermi.

From that moment, Pavese's interests were not limited to literature, but included every cultural area. Under the stimulus of the new forces active at Einaudi, even the periodicals *La Cultura* and *La Riforma Sociale* became accessible to a larger public. To those two magazines a third was added: *La Rassegna Musicale*, edited by Guido Gatti.

The Fascists had sensed danger. Around the publishing house, surveillance was intensified. In the early months of 1934, just a few days before *La Cultura* was to appear in a new format, Leone Ginzburg, who had become its editor, was arrested. The police had discovered the clandestine movement "Justice and Freedom" in which he played an important role. This was a severe blow for Einaudi and for the magazine. Unable to replace Ginzburg in his clandestine activity, Pavese intensified his work for both the publishing house and *La Cultura* in order to compensate for Leone's absence.

Among Pavese's papers I found an interesting document that dates back to 1934: it is the request he made a few months after Ginzburg's arrest, to become editor of *La Cultura*. The position fell to him because he was then the only one, among the contributors of Einaudi and of the magazine, whom the police did not suspect. His editorship lasted only one year. In 1935 he asked to be replaced because he found the responsibilities of editor too heavy, but by then his name was on the list of subversives.

While working for Einaudi, Pavese found time to organize the poems of *Work Wearies*. His fraternity friends already knew them thoroughly and were convinced that they should be published. The poems' most enthusiastic supporter was Massimo Mila who decided to take the manuscript to Florence where he had influential friends who could publish them.

In Florence was a group of young writers and critics who, led by Alberto Carocci, had founded the literary review *Solaria* in 1926. Several poems had already appeared in that magazine, among them some by Saba and Montale. Mila, who knew Carocci through their political activity, gave him Pavese's poems. Carocci asked Elio Vittorini to read them, and it was through *Work Wearies* that Pavese and Vittorini met. Vittorini, already combative, firm in his ideas, and inflexible in his polemics, read Pavese's poems with great interest. The understanding between the two writers was facilitated by their common effort to promote American literature. Furthermore, in those years, Vittorini was nearing the completion of his first novel, *The Red Carnation*, in which one could feel the same desire for renewal and the same human concern prevalent in Pavese's poetry.

Both Vittorini and Carocci favored the publication of Pavese's poems in *Solaria*. That news, brought by Mila to Turin, moved Pavese and made the entire clan of friends proud. Pavese anxiously awaited the publication, but many factors—one of which was the

Fascist censorship—prevented Carocci from issuing the volume until the end of 1936.

Meanwhile, in Turin, events came to a head. The Fascist raids against the "subversives" multiplied. With its ambition to create an empire, the regime began to mobilize for the Abyssinian War. The Fascist police kept a close watch on all the collaborators of Einaudi.

In those years Pavese's love for the woman with the hoarse voice was reciprocated. Their encounters were frequent but brief since both of them were involved in many activities. She had assumed duties of great responsibility in the clandestine work for the Communist Party. She was under strict surveillance, having already been arrested and convicted in 1926, together with her boyfriend at the time, Altiero Spinelli.

She continued to correspond with Spinelli who was still serving time in a Roman prison. Since she could not receive his letters at her home without the risk of jeopardizing herself and the entire organization, she asked to use Pavese's address. He accepted immediately, less for political conviction than for the desire to be useful to the woman he loved.

On the morning of May 13, 1935, the police raided Pavese's home. The house was ransacked, a letter from the Roman prison was found, and Pavese was arrested. Also arrested were Augusto Monti, Massimo Mila, Giulio Einaudi, Vittorio Foà, Antonicelli, Bobbio, Giua, Perelli, Cavallera, and many others. Pavese ended up in prison, where he remained for a few months. At the trial, in order to save the woman, who in fact would be released, he refused to give any explanation. When they read the sentence, condemning him to three years' exile, he showed no sign of emotion.

He was sent to Brancaleone Calabro. We can learn the history of that intense period in his life from Pavese himself, who kept in a notebook which his sister Maria was kind enough to let me read, rough copies of his letters from Brancaleone. They reveal a new Pavese, whose sense of humor was rich, even in suffering.

10

The Letters from Confinement

Pavese's writing during the period of exile began with a telegram dated August 5, 1935 to his sister Maria: "Arrived Brancaleone (Calabria). Hotel Rome. Forward money for immediate expenses. Special delivery follows. Cesare."

In a letter dated August 7, addressed to Alberto Carocci, the editor of *Solaria*, Pavese expressed his worries about the delay in the publication of *Work Wearies*. The exile and the torment of being away from the woman with the hoarse voice did not distract him from his literary interests:

Dear Carocci,

I expect you've already heard of the trouble I'm in. I'm in Brancaleone, sentenced to three years. My sister told me that my book has been given official approval, but you wish to postpone publication until October. In my opinion your reasons for this delay no longer apply, and I should be grateful if you would reconsider the matter and let me know your views. I think the volume in its definitive form, with the exclusion of "A Generation," should be sent to the Ministry of the Interior for its authorization. All I can do at present is to leave everything in your hands.

Greetings,
PAVESE

The following letter, dated August 8, is an official request addressed to the Ministry of the Interior. After the brief period of prison and exile, Pavese had already acquired the necessary bureaucratic jargon. But it is more interesting to note the subtle irony of his request; since he knew what to expect as a reply, he used a tone of "respectful" contempt.

Honorable Minister of the Interior:

The undersigned Cesare Pavese, confined under police surveillance to this commune of Brancaleone for a period of three years by the ordinance of the Royal Prefecture of Rome dated July 15, has been informed, through the Royal Prefecture of Reggio Calabria, of the Honorable Minister's decision not to grant him any subsidy for the period of his exile, "having ascertained that he has means of subsistence." He submits a respectful appeal to have his economic status re-examined. He points out to this Honorable Minister that, before being assigned to exile, he lived in Turin, via Lamarmora 35, with his sister Maria Sini and he contributed, through his profession and together with his brother-in-law, to his own support and to that of the aforesaid family. He also reminds you of the difficulty he has in practicing his own profession of Doctor of Letters, due to the isolation and the scarce resources of the locality where he now is. For that matter, any other place of confinement would not have an environment conducive to earning a living.

Please keep also in mind that until now he has been able to subsist thanks to the generosity of his sister, but that he cannot legally nor humanly expect from her that aid which is, after all, indispensable.

He therefore respectfully asks the Honorable Minister to review his own decision and, if this request seems reasonable, to grant him the minimum legal subsidy that would allow him to live not too indecorously in the commune where he is now confined.

With perfect respect,
CESARE PAVESE

The letter of August 9, addressed to his sister, shows us a different Pavese from the one who wrote the lyceum letters. His sense of humor can almost make one forget the suffering which lies under the playful words:

Dear Maria,

I reached Brancaleone at 4:00 on Sunday afternoon, to find the whole population strolling in front of the station as if they expected to see a criminal in handcuffs, escorted by two "carabinieri," emerge from the train and march firmly toward the City Hall.

My two days' journey, with handcuffs and suitcase, was first class traveling. But now our family name is definitely compromised beyond all hope of recovery. We passed through the stations in Naples and Rome at the time of most intense traffic, and you should have seen how the crowds made way for the sinister trio. In Rome a little girl asked her father, "Daddy, why don't they send an electric current through those handcuffs?" In Naples I too fell under the weight of the cross: it happened on the steps of the prison's courtyard, with handcuffs, suitcase and all. Then a good Samaritan carried my suitcase for me.

In Salerno we had to change trains, so providing an educational spectacle for the children who were watching us. It was dark when we passed through Paestum, therefore we didn't even have the pleasure of seeing the Greek temples.

We changed trains again in Santa Eufemia and in Catanzaro. What a pleasure!

Here in Brancaleone I found good people, accustomed to the worst; they try their best to be on good terms with me.

It will surely make you happy to hear that since it appears I am in a position to earn a living, the Ministry has decided not to grant me any subsidy. I shall start the usual appeal with the usual result.

I am the only prisoner confined here at present. It is a legend that here everybody is dirty: they are baked by the sun. The women comb their hair in the street, but at least all the inhabitants take baths. They carry huge pitchers on their heads. I must learn how to do that myself, then some day I'll be able to make a living in a cabaret of Turin.

Here they have no idea what "grappa"[17] is. If you were to send me about twenty bottles, I would not have any problem in drinking them.

I have received the money and I very much fear that unless at the Ministry they change their minds about my means, I shall have to ask you for the same amount twice a month.

I am still waiting for the case with the books.

I have rented a bedroom for 45 lire, but every day there is some new expense: the light, a washbowl, sugar, etc. I do my cooking, which means that I eat cold stuff. It is not pleasant to set up a household without a family.

The beach is on the Ionian Sea which resembles any other sea and is almost as good as the Po.

I have received a quantity of postcards that had been delayed.

In conclusion, I am only asking for books, money, and greetings from my friends.

Ciao,
CESARE

The detailed description of his life continues in another letter to his sister dated August 19:

Dear Maria,

I received your letters of the 10th and 12th, and have already mailed my petition to the Ministry of Education.

I have had enough of Brancaleone. I get up early in the morning, when the milkman comes, and boil my quarter litre on my little spirit stove, otherwise it would turn sour by midday. Then I go out to have coffee at the Roma café and sit over it until 10:00, trying to read or to write a poem; but the heat is so intense and my surroundings so different that I don't have much success. I skim through the *Gazzetta del Popolo*, then I go down to the sea. I used to swim, but the salt water gave me an earache, so I can no longer dive—another pleasure now lost. I stroll back to town and do my shopping: bread and fruit. At noon I drink my boiled milk and eat my bread and fruit or sometimes a boiled egg with oil that I cook in a little pan. Then I try to take a nap; if I can't sleep, I idly try to read until 4:00. I go out again to report to the "carabinieri" at 5:00. Then I stop downtown, try again to write poetry or to chitchat, though soon I am bored. If I haven't spent much that day, I go to have a beer. At 7:00 I return to my room, have supper and wash the dishes. I linger around my room until 8:00, still attempting to write poetry, then I tuck myself into bed, having first taken a quinine pill as a precaution against illness.

From 7:00 on, my room is invaded by cockroaches. There is nothing I can do about them. The "flit" spray merely fattens them, and as to another type of repellent, they pee on it. They enjoy licking my milk bowl and egg pan. They are as big as my thumb. They disappear at the first light of dawn. Since my room is at ground level, one evening I enticed a hen inside and shut her up in there, hoping she would kill them. Actually, she not only spilled my cooking alcohol, but ate a bunch of grapes I was keeping in reserve.

Once or twice a week I go out for a good lunch at the Roma restaurant to keep up my strength. Yet it is incredible, living as I do, how much I have to spend. . . . I keep a careful note of my expenses, but even so my cash just vanishes. I'm lucky that in the evening the smell of cooking alcohol, the cockroaches, the rustling noise they make and the heat ruin my appetite, thus I save on food.

I'm told that the winter here is very humid and any form of heating is quite unknown. Yet I definitely don't want to be sent anywhere else. The people here are very good, and also I am fed up with traveling as a prisoner. I'm looking forward to the "grappa" you are sending me, which will certainly help me through the winter. I've applied for a subsidy, but without much hope of getting it. Presently I have only 450 lire in my pocket. . . .

In front of my room there is a little courtyard, then the railroad tracks, then the sea. Five or six times a day (and night) I feel nostalgic when the trains pass by. On the other hand I am completely indifferent to the ships on the horizon; and the moon on the sea, with all its light, makes me think only of fried fish. Let's face it, there is nothing great about the sea.

As to my translations, I would like to do *A Storyteller's Story*, by Sherwood Anderson. Mondadori said he was interested, but so far I've heard nothing from him. If you can manage to get hold of Mr. Rusca, at the publishing house of Mondadori in Milan, make the offer to him and tell him that I would write a book better than the original (an extraordinary translation). I would do it for 1000 lire, for 800 and even for 600 if necessary. It is a deal for them. If they accept, all we'd have to do is to ask the Ministry of the Interior to give its authorization.

I've kept in my pocket some poems written last winter. One,

The house not far from the center of Santo Stefano where Pavese was born
on September 9, 1908

Eugenio Pavese (1867–1914)

Consolin Mesturini Pavese (1868–1930)

Pavese in 1915 or 1916, dressed for his first communion

Pavese (shown by arrow) with his classmates and teachers at the Gimnasio Moderno

Pavese (right) with Sturani (left) and another friend, in 1927, near the Reagli summer house

Pavese (standing) with Carlos Predella (who was also to die a suicide), on an excursion to the Langhe woods in 1924 or 1925

Pavese (kneeling in front) in 1927 with his classmates at the D'Azeglio Lyceum

Pavese on the Po River at the time he was translating *Moby-Dick*

A page from Pavese's notebook filled with synonyms

entitled "After," is my only companion, since I think of nothing else. But this is of no interest to you.

Greetings to everyone. You may show this letter to my friends.

CESARE

On August 20, in a short letter to Maria, he spoke again mainly of money and welcomed the arrival of a Latin dictionary; but in closing he expressed his feelings toward some of his friends.

Although Pavese was a political exile, he had not actually been active in politics, and at that time he did not intend to get involved. He lacked both the resignation and the silent heroism of many political activists. He never participated in any clandestine actions of the anti-Fascists, and at times he did not hesitate to make clear references in his letters, to people who were still free, but who, in his opinion, would deserve more than he to be in prison or in exile.

Here is a letter of August 20:

Dear Maria,

I received the money order for 30 lire and the package of linen. Everything was in order. I regret that you send money so loosely, because I know that on my return you will remind me daily of my debts; therefore, I want money only when I really need it. Thank you, anyway. The Latin dictionary gave me more pleasure than yesterday's meal at the Roma restaurant (for five days I had subsisted on milk and prickly pears).

With the pipes you made a mistake, for none of the used ones draws smoke. Thank Giovanna[18] for the pens. Tell my influential friends that I hope they choke on a fish bone.

CESARE

In another letter, dated August 27 and addressed to a lady friend of the family who had advised him to start an appeal for pardon, he wrote, ". . . Of course I would do what you suggest, since personally I couldn't care less, but if a man does such a thing the woman is ashamed of him."

Once again, Pavese thought of the woman with the hoarse voice, placing her feelings before his own dignity. Dated September 9, here is the draft of the only letter he sent her:

My dear,

I write with your fountain pen. In spite of the bad experience, I cannot resist the temptation of writing a letter. I don't know if the postcards I sent to your address have arrived. I have received four from you. Through the good service of this nice young boy, I send you a souvenir. It's not new, but I have nothing else.

I spend the days (the years) in that state of expectation I experienced certain afternoons at my home between 2:30 and 3:00. Always, as the first day, the morning awakes me with the sharp pain of solitude. It's impossible to describe to you my anxieties. My suffering is not what I write, it is you; and those who divided us knew it well. I don't write tendernesses; we know why; but certainly my last human remembrance is the 13th of May.

I try to imagine that all is a long, enormous afterward, but the fantasy that enabled me to write poetry so well does not help me in making anything in life tolerable.

I thank you for all the thoughts you had for me. For you I have only one and it never ends.

Yours,
C.

On September 11, he wrote to Augusto Monti:

Dear Monti,

Since I'm still unable to digest my anger that increases every day, I lack the detachment necessary to write you with proper serenity.

My health is not too good and will be worse in the winter, which they say is windy, damp, and very unpleasant.

You know how I detest the sea; I enjoy swimming, but for this the Po was much more useful to me. Besides the swimming which, by now, is already finished, I find that a contemplative spirit cannot appreciate that perennial little game of the waves on the shore, nor the low horizon, nor the smell of fish.

The townspeople here have received me very warmly, explaining that, after all, it is their custom to do so and that they act this way with everybody.

I spend my days reading a little, studying Greek for the third time, smoking my pipe, in short I try to kill time; and I am always indignant to think that with so many remarkable inventions, the Italian genius has yet to devise a drug which causes lethargy at will, in my case for three years. This should also answer your question on my intentions to remain here or not.

I now understand the writers of the Augustan age much better, and no longer impulsively call Ovid a clown. I am naturally writing my *Tristia*.

Regarding books, I accept anything that is sent to me; if you or Sturani would like to, have my relatives show you the list I sent them (which I always update) and fish from it what you want. It is good of you to assist my relatives in the expenses of my books, as they must already support me, since I do not receive any subsidy, having been declared self-sufficient.

And finally, I am only a few kilometers from the the town of Corrado Alvaro, but I preferred him through his books. . . .

I like your decision to live part of the time in the country, part in Turin and not to change cities. Therefore, we shall see one another on my return which, I repeat, will be in three years, unless one of these mornings my hand slips while making the knot in my tie, in which case I now say goodbye to you.

PAVESE

The letter of September 20, addressed to Sturani with the nickname of "Bacarozzo,"[19] shows us again an ironic Pavese who nostalgically recalls his Turin:

Dear Bacarozzo,

First of all it's useless for you to write me on the stationery of famous hotels. We know only too well the banal origin of your wealth. . . .

Bacarozzo, you are vulgar. However, ignoring you as such and considering you a friend, I was thrilled to receive your letter, and my only regret was that you waited so long to write. I became angry when you spoke about Monferini. God knows why, but I've taken a strong dislike to him. I am surprised to hear that he is alone. Is his wife a shoe box? I wish I had a wife!

I'm not living in a hotel, but in a small furnished room full of cockroaches. When it rains (as it does all winter), my room gets flooded like a boat. And tonight, with the wind, it looks like the end of the world.

I'm not too interested in the fact that in Turin you had a heat wave, but I was moved to tears to hear about the motor cruiser "Vittoria". . . .

Oh nest of my ancestors, beloved cradle! When I read what you said of via Roma, I bellowed like a calf.

The last time you came to see me, I didn't mention how shocked that gentleman[20] was when he discovered my pornographic writings. Reading some of them, he forgot everything else: his country, his duties, and his family. He took off his hat and cried like a cow.

As to the books, dear Bacarozzo, in accordance with your ostentatious financial position, you might send me the unabridged French version of *A Thousand and One Nights* (500 or 1000 francs). If, however, such an expense should provoke your sincere but plebeian objection, you can go to my family and have them show you a list of more ordinary books. But since I don't want you to find any excuse for not doing your duty toward me, your old master, I enclose a list of books which you will even be able to find secondhand, as is common with people of your station.

Won't you tell me something about your wife, my friend? Speak to me of love. Isn't she a little bit pregnant yet? She would be even lovelier if she were.

I kiss your hand, Madame. In me you see a wretched victim of fickle Lady Luck! A Ulysses without Circe, who sighs his sweet return; a Catullus whose sparrow is dead . . . I kiss your hand. And tomorrow? Where shall we be tomorrow?

> Yours very affectionately,
> PAVESE

Here is the fragment of a letter, dated November 5, to Adolfo Ruata, another classmate of the D'Azeglio Lyceum:

. . . The rest of the time I just loaf. It's impossible to do anything of significance in this limbo; all I can do is relish, in their most ludicrous quality and quantity, boredom, disgust, enervation, spleen, and bellyache.

I practice a very squalid pastime: I catch flies. I also translate Greek, abstain from looking at the sea, roam the fields, smoke, keep my diary, reread the letters from home, maintain a useless chastity.

I do not understand why so many heads of families die, leaving beautiful wreaths of inconsolable orphans, and why I, a most consoled orphan, don't drop dead. The characteristic of our Eternal Father is, evidently, a lack of tact. . . . For example: there are people who have constant bad luck. "If they sold hats, people would be born without heads." On the other hand, the Eternal Father puts into the world those who can't do anything wrong, and after making them beautiful and bright, he still has them win the lottery. And justice is done. He even invented the devil to blame him for his own excessive blunders.

In a letter of November 19 to his sister, there are new descriptions of the winter days in Brancaleone:

Dear Maria,

. . . The cold has forced me to use a brazier. But since a copper brazier would cost too much, I found a discarded basin, filled it with ashes, and in it I burn charcoal bought sparingly. It happens, however, that—as the disillusioned young seamstresses seal doors and windows, light the coals, and lie on the bed waiting to die—one can easily wake up a corpse the next morning. It is necessary, therefore, to keep the door wide open during the entire operation with the result that the benefit of the heat is dispersed into so many pernicious drafts that cause colds, rheumatisms, and asthma. Furthermore, since my bed at night gets incredibly damp, I must heat two bricks and place them under the blankets. Otherwise, I would wake up covered with mold and maidenhair. I always get up with a headache from the coal, even though my room is well ventilated, thanks to the broken windows.

I noticed that the sows, which are numerous here, seen from behind show a frightening similarity to the back of young women: high and thin heels, nervous small legs, a vivacious wiggling of the ass, and a curly tail. I am tempted to take one to bed with me to keep me company, but I don't do it because pork is an aphrodisiac.

My asthma here is so bad that the steam I make before going to bed is not enough and I must repeat it at 3:00 in the morning, after awakening with a painful suffocating sensation. I have to get out of bed in the ice cold room and, with my ass in the air, burn incense to the Eternal Father, who, obviously taking advantage of the fact that he is a pure spiritual being, could care less if someone, disgruntled, plans to break his back.

While this letter is quite cheerful, I am not.

Greetings,
CESARE

In the letter of November 27 to Sturani, Pavese talked again about books, his asthma, his aversion to the sea and the winds. He also repeated, softened with humor, his idea of suicide:

Dear Sturani,

I received news about Turin and Dan. Incidentally, you will certainly be drafted. It is no use, when a man marries or wants to get married, History always gets in his way.

So you press me to let you know which books I want; in my letter of September 20 I gave you a list from which you can always choose. I also sent a list to my family. But I discourage you from spending more money; it is not good to be too generous, for there comes a point when the recipient begins to hate the donor.

Winter has now set in, with rain, gale force winds, and humidity at night, all of which affect my asthma like pepper. This is hard to bear because, since sleeping is the only way I can pass the time without irritability, not being able to sleep every night multiplies by ten the length of the exile.

What poetry I manage to write is insipid, and I realize that the work of a poet doesn't even help to kill time, for only very rarely do I feel any real interest in the work. I spend countless hours gloomily concentrating on an idea that as yet hardly exists. I had this problem in Turin; you can imagine here.

The sea, already so unpleasant in the summer, in the winter is dreary beyond words. The shore is a yellow strip of rough sand. On the horizon the water has an edge of tender green that is irritating. And to think it is the sea of Ulysses!

The main attraction of this town is the fish, but I do not care for fish, so I eat meat which is available only once or twice a week, when someone slaughters a calf.

I bought a strong rope, made a noose, and every morning I rub
it with soap to keep it ready. With this rope I will be able to get
some meat, when the local people invite me to participate in
the hanging of the hog which is now being fattened in rigid
chastity.

Your father-in-law wrote me a card in which he promised me
some Greek books and he called me an actor. Tell him, for now,
that if I didn't have at least the comfort of playing a role, I would
have killed myself long ago.

Even you must be aware that Pinelli has written and produced a
very bawdy comedy entitled *La Pulce d'Oro* [*The Golden Flea*]. I
had read it and found it in his usual style, but amusing. It's filthy,
but so goes the world. My "He-Goat God," so full of the most
chaste resolutions, cannot be printed, and at the same time that
type of lascivious thing is allowed to be staged. Pinelli would do
better to use his present popularity to help my return home. But all
he thinks of is making children and plays: two functions he
performs with the same organs.

PAV.

The letter of December 11 to his sister reveals Pavese's spirit of
contradiction. If his family writes him to send encouragements, he
answers offensively; if they show no sympathy, he starts cursing.

Dear Maria,

I received your postcard of December first. For your information,
I drink milk—when I can find it—however, it seems to curdle in
my stomach. By now I have even forgotten what Turin is like and
I could care less if Cesarina gets bad grades. Let her keep them.

This month, between the useless decongestants, chemicals that are
poisonous, powder against asthma that I burn every two hours, and
the quinine that destroys my beautiful intelligence, I have already
spent 52 lire and 20 cents. Almost more than for food.

I don't understand why I want to return to Turin. Except for my
health, everything is fine here; my real troubles will start when I
return home, where I will have to hear you whining. I'm thinking
of getting married here and having a child who, at two, will already
say "cuckold" and "swine."

By the way, if you plan to visit me, you will need, I think, the permission of the Ministry. I tell you this to make things more difficult for you and to discourage you from coming to bother me.

I also enjoy my economic independence.

My ill regards,
CESARE

He acts the same way toward Sturani in a letter dated December 15:

Dear Mario,

Not having succeeded with your aesthetic sermons, are you turning to moral ones? Now you accuse me of putting the blame on you for my being in Brancaleone. But where, when? Moreover, if I find pleasure in cursing the sea, what business is it of yours? After all, it is not true that poets, painters, etc., all speak well of it. I, for instance, am a poet and I have always spoken ill of it.

You reproach me for being bitter with everybody. Is it possible that after knowing me for twelve years you still do not understand a fundamental element of my character? When Pavese is unhappy or bored, has indigestion or a fleabite, he cannot tolerate anyone cheerful and contented, and he does his best to spoil their peace. That's just the way he is and that's how he manages to feel well even if he is ill. . . .

I don't understand where you read that I am discouraged. What does this word mean, anyway? Torment is something else (you know it very well). It is like a woman's period; it stops when she expects a child. Do you advise me to work? I don't need advice. In four months I have written fourteen poems, seven of which are beyond praise. . . .

In strict confidence I will add that here I am well and I am treated with every courtesy. I'm being paid for doing nothing and this is my ideal life. If I have inconveniencies, they are the salt that gives me flavor and importance. And so? I lack one thing, only one thing, and it is because of this that I want to shout, and to exploit all hardships in order to obtain it. I cannot explain to a married man what this thing is. If you haven't understood it in twelve years, you never will.

To change the subject, don't you know that I enjoy laughing and complaining in my letters? And that if I had to write only to give my news, I would not bother doing it? . . .

You were saying that your wife (I kiss you with affection, Madame) found Moravia's book bad.[21] Nonsense! It's a book written with his feet, mistaken in its psychology, with a distasteful atmosphere, yet witty, tragic, captivating, phenomenal: a great feuilleton. It is better than going to the movies.

I have heard from you, your father-in-law, and my sister that you have all been sent advance notices confirming the publication of my *Work Wearies*. Let's hope so. However, I'm still not convinced that the book is coming out at all. When a man writes the finest poetry of the century, he is bound to have a long Calvary. As you can see, I contracted the persecution complex from you. But what a beautiful destiny! I suffer like Dante Alighieri, Homer, and other great men.

> Through the dark woods
> the troubadour goes alone,
> tamed by the rigor of destiny.

I am still waiting for your bawdy short poem which certainly has been inspired by *my* most recent misfortunes.

Greetings,
PAVESE

On December 17 he was notified that *Work Wearies* would be published. On the same day he wrote a letter to Irma Sini, an in-law of his sister who was trying to convince him to petition for a pardon:

Dear and kind lady,

Thank you for remembering me. Your letter and the one from my sister, dated the tenth, are full of good sense. However, if one were to live only by common sense, there would be no point in living, since the world would be so boring. It's beautiful, instead, that the world should resemble a cage of lunatics. My madness is melancholic and poetic, while others may have a madness which is violent or passionate. After all, one who has traveled handcuffed across half of Italy has every right to be a little abnormal.

At this point your advice is not to be taken lightly. When I
have six asthma attacks a day (now I have four), I promise to
reconsider your suggestion. O.K.?

I'm pleased to hear that you are anxious to read my book. I find
myself in the same situation as those authors who, when one of
their works was ready to be published, spread the news of their
premature death. There is nothing more beautiful than disappearing
when your poems are being published. Even if only out of
politeness, everyone feels obligated to speak well of you and to buy
your poems. . . .

CESARE PAVESE

In a letter of December 23 he wrote to his sister about a gypsy
woman who had told his fortune, predicting that he would be
betrayed in love:

Yesterday a pregnant gypsy came . . . and offered to read my
fortune. She said: "There are two women, one far away who is dying
of love for you, and another (unknown to you) who lives nearby and
thinks all day, 'give me a son.'" She added: "You—whorelover—give
me more money and I shall tell you everything." By then I knew
enough, therefore I didn't give her anything more and the gypsy
predicted that I would be cuckolded many times. And so, for one lira
a beautiful pregnant woman ruined my day.

Then every evening, three or four shepherds, or a group of young
men, stop in front of my door and perform a small concert with
bagpipes, fifes, and triangles in honor of the novena. On the last
day I will have to pay them. Those who see me now, wipe tears
from their eyes with the back of their hands when they think I will
spend Christmas away from home, something that for them is
worse than a blow on the head. And there are pious women who
send me sweets, or dried figs, oranges, and other things.

Then the letter of December 27:

Dear Maria,

Here is the letter of my serenity. By now I've grown used to my
destiny and I let the days pass like the man already wet who lets
the rain pummel him. I've grown used to the asthma, the loneliness,

and the uncertainty. Except for smoking, I live, if I want to, on
three lire a day. I nibble on my memories as if they were
pomegranates and think that things could be worse.

The people of these villages have a tact and a courtesy which
have only one explanation: the civilization here was once Greek.
Even the women, when they see me stretched out in the field like a
dead man, say, "There is the prisoner" with such a Hellenic cadence
that I imagine myself as Ibycus and I am quite happy.

Ibycus, for your information, is a poet of the sixth century B.C.,
born in this area. He was assassinated on the main road and is the
author of this fragment:

> And in spring the quinces
> irrigated by the currents
> of rivers, sheltering the intact
> garden of the nymphs,
> and the vineyards' gems
> grown in the shade of leaves,
> blossom: with me, instead,
> the unrequited love,
> storming from Venus
> like the Thracian north wind
> among lightnings,
> sinister, frenzied, with futile furies,
> shakes from the roots
> my reason. . . .

One should not forget that Ibycus roamed like a lost soul,
through Southern Italy and the islands, seeking hospitality. The
people of this area are still the same now: if the garden of the
nymphs has disappeared, hospitality remains intact.

It's a pleasure to read Greek poetry in the land where apart from
the medieval infiltrations, everything evokes the times when the
girls placed pitchers on their heads and slowly returned home. And
since the Greek past is now in a state of sterile ruin—a broken
column, a fragment of poetry, a meaningless name—nothing is more
Greek than these abandoned regions. The colors of the countryside
are Greek: yellow and red rocks, the light green of prickly pears
and agaves, the pink of oleanders and geraniums, in bunches
everywhere, in the fields and along the railroad tracks, and the

olive color of barren hills. Even the bagpipe, that awful instrument of Christmas, repeats the sound, something between an organ and a harp, which accompanied Paris in his times of leisure when on the plains of Mount Ida he ate the cheese from his sheep and dreamed of Helen's love.

I remember that last summer, for lack of something better to do, relying on my ephebic appearance, I undressed—as much as the regulations permitted—along the seashore and, with the "candid flower" of my "body" so exposed, I created Hellenic scenes that the geraniums of those seashores would not soon forget.

In short, I believe in metempsychosis and am convinced I'm reincarnating Ibycus, the one of the "quinces."

Sappho wrote:

> The moon is gone
> and so are the Pleiades, it is the middle
> of the night, the hour is passed:
> I lie in bed alone.

I instead, lie in the company of certain crickets attracted by my warm bed.

The crickets remind me that Carocci wrote today, telling me that *it's not possible to find the paper* to print *Work Wearies*. I knew things were going too well! This has stirred up again my rage against the embargo,[22] and if it weren't that my asthma does not allow me to walk two hundred meters without collapsing, I would already have volunteered for the war, as you advised me to do in your postcard of December 12. At any rate, I shall still be able to do it if I get better. . . .

I hope you like this letter. You must try to understand that *I am unable to provide* the news you seem to want to hear. I always forget something; however, you can easily understand, from the tone of my letters, my state of mind and therefore how I feel.

Give everyone my greetings in proportion to their love for me.

As for you, there is no need for words.

CESARE

The letter of January 5, 1936, addressed to Luigi Sini, his sister's brother-in-law, is full of humor:

Dear Luigi,

When I read your letter, I experienced the same type of amused curiosity with which one receives the visit of the parish priest who comes to arrange details of a funeral, a wedding, or a baptism. I would never have believed that the frightful Luigi was such a religious zealot. "Study is your preferred occupation . . . the little things that transform your little room into a cozy little study . . . Christian resignation . . . serenity, resignation, and hope . . ." These quotations from your letter resembled (or am I wrong?) the expressions used by the priest to console, for instance, a parishioner suffering from syphilis. And now that I think about it, I seem to recall what your sister Federica used to say: that as a child, you were playing with little altars pretending to be a priest.

Of course, I fully appreciate your good intentions toward me, but I must warn you that the ways you chose to cheer me up do not work. I have two kinds of troubles: one physical (asthma)—and it would certainly take more than a compliment to relieve me of it—and the other moral (lack of company)—which nothing but company can alleviate. But let's forget about it. I have by now decided to say that I am well and that there is nothing else to add.

I hear that you're slaving away like a dog at the office. Is it worthwhile to be such an honest citizen as you are, when you have to lead a life that makes you resemble, physically, a dried fish and morally, a prisoner? I certainly do not envy you, even from Brancaleone. My troubles are mere trifles compared to your slaving away.

You're precisely the sort of man for whom *Work Wearies* was written. Buy a copy, read it, and you will learn the many ways—all honest, of course—to have fun on the job in spite of the office manager. But how stupid of me! I was forgetting you are the office manager.

Wishing you new and legitimate advancements in your career, I thank you for your letter and send greetings to you and your doleful, sacred family.

Yours,
CESARE

On January 16 he wrote the following letter to his sister:

Dear Maria,

I received your card of the 1st as well as the two American books *Tragedy of Lynching* and *Treatment of Delinquency*. If you allow me to make a kind reproach, I would like to state that sending me such treatises on American delinquency, with vivid details of penitentiaries and electric chairs, is not the best way to cheer me up. Overcoming my instinctive repugnance, I will try, however, to read them. In so doing, I will deserve to go to Heaven. . . .

It's a month and a half now since I've been able to write any poetry, which is the worst thing that could happen to me.

Besides eating artichokes, I find much to console me here. For example, I'm collecting pretty colored stones on the beach for Maria Luisa, studying the flight of birds, waiting for the cuttlefish season to begin, and choosing a name for each of my sons, whom I shall bring up in strict chastity. Chastity is the first virtue of all: through it, races become stronger, kingdoms more powerful, the arts are perfected and souls are saved. What is a man without chastity? A rag, a twig, a feather in the wind, a drop of water in the sea, a cloud in the sky, a hair on the head of a lunatic, a locomotive without an engineer. I could write an infinite amount of things about this virtue. In Greek it is called the virtue of the lambs. Unquestionably, my sons will be chaste and handsome. . . .

CESARE

He finally received a copy of *Work Wearies* and he talked about it in this letter of February 15 to his sister:

Dear Maria,

I received your cards, a letter from Sturani and one from Monti. They meant nothing to me. Fortunately I also received the book by Stendhal, a gift that moved me deeply.

I am desperately sorry that my poems are such a success; I've been afraid of it for some time. Can a book be any good if "colleagues" here and there, "journalists," dogs and pigs of the literary world find in it "an exquisite feeling of artist and observer"? I am much more interested in your visit to the police office. . . .

Since I have not been able to correct the last proofs, due to my being so far away, my poems are full of errors. . . .

Try to console Sturani, who is depressed before my triumphs, and tell him that I would prefer being in bed with a wife, as he is, to having written this book. It is, however, a book that will last long after my generation is laid to rest. Tell him that he is the only one who understands something of it.

Also, thank Monti for his good intentions. But you should tell him that he has made an error I would never have expected from a professor like him: he has confused biography with aesthetics, praising certain poems for their documentary value, not for their merit as poetry.

I hope you have received by now, with my kisses, the copy of *Work Wearies* and my three letters which recorded a crucifixion crisis of which I am still convalescent. But the relapses will be fatal.

CESARE

On March 2 he wrote his most distressed letter. In it is the phrase: "I touch the mole on my cheek to convince myself of my own identity," which brings to mind this sentence from his diary: "I look in the mirror to keep myself company."

Dear Maria,

When a man writes letters instead of poetry, he is washed up. Memory is an ugly thing.

In the evening I stick my nose out and I see Orion, so beautiful and limpid, which reminds me of a book I read in other times.

I breathe the smell of trees, at the window, and I think of when, two years ago, I used to go to give lessons to Corradino, at the end of via Nizza.

A train passes, reminding me that tomorrow one will pass at four in the morning through the pinewoods of Viareggio.

I gaze at the distant mountains and shiver with cold, remembering the Christmas spent in Cheneil.

I undress for bed and I feel pity for my naked body, so young and beautiful and so alone.

I go out in the morning, as early as I am allowed, and remember when I used to go to the café at dawn, smoking my pipe while waiting.

I read in the *Gazzetta del Popolo* the names of Turin's movie houses and I imagine who would be watching the films at the "Statuto," at the "Alpi," or at the "Ideal". . . .

I touch the mole on my cheek to convince myself of my own identity.

I think back to the period when I was translating *Moby Dick* and everything was still to come.

I remember when I could afford not to sleep one night because of a little jealousy—I dared then to call it by this name—and I did not know yet, that being away from her could gnaw at me like a shark or cancer.

I recall how furious I was with those who insisted on coming boating with me on the Po, and I mourn for my past unhappiness.

What an utter fool I was to believe, as I did then, that personal isolation, even for a moment, would be bliss.

All day I review these litanies and other infinite ones.

CESARE

Pavese's torment in being far from the woman he loved, the hoarse-voiced woman, was emphatically repeated in four very brief letters where he begged for news from her. Was this anguished plea perhaps the foreboding of what would happen upon his return from exile?

The four letters were all written to his sister, and here are two of them. One is dated February 29:

Dear Maria,

I continue to receive nothing. . . .

If she could feel, as I do, the gnawing of distance, which is like the bite of someone starving, or of a shark or of cancer, she would write me. The book [*Work Wearies*] was sent to her.

I only ask her for a card. February 25th was her birthday.

CESARE

The other is dated March 12:

Dear Maria,

. . . When are you going to stop pretending that you do not receive my letters asking for news, news, and news about her, and for a card signed by her?

And you still have the gall to ask if I need anything. What have I been asking for an entire month? . . .

CESARE

11

From Poetry to Short Stories

His confinement in Brancaleone Calabro lasted nearly one year. Through an appeal and some outside intervention, the two remaining years of his sentence were remitted.

When Pavese learned that he was free to return to Turin, he reacted as he always did to news which should have elated him: he remained silent and detached, as if it were something that did not concern him. It was not disbelief, but rather his natural incapacity to experience happiness, as if he were convinced that nothing but sad things could occur in his life.

So instead of rejoicing at the idea of going home, he thought that, in reality, he had grown accustomed to a solitary life, even to the boredom of the sea; and Turin appeared to him as an unreal place, wrapped in a dense fog, a city no longer his. In those moments all the ties he had insisted on maintaining through his daily letters to family and friends seemed suddenly to have broken.

That was another manifestation of his contradictions and of his incapacity to face reality. He would later write in his novel *The Political Prisoner* that he "would have had more satisfaction in coming out of prison than in returning from exile, because behind bars the whole world seems beautiful, while life in exile is like any other life, only a little dirtier."

I found the following note among Pavese's papers, written on the back of an envelope: "I must return to Turin for her, immediately."

The woman with the hoarse voice continued to be his dominant thought. With her in mind, the train trip to Turin seemed endless. He was not handcuffed or escorted by policemen, but his feelings were not much different from when he had first been taken to Brancaleone Calabro.

When Pavese arrived at the station in Turin, he was seized by emotion. He carried two suitcases full of books and papers. At the exit he was greeted by the smiling face of Sturani. Pavese looked him up and down, without any exchange of words or greetings. Then suddenly, a burning question: "Where is she?" Sturani lost his smile. He did not want to answer, and tried to help him with the suitcases. Pavese stopped him, repeating, peremptorily, the question. Sturani was forced to give an answer: "Forget about her," he said. "She was married yesterday morning." Pavese turned pale; the suitcases fell from his hands and he fainted. People ran to his aid. He slowly recovered and told those who helped him that they could leave, that it was only a temporary indisposition. But the news had hit him very hard, and Sturani, confused and dismayed, could not find words to comfort him. Bent under the weight of his suitcases, Pavese walked lifelessly out of the station.

His silence would last for many days. Closed in his study on via Lamarmora, he was unapproachable, even by his sister's family. For days he did not eat; his books remained locked in the suitcases. The thought of suicide haunted him.

Abandonment by the woman with the hoarse voice destroyed Pavese's confidence in himself and in others, depriving him of any purpose. When he would slowly start to recover, it would not be to look for new human contacts, but rather to take refuge in literature, and to acquire a philosophy both bitter and inconsistent, a calculated betrayal of the reality of life.

On April 10, 1936, he wrote in his diary:

. . . Having reached utter abjection morally, the thought occurs to me that there should be material abjection as well. How fitting it would be if, for example, my shoes were full of holes.

Only this way can one explain my present suicidal state. I know that I am forever condemned to think of suicide when faced with any embarrassment or grief. This is what terrifies me: my basic principle is suicide, never committed, never to be committed, but the thought of it caresses my sensibility.

The terrible thing is that whatever is left to me now, is not enough to help me, because—betrayals aside—I was in an identical state before, without finding, even then, moral salvation. I will be no stronger this time, that much is clear.

Yet—unless infatuation deceives me, and I do not think it does—I had found the way of salvation. In spite of my basic weakness, that person was able to tie me to a discipline, to a sacrifice, through the simple gift of herself . . . By doing so, she raised me to an intuition of new duties and made them *take shape* before my eyes. Because, left to myself, as I know from experience, I am *convinced* I shall not succeed in these duties. United to her in flesh and destiny, I would have succeeded. Of that I am equally convinced. I am a coward, and she would have been able to spur me on.

Instead, what has she done! Perhaps she does not know it, or, if she does, she does not care. And that is fair, because she is herself and has her past to guide her in the future.

But this is what she has done. I had an adventure, during which I was judged and found unworthy to continue. In front of this debacle, the regret of my having lost a lover, even with all its atrocious feelings, is absolutely nothing. The awareness of this disaster becomes confused in my mind with the heavy blows I have not felt since 1934: away with aesthetics, away with poses, away with genius, away with all the nonsense! Have I ever in my life done anything that was not the action of a fool?

A fool in the most banal and irreparable sense; a man who *does not know* how to live, who has not developed morally, who is frivolous, who sustains himself with the crutch of suicide, but does not commit it.

His love tragedy in 1936 was not solely responsible for Pavese's detachment from the objectives he had nourished at the D'Azeglio Lyceum under Monti's stern guidance and later, in the stimulating contacts with his mates at the university. When he returned from confinement, Monti, Ginzburg, and Mila were still in jail. It was they who had taught him by their examples that one could not live without purpose and faith, and who would have been able to encourage him and give him confidence once again.

The exile did not transform Pavese into a political militant, since he saw it only as a long, useless period of boredom. Moreover, he was left with the bitterness and anguish of having lost his woman, with the remorse of having yielded to outside pressures instead of resisting and serving his entire sentence as his friends were then doing.

In the isolation of Brancaleone Calabro, Pavese had been unable to follow a moral regimen. On the contrary, he had accepted all the self-destructive temptations, surviving only in the hope of seeing that woman again, and in the success of his poetry.

During approximately that same period, Gramsci, who was a political prisoner too, was writing:

In prison one should never make vague and nebulous plans or promises, nor should one test one's nerves; otherwise it happens that even I, though extremely patient and capable of every inhibition, become too inflexible in the affirmation of my own will, only to demonstrate to myself that I am still alive.

Pavese had done exactly the opposite. While Pavese had grown to detest even the sea in his determination to be bitter with everything and everybody, Gramsci, who was not only tormented by asthma but physically ruined and only a few months away from death, had enough human tenderness and warmth within himself to remind his son Delio that for their goldfinch "the fresh lettuce must be chopped up into very fine pieces."

Gramsci, who was dying because there were men who had decided to destroy him, still felt enough love for his fellow man to write, as a testament to his son Delio: "Dear Delio, love the history of living men, everything that concerns men, as many men as possible, all the men in the world who unite to form a society, who work, struggle and better themselves."

After having been abandoned by the woman with the hoarse voice, Pavese suffered other bitter disappointments. The poems of *Work Wearies* found few readers. That negative response to his work of many years increased his bitterness and mistrust. Was writing still worthwhile? Was working still worthwhile?

Yet no one as much as he, was then aware of the importance of those poems to his artistic experience. They were significant, among other things, because with the new style he used in them, he intended to challenge the methods of poetry fashionable in Italy at that time.

His certainty about the value of his work, together with a new friendship, provided him with the strength he needed to regain his vitality. During that period, Mr. and Mrs. Roata, to whom he would remain close until his death, introduced to him a young clerk who needed lessons in Greek and Latin literature. His name was Paolo Cinanni and he had come from Calabria to settle in Turin.

Pavese gladly accepted the opportunity to work and immediately liked his pupil, above all because he was Calabrian. He told him he had fond memories of the people in Brancaleone and showed him the letters and postcards he continued to receive from his friends there. Every morning, from 7:30 to 8:30, Cinanni would go to Pavese's home for his lesson.

After a month, when Pavese collected the fifty lire agreed upon, he invited Cinanni to accompany him to the Lattes Bookstore, in the center of town, and showed him a volume of Pirandello's short stories that cost eighty lire. To his pupil's astonishment, he added thirty lire to the fifty he had just received, and paid for the book, saying: "Read these short stories, they're interesting, then tell me what you think."

Cinanni intended to take the Classical Lyceum final exam. He was a hot-headed youth, with revolutionary political ideas, and had already been arrested because he listened to the clandestine Communist radio and reported what he heard to his colleagues in the office. Discovered by his supervisor, he had spent a few days in prison.

As Pavese and Cinanni became closer, the exchange of their political ideas intensified. Pavese gave Cinanni, as a present, a copy of *Das Kapital* and some books on the Soviet Union. He often repeated his gratitude to his young pupil and friend for having made him love life again, by coming to wake him up for his lesson each morning, by forcing him to work, to study, to read Dante and Lucretius again. Cinanni had distracted him from his thoughts of suicide.

Cinanni still remembers how Pavese would read with passion Lucretius' *Ode to Venus*, commenting immediately afterwards, quite sadly, that there were no Venuses on earth, and if some did exist, they would not be worthy of odes. Pavese and Cinanni met every day until the eve of the Partisan War. In those months Pavese also resumed his assiduous collaboration with the Einaudi Publishing House, another source of employment and another step toward reconciliation with life.

In Italy meanwhile, the crisis of ideas grew more dramatic. Croce himself was affected by the problems of Italian liberalism, and all the literary movements, as well as the state school system, were succumbing to the Fascist regime. Luigi Einaudi kept silent. Those who continued to think in a manner contrary to the regime did so within prison walls. It became particularly difficult to remain faithful to tradition without falling into provincialism, or to combat nationalism without yielding to anarchy.

With no guide except his desire to learn and to discover, Pavese read and read, translated, and always searched for new material, thus risking the eclecticism he so dreaded. Mysticism attracted many writers. Pavese was not a believer, yet he had a religious sense of life, and in those years he developed certain doubts that continued to torment him for a long time. The collapse of all cultural organizations, together with the exasperation of Crocean idealism, led to the abandonment of every humanistic message, and discouraged every serious effort at inquiry. After overcoming his human anguish, Pavese was faced by literary anguish.

It was then he formed the conviction that salvation could only be reached by one who knew how to stay alone in his literary trench. Attracted by the most dangerous elements of irrationalism, he was approaching decadence. His theory of suicide was the inevitable consequence. In his diary, he expressed he had the need to "isolate himself" and feel like a "leaf in the wind."

During that period Pavese consolidated his theory of self-destruction, exalting the poetics of escape from reality. Reality, he said, was "a prison where one vegetates and always will." Suffering from irresolutions, morbid tendencies, inferiority complexes, and from anxieties that were idyllic and tragic at the same time, he tended, during those years, to resemble Hamlet. All this expressed the involution of Pavese's generation, but was later exploited by those who, believing they understood him, had, in reality, ignored his most important virtues.

Those who emphasize Pavese's boredom with life do not completely follow his struggle, and ignore that he managed, once again, to overcome his crisis. At that time, he resumed his study of the value and meaning of words. He returned to filling his notebooks with synonyms, the result of constant and rigorous research. He was even able to control his asthma and could smoke a pipe. Thus, he succeeded in defeating his moral and physical shortcomings.

At night, in his room on via Lamormora, Pavese returned to ponder the poems in *Work Wearies*. He continued to believe in his creations, and, more importantly, he was convinced that he needed to return to a world of hills and clear skies, like his Langhe, in order to breathe some pure air again. Since his disappointment in love, he had relied more on intelligence than on feeling, and could now appraise his poems more objectively. That detached evaluation inspired the comments he added to the new edition of *Work Wearies* published by Einaudi. In exile he had already written some of the most lucid pages of his diary on the theme of his poetry:

Chance made me begin and finish *Work Wearies* with poems about Turin—more precisely Turin as a place from where one returns, Turin as a place to which one will return. One could say that this book is the enlargement of Santo Stefano and its conquest of Turin. Among the many explanations of this collection of poems, this is one. The village becomes city, nature becomes human life, the boy becomes man. As I see it, "from Santo Stefano to Turin" is a myth of all the possible meanings of this book.

Work Wearies was, therefore, the reflection of this transition, the broadening of Pavese's horizons both in imagination and in reality.

In the poem "South Seas" for instance, the return of a cousin from America is significant precisely because the cousin has come back to his town strengthened by the new world he has seen, with the ability to recreate that world on his own land. To the romanticism of the country is added the realism of the city: weary women, casual loves, cafés, factories, prisons, a world populated with characters determined to live in spite of their suffering, daily turmoil, and inevitable disillusionments.

The vivid and picturesque atmosphere of Santo Stefano's landscapes prepared Pavese's imagination for his first encounter with mythology, while the intense and laborious atmosphere of the city directed him toward a research of style through the classics.

In 1934, Pavese had elaborated his poetic theses in the essay "The Poet's Craft" where he explained that his attempt at narrative poetry derived from the American authors he translated, from his experiments in writing short stories, and from his exercises with the Piedmontese dialect in order to revive a language that was threatened by the invasion of so many official words.

He also explained that his narrative verse had originally been instinctive. As a child, he had repeated with a humming sound, the emphatic cadences of the sentences he read that most impressed him. Now, he rhymed his poems by humming their cadences. This of course was a departure from the traditional poetic meter, as well as from the free verse of Whitman whom, nevertheless, he deeply loved.

He added that his poetry was influenced by two other elements: his painstaking study of Shakespeare, and paintings by his friend Sturani and by Spazzapan that provided him with examples of images presented in rarefied settings.

Pavese's literary activity of those years was dedicated to poetry. From 1928 to 1932 he was occupied primarily with his translations and essays; from 1932 to 1937 with poetry; from 1937 to his death, with narrative prose, except for the final poetic parenthesis of *Death Will Come and It Will Have Your Eyes.*

In the preface to the second edition of *Work Wearies*, Pavese declared that the time had come for him to abandon narrative poetry, because he doubted he could completely realize the fantastic rapport between image and reality. Already rooted in him was the fear that a direct association with reality would lead him to naturalism, rather than helping him to maintain the balance he always intended between realism and symbolism.

It was then that he formulated his creed: "Events will occur not because reality wants it so, but because intelligence so decides."

The discovery of the symbol tempted Pavese precisely because of his need to escape his real, bitter, and solitary life. The political confinement had driven him to doubt everyone's loyalty. The betrayal suffered in his private life left him even more resentful toward others. This literary refuge into the symbol, his resort to the irrational and the arbitrary became necessary in order to find significance in his life and work. Fortunately, the human warmth of a very few friends would prevent him from turning this escape creed into a constant method of life and work.

He began to write short stories, some brief and without a plot, others longer and close to the structure of a novel. He needed to speak about himself, and his diary was not sufficient. He wrote it only to be read after his death, almost with the intention of degrading himself and appearing unrecognizable to those who professed to have understood him when he was alive.

To those short stories, Pavese entrusted his true self. He sought refuge in some of the characters, finding in them a greater space for expression than was bound to any confession. The stories would be published posthumously, in 1953, with the title *Festival Night*. Perhaps Pavese did not want to see them published in his lifetime because, like his lyceum letters and those written during his confinement, they introduce us to his true biography. In "Suicides," written in 1938, he said:

> There are days when the city where I live, the people, the traffic, the trees, everything wakes up in the morning with a strange look, familiar and at the same time unrecognizable, like those moments when one looks at oneself in the mirror and asks: "Who is that man?" For me, those are the only days in the whole year I really enjoy.
>
> On such mornings I get away from the office a little early, if I can, and go

down into the streets to mingle with the crowd, staring freely at everyone who goes by, as perhaps some of them do at me; in such moments I really do feel a self-confidence that makes me quite a different man.

I am convinced that never in my whole life shall I have anything more precious than the revelation of how I can obtain these moments at will. One way of prolonging them that I have sometimes found successful is to sit in a modern café with wide, clear windows, and from there grasp the bustle of the traffic and of the street, the reflections of colors and voices, and the inner peace that regulates all this commotion.

Pavese was already fleeing from solitude, searching for people, for the movement and sounds of life, and in the middle of this bustle we can recognize his inner calm. It is true that between himself and people he placed the window of a "modern café," but even behind that window he perceived life and looked for it. Moreover, in the same short story, he exposed the innate flaw in his character:

For some years now, I have suffered from delusions and the most bitter remorse, yet I can affirm that my most cordial wish is only for this peace, this serenity. I am not made for storms or struggles; even if on certain mornings I go down, all daring, in the streets, and my pace seems a challenge, I repeat that I ask nothing more of life than to be allowed to watch it.

We are aware of the delusions of which he spoke; and remorse came to him as he observed the dignified and virile example of his friends, Monti, Mila, Bobbio, Foà, and the Pajettas, who were more harshly sentenced than he and who spent the best years of their lives in prison.

That remorse would culminate during the Partisan War when peculiar and unpredictable events would draw him away from any commitment and risk, causing him to suffer greatly as he limited himself to watching life rather than living it.

In his diary, during those years, he pushed his sincerity to an excess of self-destruction:

Naturally, everybody says to you, "What does it matter? That's not the only thing. Life is full of variety. A man can be good for something else," but no one—not even men—will look at you unless you have that power that radiates. And women say to you, "What does it matter?" and so on, but they marry someone else. And to marry means building a life, a thing you will never do. Which means that you have remained a child too long.

But in 1938, thanks to his work, to Cinanni's faithful friendship, and to the fraternal exhortation of Geymonat, Mila, and Bobbio, Pavese seemed to resume contact with life.

12

From *The Political Prisoner*
to *The Harvesters*

As a former political prisoner, Pavese knew he was under police surveillance. The fact that he was working at Einaudi, considered a cove of anti-Fascist intellectuals, certainly was not favorable to him. However, neither in his diary nor in the works he wrote during that period do we find an open reference to this surveillance. He would allude to political situations only rarely and briefly. And yet there were political and military events that affected him deeply; the Spanish Civil War was one. It was the subject of many conversations at Einaudi, and Cinanni, too, often spoke about it. The names of those who had left Turin to volunteer in the fight against Franco were often mentioned. Those names soon became legendary: Togliatti, Pajetta, Negarville, Leone, Ravera, Longo, Montagnana, Giua, Calosso, etc.

The news that affected Pavese most deeply was the death of Renzo Giua who had been a student at the D'Azeglio and was a member of the fraternity of Monti's ex-students. When Renzo died fighting in Spain, his father, who was in prison because of his anti-Fascism, received the news without shedding a tear. Pavese was shocked and impressed by this. It was one of the events that most notably led him to reflect on his own way of life. Then there was Cinanni who continued to accompany him each night to friends' houses where the anti-Fascist conspirators met. Pavese frequented two of these homes in particular: his friend Geymonat's and that of Guaita, a Communist. On other evenings Pavese, who was a tireless walker, would stroll with Cinanni, especially through the working-class neighborhoods.

Cinanni often brought him to Borgo San Paolo where lived the families of those Communist conspirators who were in prison or had been forced to emigrate. Cinanni pointed out to him the houses of the Montagnanas, the Negarvilles, and the Longos. That was the part of Turin which never bent to Fascism.

Pavese listened very intently to Cinanni. And when in the summer he would take short trips to Santo Stefano, he was already prepared to understand how even there Fascism had not made proselytes, but only victims. The peasants were not as talkative as they used to be; the poverty had worsened and illiteracy remained an incurable wound despite the many promises of the various Ministers of Education.

In Santo Stefano, Pavese visited the home of Scaglione (Nuto) who was against Fascism and spoke to him of the very difficult conditions of the peasants, just as Cinanni and other friends would speak to him, during the evening discussions in Turin, of the serious situation of the city workers. He learned that many young peasants who had tried to find work in the city had been sent back to the country because of the Fascist aversion to urbanization.

Nuto would take him to the hills to talk with the peasants. Pavese felt more at ease there with them than he did in the city. And his statements were so openly anti-Fascist that one day Nuto asked him if he was a Communist. Pavese answered no, shaking his head. He was, in fact, not a Communist, even if his method of judging the situation was the same as Cinanni's.

The consequences of that political awareness became soon evident in his work as a writer. The short story no longer offered him the means to narrate adequately the political facts he so deeply understood. Nor did he believe that the translation of American novels continued to be useful to Italian readers. He felt that the time had come to present as protagonists the farmers and workers of his country, since even in Italy one could by then feel the ferment of revolt.

Politics had already entered some of his short stories. In the one entitled "Friends" the protagonist is an unemployed veteran of the Abyssinian War. Unemployment was the only legacy left him by the war, but at the same time he had learned to understand the futility of those massacres.

> "Have you done any killing yourself?" asked Celestino, rising to his feet.
> "I don't know. Nobody knows. I've seen dead bodies, that's for sure."
> "The rule of war. Shall we go?"
> Rosso remained seated, his head raised, confused.

In the same short story is an awareness that war had increased the poverty in Italy and that the Southerners had to migrate to Turin to avoid suffering from hunger:

> Rosso planted both elbows on the table and stared at his friend. "This wine is like Turin," he began. "There's more Southern than Piedmontese wine in it. Still it's warming, that's the main thing. Would you believe that the Southerners, when you live with them, are much the same as us? Rotters are rotters wherever you find them, but the right sort make the best friends you could ever imagine."

Already alive in Pavese were a political concern and the world of his favorite heroes.

He wrote his first novel, *The Political Prisoner*, between November 27, 1938 and April 16, 1939. It would be published several years later together with another novel, *The House on the Hill*, under the title *Before the Cock Crows*.

Since Pavese would later be accused of imitating American authors, it is important to stress the fact that *The Political Prisoner*, although it is his first novel and followed many important translations of the Americans, has an originality of style and a way of constructing the plot which have nothing in common with the American novel.

The story related to Pavese's political confinement. However, in Stefano, the protagonist of *The Political Prisoner*, Pavese did not want to project himself as he had been at the time of his exile, with his torments, his weaknesses, and his remorse; he wanted to appear as the Pavese of the period when he wrote the novel, spiritually strengthened and calm. The irony and the despairing sense of abandonment that had pervaded his letters from confinement are absent. Stefano resembles Pavese in only a few particulars, most notably in his way of treating women. When women appear in the novel, Stefano suffers the same torments as Pavese, and for Stefano too, women are only objects of compassion or revenge.

The politics expressed in the novel differ greatly from those of the irritated letters from confinement. The conversations with Gey-monat and Cinanni, the memory of Renzo Giua, the walks to Borgo San Paolo, had all had an impact on Pavese. The exile, who is called "anarchist" by the people in the village, not only has a symbolic value, but also expressed Pavese's new political reality:

> Stefano was now passing in front of Concia's house and thought of the prison up there . . . Another wall had added itself to his prison, a wall made of vague terror, of a guilty anxiety. Up there, on that lower parapet, sat a man, an abandoned comrade. It would not involve much risk to say a word to him, to visit him. . . . Stefano admitted to being a great coward.

This harsh self-criticism was already an act of courage.

From June 3 to August 16, 1939, Pavese wrote *The Harvesters*, a book of denunciation and revolt. Meanwhile he had returned several times to Santo Stefano, and Scaglione had described to him once more the increasingly wretched conditions of the peasants. There was a gloomy atmosphere on his hills and among his people. Work offered no reward. The young men were called to arms and had to be always prepared for war. In this climate Pavese wrote *The Harvesters*, and he wanted his new novel to reflect the mood of the people, their language charged with anguish and violence.

In *The Political Prisoner*, the protagonist Stefano is an intellectual who endeavors to protect his solitude so that he can better taste his suffering. The prose is soft, slow, and fluid. When there is political and social content, it is immediately subdued and fused in the ecstasy of memories, in the daily chores of a man who refuses to fight and loathes heroic gestures.

In *The Harvesters*, however, the social content takes control, giving the style a polemical and violent character. The tragic conditions of the Langhe are reflected in this novel which marked another return by Pavese to his beloved Piedmont. In Alba I found a letter written by Pavese on June 23, 1949 to Professor Nicola Enrichens who was a school principal in Santo Stefano. Here is the most interesting part of the letter:

> I will cite my case: I arrived at the land (whichever it may be) of *The Harvesters* and of *Work Wearies* after going through very violent literary attachments to "The South Seas" (Oceania of the nineteenth century and America of the twentieth century). I *literally* discovered myself in those remote people and places. Besides, all of us learned in school that Alfieri discovered himself and Italy traveling around the world. You cannot imagine the great wealth one rediscovers in our own classics and in the Greek classics, when one approaches them after returning from the American, German, or Russian twentieth century. It is the same feeling one experiences for the family and the country. I am madly in love with Santo Stefano, but only because I come from far away.

By then his past experiences, both human and literary, allowed him to rediscover his land without any shade of prejudice and to see in his hills not their picturesque fascination, but their tragic humanity.

With *The Harvesters*, Pavese also wanted to shatter the literary fashions of the period based on conventional, idyllic plots. *The Harvesters*, instead, is built on the incestuous passion of Talino for his sister Gisella. Pavese, therefore, proposed a classical Greek theme, to which he had already made allusions in his letters from confinement.

The Harvesters is the fruit of a new political conviction. Pavese had surpassed the confession of his own cowardice and had finally arrived at a recognition of the validity of class struggle. He abandoned his attitude of proud detachment and became more active, at least in his writing, in the fight against Fascism.

The novel begins at the gates of a Turin prison where those peasants who have tried to leave the country for the city are locked up together with the workers—as if Pavese wanted to demonstrate that whoever desired freedom, in those years, would only end up in jail. Berto's escape from the city is symbolically identified with his escape from prison. The political significance is obvious even if in Pavese's novel, Berto and Talino do not go to jail for political reasons. We must not forget that *The Harvesters,* written in 1939, was published in 1941, at the height of Fascism, and therefore certain precautions were necessary.

The condemnation of the poverty and the wretched life of the country people, whose only contacts with the state are through the police, the tax collector, and the draft calling their sons to war, grows page after page. Here is Berto's first encounter with Talino's father, the old man Vinverra:

> "There's always work to be done in the country, eh?" I told him.
>
> "Every man has his own. But the land eats more than we do."
>
> "What do you mean?"
>
> "I mean that hard work is not enough. What little we make we have to put back into the land, to get it ready for the next year."
>
> "Then there is some profit."
>
> "There would be, if they didn't take our sons away for some silly reasons, just when the work is pushing us hardest. What we need is money."

And later there is this comparison between the city and the country:

> . . . As I watched him coming toward me in the bright sun, the thought struck me that the sight of blood seemed less shocking in the country than in the shadow of a house in Turin. Once I had seen blood on the tracks of a tram after an accident, and it was terrifying. But here the idea of someone bent over and bleeding on the stubble seems more natural, as in a slaughterhouse.

Throughout the entire novel we find blood and misery, selfishness and illiteracy, taxes, hard work, and the police. Women are brutalized more than men, and sex explodes savagely under the hot sun.

When many years later, I had occasion to accompany Pavese around the countryside, from my home in Vinchio to Santo Stefano, I remember we spent an entire afternoon talking only about *The Harvesters*. We had seen a farmyard on the Vinchio hills where the threshing of wheat was taking place with its usual fervor. It was like the world of the Grangia farm described in *The Harvesters*. Among the women and men working in the dust and the sweltering heat, one could almost recognize the characters of Miliota, Gisella, Talino, Vinverra, and Berto.

As we left that yard, I remember Pavese said to me: "I needed this walk and this return to the climate and the setting of *The Harvesters*. You don't know how many times I would have liked to experience the same fury I felt when I wrote that short novel!"

The fury also found expression in violations of syntax and in a dialectal tempo giving great vivacity to the action. It is not a dialect prose, but rather an attempt, mainly successful, to create a more immediate and incisive language to be spoken through the protagonist. In fact, it is only the protagonist who speaks and thinks.

An innovation in expression and style is, therefore, at the base of *The Harvesters,* together with positive social and political contents. With regard to the language, Paolo Cinanni showed me this passage from Svevo's *Profilo Autobiografico* which particularly impressed Pavese: "He knew quite well that his language could not be adorned with words he did not feel. One can only effectively narrate in a language which is alive, and his living language could only be the one spoken in Trieste. . . . He remembered with veneration and gratitude a certain Faldella who wrote in an Italian into which he was trying to put as much Piedmontese dialect as one could understand."

Through a letter written to Mario Alicata, we know what Pavese thought of his book and how he reacted to the many reviews, for the most part favorable, of *The Harvesters*. Mario Alicata had written one particularly praising the interpretation of the landscape and the people. Here is Pavese's letter:

Dear Alicata,

I like your review, especially the historical part—the first—which is the most comprehensive to appear so far. The comparison with the Americans and, more importantly, with *Work Wearies,* is well balanced. You are exactly right in stating that "my presence" is a permanent necessity.

There are some errors when you paraphrase my world—my tramps are not stowaways, nor are my women blonde. This is not pedantry, because with your incorrect interpretations you tend to give my world a playful tone, making it "idle . . . laughing . . . excited," which is very far from reality—as I will better demonstrate, I hope, in the future.

In any case, I want to thank you for the great attention with which you read my work and for the warmth you showed.

Cordially,
PAVESE

At the same time, Alicata received a letter from Elio Vittorini who expressed a positive opinion of *The Harvesters*:

Dear Alicata,

I am pleased with your article. And I was happy to see that you praised Pavese, since many people are critical of his book *The Harvesters,* while it seems to me a work worth publishing. I would ask a little more from the critics: answers, not only opinions, since books are full of questions. But perhaps it is necessary to wait for more relaxed times. We will have the opportunity to talk.

With my best greetings,

Affectionately yours,
VITTORINI

On July 26, 1949, Pavese wrote to Nicola Enrichens a letter in which he talked again about the world of the American writers and that of *The Harvesters*:

Dear Enrichens,

I have read and thought about your manuscript. I found it moving because there are parts that resemble some of my remarks and emotions from when I was not yet thirty.

It is, without question, better than your poetry. You are by nature more a prose writer than a poet: you tend toward a lean and direct prose, while in your verses you are often rhetorical. . . .

Now let's examine the core of your letter, in which you accuse some Italian literary trends of being gratuitously foreign oriented. I insist on my thesis: when we are sad, cynical, skeptical, and indifferent, if we want to regain confidence we must look around us and, in the realm of culture, we must look to past or foreign cultures. In Italy today we are provincial; all the concepts which govern our political, scientific, philosophic life are of foreign origin (democratism, idealism, historicism, etc.). The only thing to do is to study these fields well and acquire a critical understanding of them instead of accepting the presentation of the journalists, and so deluding ourselves in the belief that we are ancient Romans. *Today* an Italian culture does not exist. A European, or perhaps a world-wide culture, does exist; and we can say a valid word only after digesting all that is contemporary.

If you will allow me the comparison, I was once able to recover from a spiritual and literary situation analogous to yours by taking an interest in American culture, the Greek classics, the history of primitive religions. This does not make me feel less Italian, as I do not feel less Piedmontese because I write in Italian and love madly the city of Rome.

My cordial greetings, and I look forward to seeing you again soon.

PAVESE

The recovery mentioned by Pavese in his letter to Enrichens is also revealed in the pages of the diary written at the time he worked on *The Political Prisoner* and *The Harvesters*. During those years, the expressions of anguish for his lost love and resentment toward women progressively disappeared from his diary. He was slowly healing through study, work, and writing. We quote from his diary of May 4, 1939:

. . . Serenity comes from doing something which is not an end in itself (as suffering and pleasure are), but from doing something which is applied to a work, because this interrupts boredom without involving us in the *passive* sequence of feelings; it is a process that allows us instead to take a detached view (*serenity*) of a structure that accepts our laws (our work).

This statement would become ever more important in Pavese's life. He attempted to replace women and love with the written work. As long as that creative fire lasted, he would not even attempt to reattach himself to a woman and to find love again. This does not mean that he advocated total solitude. On May 15, 1939 he wrote:

The greatest misfortune is loneliness. This is so true that the highest form of consolation—religion—consists in finding a friend who will never let you down: God. Prayer is opening one's heart, as with a friend. Work is equivalent to prayer, since ideally it puts us in contact with those who will benefit by it. The whole problem of life then, is this: how to break out of one's own loneliness, how to communicate with others. That explains the persistence of marriage, fatherhood, friendships. . . .

He was concerned with loneliness, but his main interest, especially during the last months of 1939, was literary. On October 29, 1939, he wrote:

It is not true that novels are not written in our time because we no longer believe in the stability of the world. It cannot be true, for the nineteenth-century novel was born while a world was crumbling, and even served as a substitite for the stability the world was losing. Now the novel is seeking a new structure in a world which is renovating itself, and it cannot be satisfied with moving in this new world according to the old dimension.

On December 12, 1939:

Every artist tries to dismantle the mechanism of his technique to see how it is made. Nevertheless, a work of art is successful only when it has a certain element of mystery for the artist. This is quite natural: the story of an artist is the improvement upon the technique employed in his previous work, with a creation that implies a more complex aesthetic law. Self-criticism is a means of self-improvement. The artist who is not continually analyzing and destroying his own technique is a poor devil.

The same thing happens in all activities. It is the dialectic of historical life. But both in art and in life, since the beginning of Romanticism an ever-present danger has existed in this dialectic: that of deliberately setting up the field of mystery, in order to guarantee oneself the desired creative urge . . . But the mystery that stimulates creation must be born by itself through an obstacle encountered unintentionally during the course of our very effort at clarification. Nothing is more obscene than an artist or a politician who *coldly* plays with his own mysterious irrationality.

These excerpts from his diary reveal a most conscious Pavese as he treated life and imagination, art and politics, mystery and the effort of clarification. His wound seemed to have healed. Even his "absurd vice" was no longer insistent. His artistic choice was clearly expressed in the diary of December 14, 1939: "It is necessary to have realism's wealth of experience and symbolism's depth of feeling. All art is a problem of balance between two opposites."

The years 1938 and 1939 were very fertile ones for Pavese. On January 1, 1940 he wrote with pride:

I close the year 1939 in a state of exaltation, with confidence in myself and a tension similar to that of a cat lying in wait for its prey. Intellectually I have the same agility and the controlled energy of the cat.

I am no longer agitated. I have lived to create: this is certain. On the other hand I have been very afraid of death and terrified that my body might let me down.

This has been the first year I have lived with dignity, because I have applied myself to a program.

13

Turin During the War

Beginning in 1939, the clandestine activities of the anti-Fascist groups grew in strength and in number. Many homes in Turin became centers for political and military meetings. The groups represented different political parties and were not always in agreement on everything. However, in each group there were men and women who worked for unity of action. The more Fascism involved itself in war, the more it offered these supporters of unity a motive to spread their influence.

After the repeated arrests that had practically destroyed it, the "Justice and Freedom" movement succeeded in resuming contact with the activists who had fled to France. After their release from prison, Mila and Ginzburg returned to work with intensity, in spite of the surveillance to which they were subjected. At the same time, the Communist organization attracted more members, especially among young workers and intellectuals. Its most qualified leader was Capriolo, a worker who had just returned from prison. In 1939 Pavese and Cinanni were introduced to Capriolo by Geymonat. Capriolo had both the frank nature of a worker and a sense of culture acquired while he was in prison. He was a simple and courageous man who spoke without rhetoric and gave the impression that his words were already actions.

Although Cinanni was aware that Pavese was not a member of the party and had never expressed the intention of becoming one, Pavese met more and more frequently with Cinanni and other Communists. He continued to frequent the group of Ginzburg and Mila, that of Antonicelli and others. He listened to the discussions, intervening only on artistic and cultural topics, but never in political matters.

Meanwhile, Pavese's cultural and political contacts had spread throughout Italy. He received many letters, mainly from young poets, writers, and critics. He answered all of them with advice and criticism, often severe, but always useful and sincere. Every Saturday evening Cinanni, who also lived on via Lamarmora, would stop by Pavese's home to accompany him to the political meeting, which was held at Guaita's home. At first the participants were all Communists, but later they were joined by the exponents of other political currents; together they came to represent an embryo of the future "Committees for National Liberation."

The political discussions at Guaita's home often lasted until 2:00 or 3:00 in the morning; and Pavese, although generally remaining silent, did not miss one sentence. After the meetings ended, he would wander with Cinanni through the streets of Turin until 5:00 or 6:00 in the morning.

Cinanni told me that as soon as they left the meetings, Pavese became very talkative. He would go over all the political topics previously discussed one by one, analyzing them carefully. He loved to play the role of the sage who was able to see both the positive and negative sides of every position, and he never sided decisively with one thesis. Entangled in his own paradoxes, he would often refute the most logical opinions and choose those less convincing. Cinanni let him talk, but then, at home, he wrote long notes with his points of disagreement and, the next day, he gave those written opinions to Pavese who, after reading them carefully, recognized his own errors.

Often during those nights, Pavese would suddenly stop talking and invite Cinanni to look at the moon and its reflection on the streets, amid the shadows of the buildings and the trees. Pavese would then begin to talk about Thomas Mann with great enthusiasm not only for his novels and their style, but also for Mann's political, social, and historical ideas. Thomas Mann was his gospel, an important name to remember among those of Pavese's masters.

Through those meetings and discussions with Cinanni and other anti-Fascists, Pavese seemed to have found a new faith in life. It was like old times at the D'Azeglio and at the university.

Italy's declaration of war was another factor in reinforcing Pavese's sensitivity for life. On June 5, 1940 he wrote in his diary:

> Grief makes us live in a dream-like world, where banal, everyday things assume a bewildering and *thrilling* aspect not always displeasing. It makes us aware of the gap between spirit and reality; it uplifts us, making us perceive reality and our bodies as something remote and strange. Herein lies its educational effectiveness.
>
> The reality of war suggests this simple thought: it is not sad to die when so many of our friends are dying. War creates the sense of group. That is a welcome feeling.

And on June 12, 1940:

> War raises the tone of life because it organizes everyone's inner life around a very simple pattern—the two opposing camps—and, implying the idea that death is always imminent, impresses even on the most banal actions a seal of gravity more than human.

Pavese, in those years, abandoned almost completely his reference to his mania for suicide, to his "absurd vice." A new encouragement to his physical and moral rebirth was the encounter with Giaime Pintor, a very young officer who had arrived in Turin at the end of 1939. A Sardinian, open and loyal, Pintor was just twenty years old, but had already demonstrated through his articles an attachment to the cause of freedom. Although he was known in Rome as an anti-Fascist, he was not readily accepted in the anti-Fascist circles of Turin because of his name. General Pintor, former commander of the Italian troops in the war with France and then president of the "Commission for the Armistice" in Turin, was his uncle. Giaime Pintor's Roman anti-Fascist friends, Alicata, Muscetta, Lucio Lombardo Radice, had recommended him to Einaudi, but there were still reservations due to his relationship with the General. Pavese was the first to approach Pintor, to trust him, and to support him with his political friends.

Pavese had also been the first to call on Ginzburg and Mila upon their return from prison when they were still under constant police surveillance. Actions such as these must be mentioned because they demonstrate that he did not lack courage, even though later he failed to take up arms and fight like his friends.

Because of his youth and lack of experience, Pintor did not have a solid cultural formation upon his arrival in Turin. Like Pavese however, he soon understood that those intellectuals who sought escape from Fascism through an autonomous life in the world of art and culture, were taking the wrong route. It was impossible to separate culture from politics. It had taken Pavese many years to convince himself of this; Pintor, with his vivacity of character and sense of human solidarity, had arrived at it spontaneously.

One can better understand both the differences and the similarities of these two men by comparing Pavese's writing on war with what Pintor wrote in a letter to his brother Luigi shortly before facing death in combat:

> The war has materially diverted men from their habits, it has forced
> them to realize with their hands and eyes the dangers which
> threaten the essence of each individual life; it has convinced them
> that there is no possibility for salvation in neutrality and isolation.
> Some of my friends better prepared to immediately feel the public
> facts had dedicated themselves for years to the struggle against
> Fascism. Although I feel closer and closer to them, I don't know if I
> would have decided to totally commit myself in that direction.
> Down deep I was too independent, indifferent, and critical to
> sacrifice all these feelings for a collective faith. Only war has
> resolved this situation, sweeping away certain obstacles and brutally
> putting me in contact with an unmistakable world.

That contact had found a particular reinforcement in Turin, at Einaudi, among Ginzburg, Pavese, Mila, Geymonat, and Antonicelli, as well as in the encounters with Capriolo and other anti-Fascists. Another point that Pintor and Pavese had in common was their indiscriminate acceptance of every political movement as long as it was engaged in the fight against Fascism.

At that time Pintor, like Pavese, contributed to several literary magazines; he also translated from German and was a literary consultant for Einaudi. He often met with Pavese in the cafés and they discussed the cultural situation of Europe and Italy.

During that period, Pavese felt an even greater need to write. More precisely, he wanted to explore those places he had frequented in his university years when, with Monti and the other friends of the fraternity, he would spend evenings in Sturani's study.

He wanted to know what had happened, in the turbulence of the war, to those seamstresses, models, and other working girls he had known as a student. The corruption of society, perpetrated by Fascism, had already overwhelmed those women. With these questions in mind, in 1940, Pavese wrote *The Beautiful Summer* which would be published much later, in 1947, together with two other short novels, *The Devil in the Hills* and *Among Women Only*. It may appear strange that during the time of his most active social and cultural participation, he dedicated himself to a novel seemingly so distant from the new reality.

The Beautiful Summer was in fact considered by some critics a decadent work in a human and literary sense. But it is not difficult to understand Pavese's denunciation in this novel of the corruption Fascism had brought to the middle class and, in some areas, to the workers.

In the background of the novel is also the anguish caused him by the woman with the hoarse voice; his anger is reflected in the hopeless pessimism of the characters in the novel.

In *The Beautiful Summer,* Pavese tried a new style. The monologue of *The Harvesters* is replaced by conversation; the entire story is based on a continuous dialogue. Here men and women carry on their lives and loves in an alternation of feverishness and languor. Pavese's ability to understand his characters, especially the women, is matched by a probing description of the surroundings and the events. He also knew how to avoid a moralistic tone.

The protagonists are all women. In a previous chapter, I discussed the sad fate of women in Pavese's works. However, they are characters who are not easily forgotten, even if it is their feelings and not their physical traits or the daily events of their lives that the author chose to reveal. He usually did so with quick sketches, as in the following passage:

> Amelia began to laugh. "No way. The cleverest models are the ones who drive the artist mad. If you don't move once in awhile, he forgets you are a model and treats you as if you were a maid. Behave like a sheep and the wolf will eat you."

The novel also gives us an exemplary portrait of Turin. There is Turin in the summer with dances in the hills, and Turin in the winter under the snow, in the cafés. Pavese had a debt to pay to his city and to the environment of his younger years.

His memories of Santo Stefano were then less intense. The difficulties of the war, the demands of his work, and the fervor of political friendships kept Pavese away from the country. Even when he was able to take a few weeks vacation, he went to the sea, to the beach of Varigotti. The change of lifestyle and the encounters with the sea—so different from those of his exile—prompted Pavese to write *The Beach*. This novel was also to serve as an outlet for his irony toward his friends, particularly Sturani, who were married. Once again his jealousy and near anger were provoked by the ever present and tormenting desire to have a wife. But from that beginning—subjective and a little mischievous—the book is an intriguing inquest into new social environments, characters who have nothing in common with Pavese. The plot is based on daily boredom and develops subtly, without any explosions of tragedy, without clashes. After the first few pages, Pavese himself seems to be ill at ease with that rarefied atmosphere and he takes his characters away from the sea, in an excursion into the country among the trees and the hills familiar to him. But feeling that the contrast is too abrupt, he quickly returns them to the beach, to their lazy love games by the sea, to their encounters and words as futile as the breaking of the waves against the rocks.

With *The Beach* Pavese wanted to construct a world which was completely different from his own. He noted in his diary the date he completed his novel, something he had not done with any other previous work, almost as if he had fulfilled some binding obligation. In 1946 he would give the following judgment of his book:

The Beach . . . a novel which is neither brutal, nor proletarian, nor American—fortunately only a few have read it—is not a splinter from the monolith. It represents a distraction, even human; in short, I would be ashamed of it if doing so had any significance. It is what you call a frank stylistic research.

When Pavese is his own critic, he often enjoys mortifying himself more than necessary. Later on he gives, instead, a valid opinion of *The Beach* in the diary: "I salvaged *The Beach* by grafting it with youths who discover the life of discussion, the mythic reality."

At the time he wrote the novel, Pavese seemed more interested in his diary than in the works he was preparing for publication. On January 9, 1940 he wrote:

The proof of your own lack of interest in politics is that, believing in liberalism (i.e., the possibility of ignoring political life), you would like to enforce it tyrannically. You are conscious of political life only at times of totalitarian crises; then you grow heated and run counter to your own liberalism in the hope of quickly bringing about the liberal conditions in which you can live without bothering about politics.

On April 19:

Generations do not age. Every youth of any period, of any civilization, has the same possibilities as always.

The Empire did not fall due to the decadence of the race (in fact, the generations that witnessed the fall, and those which followed, have built out of it a spiritual empire—the Catholic Church), but due to changed economic and social conditions . . .

On June 21:

. . . The point linking your work to life is in the *need* of your work *for expression* and in the *need* of life *for human contact*.

As long as there is a man who is hated, unrecognized, ignored, there will be something to do in life: to draw close to him.

The dangers of war threatening everybody drew Pavese closer to people and inspired him to write phrases of sincerity and generosity. He also learned to judge his own poetry with more lucidity. Again on June 21 he wrote:

Your poetry is necessarily dramatic because its message is the meeting of two people—the mystery, the charm, and the adventure of such encounters—not the confession of your soul.

Until now you have preferred contrasts of environment (north against south, city against country) because they vividly express the contrasts between two people.

He made political judgments, as in his diary of July 10, 1940:

In this war there have been perhaps more *betrayals* than in any other; which signifies a revolutionary climate, a climate where the initial state of things is gradually changing, and where one's criterion of judgment *becomes* different from that of the political group to which one belongs.

In 1940 a second woman entered Pavese's life and she would occupy an important place in it for over five years. She was a young student from Turin—Fernanda Pivano—who had been in his class during the few months he taught as a substitute at the D'Azeglio.

The very young teacher, both brilliant and shy, soon attracted special attention from all his students, especially from the girls. He provoked a general curiosity with the frequent phone calls he ran to make between classes. He was calling the woman with the hoarse voice, and his students, without knowing anything about his life, could tell by the expression on his face that their shy professor had a secret love.

After the brief term he spent as a substitute at the D'Azeglio, Pavese no longer had the opportunity to meet with his students. It was after a few years that he again saw Fernanda Pivano, who had come to the public swimming pool with her friend Norberto Bobbio. By then she had developed into a beautiful, talkative, elegant, and happy woman. It was she who reminded him that she was his student at the lyceum. After that meeting, Pavese would see Fernanda every day.

Determined to conquer her intellectually, Pavese never tried to kiss Fernanda in five years. Each morning he would wait for her on Stupinigi Boulevard. He would sit with her on a bench and read her poems by Montale and Ungaretti and sometimes even his own. Under his influence, she became less frivolous and more devoted to her studies.

Then one day while they were still on very formal terms, Pavese suddenly asked Fernanda to marry him. She did not answer either yes or no.

Meanwhile, without telling Pavese, Fernanda had begun to translate *Spoon River Anthology*. When he read the translation, during a visit to her home, he thanked her as if she had given him a demonstration of affection.

To keep his appointments with Fernanda, Pavese had bought a bicycle, and he convinced her to do the same so they could take long rides together on the banks of the Po or the Sangone.

But even this relationship ended in failure. On the title page of *August Holiday* are two dates—July 26, 1940 and July 10, 1945—with a cross and the words "In memory," to signify, in a funereal way, the period of the relationship.

Fernanda Pivano maintains the fondest memories of Pavese. After much hesitation, and only in the hope that they would help to complete his biography, she was kind enough to let me publish the letters he wrote to her. They complement Pavese's diary, forming a special autobiography of Pavese as a man and as a writer.

The first letter to Fernanda—dated August 22, 1940—was accompanied by a note saying: "Nando's friend is stupid. Five days ago, for the second time in his life, he managed to put himself in prison."

It is not difficult to understand that Nando is Fernanda and that her "stupid" friend is Cesare.

Here is the letter, playfully written as a school essay:

Home Assignment

Topic: Describe how you spend your holidays and state your plans for the future.

How beautiful are our bicycle rides in the countryside around Turin! Every morning, as soon as I wake up, I telephone my friend Nando and then we meet at 10:30, the time he infallibly comes down from his apartment. I like to see him come out of his front door, almost always wearing something different from the last time. The colors that suit him best, I think, are white and bright red. We mount our bicycles and Nando, who is tidier than I am, always carefully rolls up the bottoms of his trousers. Then we make our way toward the open country around Turin, pedaling away with all the breath we have and talking mostly about our schoolwork, for we, during our vacations, continue to study and especially Nando likes to reminisce about our pleasant school days. I go with Nando because I know I can learn a thousand good things from him: he never says those inappropriate and filthy things that unfortunately poison the souls of so many boys of our age. With Nando, instead, the subjects of discussion are our professors and what happened at school. Though we know one shouldn't find pleasure in other people's misfortunes, we sometimes have a good laugh at those friends of ours who, not having studied all year, now must spend their vacation closed in, trying to catch up. How beautiful it is to have passed all the exams!

But Nando also confides in me, especially after a long ride when we stop to rest, sitting on a low wall at the edge of a wood, which we already call "our" little wall. There we stay, close to the road and in full view of the passers-by. What would they say if they saw us disappear among the trees? One must avoid even the appearance of evil; people are only too ready to spread malicious gossip. . . . Nando and I have decided, once and for all, never to hide away, and to do everything openly.

As I was saying, Nando talks to me confidentially, as I do to him; it is one of the most beautiful points in our friendship. He tells me things that amaze me. For instance . . . he would like to have his parents stop worrying about him and he would also like to take refuge from the perils of life. He talks of marriage, and feels he has

wasted too much time already. I tell him to wait at least another
year and to finish his studies, but Nando begins to fret and insists
he will do as he says. I am well aware that young men like us get
strange ideas, because we are going through adolescence, a period
full of dangers and temptations; lucky are those who can make it—
like Nando and I. But the idea of marrying has never occurred to
me. I ask him with a smile if he already knows whom he would
like to marry and I try to distract him. He lowers his brown eyes
and becomes thoughtful. "It's a difficult choice," he says, "it
involves a whole life." I was shaken by one of his ideas. He would
like to see at school, among the regular courses, one on marriage
taught by a good and paternal professor, like the one who teaches
us Italian literature, or like our principal. The course ought to be
organized in such a way that its best students, while continuing the
other regular classes, at the end of the year would find themselves
married. "Think how beautiful it would be!" he says. However, he
would not want women teachers and I agree with this because
women of any age and status can do nothing but harm to an
adolescent. Now I must confess a thought of mine. I'm doing it
since our professor never ceases to inculcate in us the importance of
sincerity, above all with ourselves. The thought is this: I wish I
could change my sex and become Nando's girlfriend so that I could
marry him, such is my love for him. But I think that if I were a girl I
would not be able to go bicycling with him, so it is better this way.
After all, Nando will certainly change his mind since he has so
much life ahead of him. And I tell him that he must study in order
to compensate his family and his teachers for the sacrifices they are
making for him, and that someday his parents will find him a wife.
When I say this, Nando makes faces but actually he is happy.

How beautiful it is to cross the countryside on a bicycle! In the
fields the daisies invitingly wink at us, the road runs smoothly
amid the green, and the blue sky reflects the serenity of our
thoughts. Occasionally other riders—soldiers, workers, or family
groups—pass by and always when they see us they hurl a cheerful
shout which has the power to make Nando lean over the handlebar
and turn red with joy.

But I realize that you do not know Nando, so I will describe
him. He is a pleasant, intelligent fellow who, seen in profile, looks
already like a man, but face to face looks very young because of

his great brown eyes which are innocent and always smiling. He is always clean and well groomed; I, instead, sometimes even forget to comb my hair. Just by looking at him I feel a better person, more active and eager to show myself worthy of him. I shall, therefore, always study very hard, and next year, if the devil does not interfere, I shall pass my exams with honors! Then we can spend our vacations together again, learn many things, and be happy.

CESARE PAVESE

The second letter, dated October 25, 1940, is a rare document: Pavese's self-portrait during those years. It is accompanied by a brief, affectionate dedication dated November 5, 1940:

Dear Fernanda,

You can take comfort in the fact that we all have our problems. I want you to read the self-analysis I made during my worst days of this October—so you will see how it is possible to find peace and relief simply in trying to *understand* what happens to us.

If at times you have felt that my frank comments have been like blasts of cold water on you, try to see how one must, above all, administer these showers to oneself. This is what keeps us going. In these pages I shall try to tell you things so shameful that you will quite understand that I wrote you with no ulterior motive. I did it out of friendship, because I am also and very much

Your friend,
PAVESE

Here is the letter:

Analysis of P.

P. is without doubt an unusual man, which does not yet mean a man of special merit. He has the most obvious traits of a failure— lack of any social *routine* and a readiness to disengage himself—but at the same time he has the capacity to concentrate his energies on one particular thing—be it work or passion—something which has enabled him, between periods of confusion, to achieve a few results and some degree of self-confidence.

His basic inclination is to give his actions a significance that transcends their actual worth; that is, to regard his days as a gallery of unique and absolute moments. Hence, in anything he does or says, P. reveals his dual personality, and, while appearing to take part in the human drama, privately he has other intentions and he already moves in a different atmosphere which transpires through his actions as symbolic intention. This apparent duplicity is rather an inevitable reflection of his capacity to be—before a sheet of paper—a poet. As much as P. is convinced that art and life must be kept clearly distinct, that writing is an occupation like any other, like selling buttons or farming, he can only regard his life as a gigantic spectacle in which *he* performs. The comparison of life to a spectacle usually implies that life must not be taken seriously, that it is merely a joke. P. does, however, perform with tremendous seriousness. In every major scene of his life, he displays such an abundance of passion and self-revelation that he resembles a tragic poet who climbs on stage among his characters to kill or be killed. . . .

Undoubtedly, P. is a loner, for as he grew up, he learned that nothing of any value can be accomplished unless one is isolated from the business of the world. He is the living martyr of these contrasting needs. He wants to be alone—and he *is* alone—yet, at the same time, he yearns to be in the center of a group which is conscious of his solitude. He wants to feel—and he does feel—for certain persons, profound attachments which no word expresses; but he torments himself day and night, and he torments the very persons to whom he is attached in an effort to find the precise word to express his feelings. All of this is without a doubt sincere, and unfortunately entangled with the need for expression which his poetic nature demands. P. even refers to all these feelings as a need for communication, for communion, and to their absence as tragic loneliness, spiritual incommunicability, and so forth.

What will such a man do when confronted with love? The answer is obvious: nothing, that is, an endless number of extravagant things that amount to nothing. Once he is in love, P. will be ruled by his temperament. This is precisely what should be avoided. He will let it be known, first of all, that he is no longer his own master, that nothing in the day holds as much importance for him as the moment he meets her; he will want to confess all the most secret thoughts passing through his mind; he will always neglect to put the woman in a position in which she would be risking her reputation by leaving him. This, the first elementary precaution taken by the libertine (the only one who impeccably applies the strategy of love), is in P.'s case completely reversed. P. forgets to make the woman in question fall in love with him; instead, he is preoccupied with offering his whole soul to her, while filling every molecule of his own spirit with love for her. In short, he burns every bridge behind him. He has confessed that, when in love, he finds it physically impossible to approach other women—a weakness no woman, not even the loved one, can forgive. Why so much naïveté? It is evident: P. takes things too seriously, he *performs* in earnest, he gets worked up in the manner of an old school actor or that actor in the D'Annunzio tragedy who demanded that even Atreus' gilt mask be made of pure gold. Here is that mania for the absolute, for the symbolic, discussed in the beginning. P. plays his lovelorn part to the very end: first, because of his fierce need to escape from his solitude; second, because of his need to believe unquestioningly in the passion he suffers. He is stricken with terror at the thought of living in a purely physiological state, of being no more than the protagonist in a frivolous adventure. P. wants his feelings to be *noble,* to *symbolize* a nobility that is in and around him. These feelings finally become for P. an idol, to which it is worth the pain of sacrificing even life or the mind—a mind P. knows to be great.

But who expects him to sacrifice his mind or life? Which woman asks a man to lose himself completely and to love her with the useless cosmic intensity of a summer storm? What woman, if not the *vamp*? As a matter of fact, P. has the gift of transforming into *vamps*, girls who have never dreamed of being such, thereby bringing total destruction upon himself. Then, after the ruins have fallen and he finds himself alone again, the *vamp* suddenly feels remorse and returns to look for him with a melancholic and motherly gesture. At this point, P., feeling shame and anger, returns to his solitude. A natural tragedy: P. has, or can have, any kind of love from women except the very one which he, like all men who are failures, desires from the bottom of his heart: the love of a wife.

This craving for a home and a life he will never know was once uttered by P. in the heat of his now famous passion. He said: "The only women worth marrying are those you cannot trust to marry."

It's all here: the *vamp* and the fury, the wife and the perpetual dream. It's like saying that P. is crucified upon this dream. Nothing is more pathetic than his frenzied attempts to unnail his hands. Knowing that he can nail himself in this manner and knowing the impossibility of freeing or defending himself, he trembles with fear at every approach of new passions.

P. has a vivid imagination, and all he has to do is envision himself in a painful pose—like his crucifixion—to suffer *physical* torture. Usually, the exasperating sensitivity of types such as P. lasts only for a short while. . . . But P. is not an ordinary man. Years ago he carried this image of the cross in his system for *over three consecutive months,* together with another image he calls the uprooting, that is, the sensation of having his breast and heart lacerated and bleeding from the violent tearing out of the thousand roots a woman had implanted there. That's what happens in the course of passion, which is only natural. The same need for symbolic nobility, which is so important at the onset of his passions, further reveals itself in the strength with which these feelings endure. Moreover, P. has unconsciously based his feelings on such a solid foundation that even the bitterness of their proven futility cannot destroy them. It must be pointed out here that with P., passion is intertwined with his poetry; it becomes the *flesh of poetry*, and, as such, it is identified with the language, sight, and breath of the imagination.

For a long period of time, P. achieved a kind of stoical ataraxia through the total renunciation of every human bond, except that one abstract tie with his writing. He felt as if he were in a daze, hanging his head and trying to write. But as months and years went by, he wrote less and less: the life within was drying up, he was becoming a phantom. Still, P. held on, knowing that for him a weakening of his attitude toward people, any people, would be only a relapse, not a rebirth. Another of his memorable sayings is "all or nothing"—"Aut Caesar aut nihil"—P. never stops halfway.

Instead, the weakening has happened. P. tried to stop halfway, but he did not succeed. Now he must pay for every moment of the fictional isolation he created for himself. Life takes its vengeance with real solitude. Let it be as life intends it.

The third letter, dated March 15, 1941, begins with an introduction in English and continues with a portrait of Fernanda:

Since you have seen the jottings, you may as well have the whole. You can treat it like a "Chopin" and needn't pretend to have read it. In any case don't be affected, it is not worthwhile, but keep in mind I was younger when I wrote it.

So long,
PAVESE

The Fears of F.

F. lets it often be understood that there were two distinct periods in her life, a former and a later, a then and a now, and, naturally, she explains no more. She loves very much to dualize, namely to let people perceive in every facet of her own nature and activity two contrasting moments, marked by a crisis: when she was in Genoa and now that she is in Turin, when she was wealthy and now that she is poor, when she was an intellectual and now that she is active, when she was silly and now that she is masculinized, etc. She does not speak of the crisis in question, but one understands immediately that, because of her nature, this crisis cannot be a single event fixed in time. F. speaks of her transformation with an apparent indifference, and one needs some time to realize that this transformation, rather than being a recollection, is a desire, a decision, a program, a present state of mind that projects itself into the past and splits it.

Notwithstanding certain apparent intimacies, F. does not confide in anyone (this is proven by the fact that of her many friends probably all receive F.'s confessions which, told to one person only, would be a sign of trusting devotion—told to many, merely "interesting" conversation). One must therefore auscultate her "talks at random" in the event that some of her words might send an echo of unknown depth. Whoever, encouraged by the easiness with which F. treats erotic subjects, should feel that this is a good area to dwell on, would err: the reason being that evidently F. watches and inhibits herself with total awareness and allows very little of her true nature to be understood. The key—if a key exists—must be sought elsewhere.

For example, about her fears, F. said one of the truest things once, during a summer in the country, in front of a group of still trees in the evening: "When trees remain perfectly still they are frightening." She also says that she even now fears the dark; and one day she referred, shivering, to the anguish she would feel when she was a child, as she talked all alone behind a curtain, to a light switch. Who then saw her suffering real fits of terror, shaking like a mouse with eyes wide open, at the idea that in her house something loathsome was taking place, but who also recalls her stating, cheerfully, that she is not afraid of an air raid, would begin to discover a constant in these characteristics: that F. suffers more from anguish than from fears. Which means that F.'s inner life (since childhood) is made up of moments during which she has been waiting, painfully waiting, for an "unknown" that is both desired and rejected. . . . It is necessary to remember that, although intellectually not inactive, F. has purposely limited her contemplative life to the enjoyment of music—a taste that requires precisely the capacity for anguish that for some is a corrective, while for others is a sublimation.

Now, in accordance with the picture of her anguish, F. confesses to having experienced since the age of twelve a sullen repulsion for every "stranger." How is it that the moody and sensitive child (what makes one hard and even violent is the thirst for tenderness), solitary and imaginative, awkward and domestic, could turn into a woman "répandue" and self-assured, positive and active, crystalline and cordial, with whom sculptors, musicians, and poets think they can flirt? Above all, how is it that the child who could be easily enchanted and who still today has remained the virgin who shivers at the idea of rape—how is it that this woman lives an ideal of virile sociability, and has only male friends whom she seeks with boldness and dominates effortlessly, to the point where he who does not know her with love suspects that she is a "viveuse" and treats her as such? The key to this secret can be found in one of her naïve confessions which is wrong to consider simply as a whim of a saucy young woman (as our friend Bobbio does) or as a rash excuse of a "dévergondée" (as her worldly rivals and, it seems, the musicians think). The confession is the banal line, repeated by F. a thousand times, that she is a masculinized woman. It means that F. tends to *identify* with men or, better still, with a definite type of man who evidently represents her ideal. F. is naïve enough to let it be understood that she lives this diverse and active life out of desperation, of absurdity, or as a calculated choice—which turns out to be the same thing. This is, in substance, the *second* period of her life, that period which contrasts, in F.'s desire, with a not well-confessed or specified first period in which she seemed to do the complete opposite.

This explains why the idea of a certain *crisis* and of a conversion to a new life is unacceptable. When one says *identification*, one means a repressed psychological complex which seeks its outlet in a new myth of behavior. One says, therefore, that it is a split personality, not subsequent but simultaneous. F. is still the anguished child, just as she lives her myth of a dynamic practical life.

It went like this. Like all the adolescences of this world, that of F. involved the painful and humiliating awareness of sex. Few things are as distressing as the lewd, frenetic, and inexorable discovery of the sexual destiny of the flesh in those years, when one is not yet aware of its possible rewards. Furthermore, F. did not have, in those years, the inevitable mystical crisis that distracts one from sex (in reality it is only a phase of its course) and discharges the wave of one's indignations and rebellions into the sweet atmosphere of the heart and conscience. Isn't it strange that with such a capacity to feel *anguish*— the state typically pre-religious—F. has not felt at least for a year, for six months, the religious transport? It is not at all strange and, if we remember her experience at the age of ten—the confessor who revolted her by teaching her *the* filthy things—we will understand how her very anguish was born and *has remained* in the area of sex, naturally as an ambivalence—horror of the human contact and at the same time a longing for it, a sullen physical reserve together with a fear of solitude. Again today, although she understands herself and others better, F. continues to shiver at the idea of rape—naturally in fictional and exaggerated forms. This is both the most ancient and the newest of her anguishes. When she speaks of it, she even becomes sincere and forgets the myth of masculinization. Or better still, she discovers the true face of this myth: an identification born from a repressed instinct. What does F. fear in rape? Joking, she imagines it with an entire retinue of horrors—revolution and civil war—but I suspect that she fears it in its pure state, in its simple physiological necessity. In short, she is in the same condition as those youths who cannot decide to "livrer leur force à une femme," in the condition, that is, of one of her friends, V., about whom she often speaks. The massacre, the blood, the machine guns, which in her sarcastic fantasies should accompany the ceremony, are also here a myth of a simpler and more human repugnance: F., just like V., cannot resign herself to the idea of being subjected to the revelation of the reality of another sex. To her this is pure anguish.

One must insist. F. *is not afraid*, she does not fear pain (remember the case of the air raids), on the contrary, if she thinks of marrying, she thinks immediately of children (another proof that she has still not been able to see in sex a possible voluptuous reality). What she fears is the insult to her narcissistic reserve, it is the violent shattering of her sphere of solitary anguish we can trace back to her childhood talk with the light switch, or to her understanding of the metaphysical horror of still trees.

At this point one understands better, in its melancholic reality, the cause of her identification with the other sex.

A young man who systematically seeks the company of females, not to make love, but rather to find in them a model, and who feels their influence on his tastes, manners, and moods, is a homosexual who is not aware of his true identity. Later he might marry and become a happy husband and father. However this does not exclude his original inclination toward a completely different life. He probably saved himself unconsciously—by chance, by a fortunate encounter; but he walked on the razorblade and his destiny was different.

The same must be said for a girl who demonstrates a resolute taste for the company of males and who makes an ideal of asexual life through this company. In both cases a process of identification with the opposite sex has begun, and it is evident that—at the first occasion that shatters the last inhibitions of conscience and habit—it will happen that the feminized young man and the masculinized girl will find it conceivable to free their inverted instinct through homosexual activity. It goes without saying that the individuals who arrive at a declared homosexuality are as rare, when compared with latent homosexuals, as the actual murderers compared to the potential ones (who among us has not dreamed at least once of killing someone?). This inquiry—let it be clear—does not aim at discovering in F. an inexorable destiny, but only at tracing a tendency in her, at clarifying for her the possible meaning, which perhaps escapes her, of an attitude in itself innocent.

Nevertheless, the homosexual inversion is such a violent thing that it cannot be provoked merely by a state of diffused anguish but—as psychoanalysis teaches—by a well-defined psychic trauma. Does this trauma exist in F.'s childhood? The entire problem is here, and naturally only F. could answer it by exploring her own self.

In the three letters that follow, written to Pivano from June to August 1942, Pavese returns to analyzing himself, and especially his feelings as a writer:

June 25, 1942

Dear Fernanda,

If you ignore the smell of wheat, I mean the wheat still on its stalks in the field, ripe, swaying, under the summer clouds and rain, you are unfortunate and I feel sorry for you. Just think that I had never smelled the grain in the field, because I always arrived in the country in mid-July, when it had already been reaped. This time, instead, it was similar to when a husband, away for years from his wife, returns to visit her and now he sees her as a mistress—she has words, gestures, and moments unknown to him, since he had not noticed them at the time of their passionate love, but now they seem to reveal to him all the tenderness of their first love.

So this morning I set out along the routes of my childhood and carefully observe again the great hills—all of them—the one enormous and fertile as a woman's large breast, the other steep and pointed, where we would have our great bonfires, and those sheer hills which seemed to hang over the sea—but under them is the road, the road which circles around my old vineyards and disappears, at the curve, like a leap into a void.

I never went beyond the point of that leap . . . I had always arrived only as far as this horizon . . . but I sensed that beyond that leap, quite far away, after the valley which stretches out like a sea, I would find a remote barrier (so remote, that it is tiny), of exotic, sun-drenched hills in bloom. That was my Paradise, my South Seas, my Great Prairie, the corals, Ophir, the White Elephant, etc.

And so this morning, now that I am no longer a child and that I have understood these places in no time at all, I set out along this road, headed toward the curve of the leap. I caught a glimpse of the distant hills, recapturing my childhood at the point I had interrupted it. My valley was misty, with spots of sun and wheat fields, and it was what the body of the woman one loves must be like, when she is blonde. Naturally it is no longer the child who speaks, but rather a man who was that child and now is happy to be a man and to remember Fernanda.

Ciao,
PAVESE

June 27, 1942

Dear Fernanda,

I send you greetings and good wishes immediately, in case I forget later. I have to talk about myself.

So it happens that I have a burning love for the *Georgics*. Here is why:

Always, but this time more than ever, I am deeply moved to find myself again among my native hills. You have to think that primordial images—that is the tree, the house, the vineyard, the path, the evening, the bread, the fruit, etc.—opened themselves to me in these places. To be more precise, it happened at a certain fork in the road where there is a huge house, with a red gate that creaks, and a terrace green with verdigris forever dropping from the pergola; my knees were always dirty from it when I was a boy. Seeing again these trees, houses, vineyards, paths, etc. gives me a sense of extraordinary imaginary power, as if the absolute image of them were quickening to life within me now as if I were a child, but a child who brings in his discovery a wealth of echoes, moods, words, returns, in short, of an imagination which is truly immeasurable! I have not lived another twenty years for nothing. (This should also console you who cry over Bardi and the Cervara; your imagination was born in those places and it can be born again each time you return there—in body or in spirit—and the years in between can only help.)

Now, this state of primordial virginity that I'm enjoying makes me suffer, because I know that my work consists of transforming everything into "poetry." Which is not easy. To the contrary, my first idea was that what I had been writing was foolish, inspired by patterns which do not have any savor of the tree, the house, the vineyard, the path, etc. as I know them. While walking along the

road of the leap into the void, I would in fact understand that I
needed very different words, echoes, and imagination. In short, it is
necessary to have a myth. I need myths, universal and fantastic, to
express in depth and unforgettably this experience which is my
place in the world. I thought that still it was not enough to write
stories of peasants (although psychoanalized and transfigured). And
then to describe landscapes is foolish. The landscapes—or better yet,
the places, namely the tree, the house, the vineyard, the path, the
ravine, etc.—must live as people, as peasants, and be therefore
mythical. The great hill, shaped like a woman's breast, ought to be
the body of the goddess to whom, on St. John's night, we could
pay a tribute, as part of a cult, by lighting bonfires of stubble. The
sweet line of hilltops rushing toward the leap into the void would
be the road taken by the civilizing hero (a Hercules, an Adonis)
when, after benefiting the people, he departs for an unknown
venture. The barren and awesome field on the summit of the
highest and most desolate hill, beyond the trees and the houses,
would be a kind of altar upon which the clouds descend and
celebrate their union with the most intelligent mortals. Etcetera.
Certainly we ought not recreate the Greek myths, but we should
follow their imaginative structure. (It is needless to say that it is
impossible, considering these times of "enlightment"—and this is
why I grit my teeth and bite my nails.) But I have understood the
Georgics.

The *Georgics* are beautiful not because of their sensitive
presentation of country life—as I bet one of our acquaintances
would say—but because they imbue the entire countryside with
secret mythical realities, and they go beyond the appearance,
showing, even in such gestures as studying the weather or
sharpening a scythe, the traces of a god who did it or taught it.

Ciao,
PAVESE

August 30, 1942

Dear Fernanda,

Some beautiful thoughts come to my mind, and there is no
reason for not relating them to you. It is the usual problem of how
much imagination one place can contain. I am here before a steep

mountain-face covered with pine trees (or perhaps firs); it is immense, impervious, streaked by an inaccessible small white cascade which now looks like a rivulet of perspiration, but all night made me believe that it was pouring rain.

I have never seen places like these except, refined, in the background of some Tuscan painting. I wonder what I can do with them, in my imagination of course. I could, for instance, narrate something somehow conditioned by this mountain. A mysterious adventure taking place here, with the pines, the small cascade, the meadows suspended in midair, the dark-red scars of the rock as the *setting*, the precedent, the reality, the "memory" in the inner life of the people. The characters of a story must be rooted, in their surrounding reality, by innumerable roots that are *their* memories, *their* imaginative life. Now I have no memories of these places, of this nature, of this reality: for me it is a gratuitous world, empty, objective, like a person seen for the first time. It's obvious I have nothing to say about it.

So why does everyone extol unusual and beautiful places and landscapes which would constitute so-called "natural beauty"? Does one move and travel to find and admire some of them? It is undeniable that I find an interest in this unheard-of view, and a creative interest, remember, consisting in the effort to develop these impressions into a story, a fantasy. Something that, at least now, I am incapable of doing.

I want to conclude. It is not that the sensations of beauty, of stimulation in nature do not exist. Sensations are the most unsuppressible reality of this world. But whether it be landscapes or people, gestures, colors, the entire realm, it must be said that we observe them in a state of continuous tension and effort in order to transform what to us is unheard of, surprising, new, into a set of memories which are only our own. External reality lives for us only as memory. The word *beauty*, therefore, ought to be banished from the field of aesthetics which should, instead, be a scientific effort to transform what is the unheard of, the surprising, etc. (= the beautiful) into a complex and meaningful set of memories. We say that people are *beautiful* the first time we see them; then we begin to find them *dear* as they become fixed in our memory; finally we fall in love with them (with your permission, *madame*!) when their reality is already part of ours in a meaningful system of relationships which is, in the practical world, what a work of poetry is in the spiritual one. Am I right?

But he who was born to create stories or poems is not satisfied with falling in love, since love lacks the autonomous intellectual construction it needs to be a work of art. In a work, memories are purely intellectual relations; the more inexpressible they are, the more they are translatable into language, because then they are expressed in symbols (the height of art). In life this symbolic element is limited to the celebration of anniversaries or to the cult of relics (hair, objects, words that were said, etc.) which never have the autonomy of pure creation. The truly loving creation—the offspring—is the end of every autonomy on the part of the creator.

I shall end here. If then someone should remark that the essence of my exposition is this: "Let's make art, let's make love, but let's not make children," he must know that I shall not lower myself to answer him.

Keep well,
PAVESE

This was the time when Pavese's presence became more and more indispensable at Einaudi where all the series carried the mark of his interest, inventiveness, and rigorous work. He also continued to attend the anti-Fascist political meetings. Pintor, who often went abroad, was establishing contacts with the anti-Fascists and anti-Nazis of other countries, and when he returned to Turin he reported all the news at the evening meetings after having discussed them at length with Pavese. In the meantime, the group of organizers and collaborators at Einaudi had expanded, and now included Felice Balbo, Natalia Ginzburg, the wife of Leone, Norberto Bobbio, and others.

At the same time, *The Harvesters* obtained an unexpected success among the public and the critics. Every magazine and newspaper wrote about Pavese and the majority of critics agreed that his book was a literary event of prime interest. Only the intransigent Fascists accused him of offending his country, but this criticism, rather than worrying him, galvanized him and inspired his humor.

Here are two previously unpublished letters of that period which are particularly significant. Both are addressed to Pavese's friend

Giulio Einaudi, with whom he jocularly uses a formal tone of affected respect. The first letter refers to the publication of *The Harvesters*, and the second to the new edition of *Work Wearies*.

The first letter is dated May 2, 1941:

Most Esteemed Publisher Einaudi,

I accept the conditions you offer me for the edition of my story *The Harvesters*. I would appreciate receiving, as a symbolical advance, a pipe, so that I could smoke it and serenely prepare other and more seductive stories.

Your most devoted,
CESARE PAVESE

The date of the second letter is June 8, 1941:

Most Esteemed Einaudi Publishing House:

With this letter I am offering you the opportunity to publish a book of verses which has already had, in its first edition with the Parenti brothers of Florence, some failure, and could certainly have another.

Which means that it would have another failure if another publisher is interested in my offer. But I am too well aware of the proportions recently reached by your House, to ignore the fact that a launching promoted by you would reach catastrophic proportions and rob all Italian readers of their peace.

But enough with preambles: you cannot and should not miss this new opportunity to pay homage to a major living poet, who, if rejected by you, could turn to some other publishing house, causing you a perfidious and most serious damage. I say this not to blackmail you, but to confirm once again the reputation as a great publisher you enjoy with everybody. The undersigned does not ignore that you host in your series such books as would embarrass any printer or booklover. He assures you of his diligent help, *without compensation*, in the correction of the proofs, so that the pages of his book are not disfigured by too many errors.

Once again, let's put a stop to the preambles. I am offering you the volume *Work Wearies* newly enriched with unpublished poems and with appendixes in prose explaining the poetics of the author.

He states his willingness to provide you with the manuscript free of postal charges, and possibly including new poems.

Sir, you are good and charitable, and I have been informed that you protect young people. Sir, I am young, not unknown and I have some support. I declare myself ready to relieve you of about fifty free copies for my own use. . . .

Expectantly, I am your most devoted

CESARE PAVESE

From the tone of these letters one gathers that it was a happy time in Pavese's life. Around him was a fervor of cultural as well as political activity. In 1942, Pintor published Pisacane's *The Essay on Revolution* and his own translations of Rilke's poetry. It was in fact with Pintor that Pavese's discussions on literary themes and political problems grew more intense. Pintor's courageous articles in *Primato*, the well-known periodical of the Fascist minister Bottai (in which he dared to openly defend Croce, maintaining that university and culture ought to oppose Fascist rhetoric and excessive nationalism), convinced Pavese that his friend had the ability to combine, at every possible opportunity, culture and politics. Their opinions often coincided in the analysis of works by writers such as Thomas Mann, Montale, and Vittorini.

Soon after *The Harvesters*, another very significant book was published: it was Vittorini's *In Sicily* which sparked endless discussions. To defend Vittorini in the magazine *Prospettive*, Pintor wrote: "In that journey the first signs of Sicily are announced: 'a little malaria, a little tuberculosis.' To complement these signs, the first human figures intervene. They are men and women stricken by poverty, Sicilian men with soft peaked caps on their noses, Sicilian women wrapped in shawls, but their rigid gestures and abstract words (whether they say New York or 'pesceduovo') surely are an introduction to allegory."

Both Pavese and Pintor had understood, above all, the cry of the offended man which Vittorini made erupt from Sicily; Pavese had the same cry arise from the Piedmontese countryside in *The Harvesters*, with a different style, but with the same intentions.

When Vittorini published *Americana*, an anthology of the most representative authors of the United States, Pintor wrote: "This America does not need Columbus; it is discovered within us, it is the land for which one longs with the same hope and confidence as the first emigrants and of whoever is determined to defend, at the cost of fatigue and errors, the dignity of the human condition." With equal admiration, on May 27, 1942 Pavese wrote Vittorini the following letter, which also appears in his diary:

Dear Vittorini,

I owe you this letter because I think you'll be pleased to hear that we are all in solidarity with you. . . . The whole value and significance of *Americana* depend on your notes. In the ten years I've been studying that literature I never came across a synthesis so accurate and enlightening. I want to tell you this because when your notes become known around the world, someone is sure to jump up and say that they are highly original, yes, but fantastic. Now it should be shouted that it is precisely because they are like a short story, a novel if you will, something invented, that they are so illuminating. Leaving aside the soundness of the individual judgments resulting from just as many very well-informed, intimate monographs, I want to speak of your thematic approach and of the drama of corruption, purity, ferocity, and innocence you have established in that history. It is neither by chance nor by choice that you start it with the "abstract ravings"[23] since its implied conclusion is *In Sicily*. In this sense it is a great thing that you have brought to it the tension and the excited cries of discovery of *your own* poetic history; and since this history of yours has not been a chasing of rainbows but a confrontation with world literature (that world literature which, in universality, is implicit in American literature, if I understood clearly), the result is that the entire century and a half of America is reduced to the essential evidence of a myth we have all lived through and which you now relate to us.

In the company of Pintor, Cinanni, and Capriolo, Pavese was completely transformed. He was no longer concerned with concealing his interest in politics, in fact he exhibited it. Above all, his discussions with Capriolo appeared to have convinced him to take a position. The worker and the intellectual had found a common ground, even if Pavese still hesitated before Marxism.

Cinanni had become totally involved in clandestine work. A special section of Communist leaders and intellectuals had been formed; it held its meetings each Sunday morning at the Pajettas' house, in Borgo San Paolo. Members of this section were Capriolo, Cinanni, Guaita, Mrs. Pajetta, and her son Gaspare, the youngest Communist in Turin whose two older brothers, Giancarlo and Giuliano, had been forced for years by the Fascists to remain away from home: the first in prison, the second in a concentration camp. Gaspare was not yet sixteen, but with his own insistence and with Pavese's support, he had been able to convince his mother to let him participate in the political activity. Pavese tutored Gaspare in Greek and Latin. During the lessons, as well as when he was invited to dinner at the Pajettas' home, Pavese did not talk with Gaspare only about literature, but also about politics and the serious human problems that troubled Italy. Gaspare grew so fond of Pavese that he began to imitate his gestures and repeat his words. One day he was telling his mother that Pavese had taught him to admire Dostoyevsky more than Tolstoy; another time that only Pavese could teach how to appreciate poems of chivalry and to distrust Napoleon. At times Gaspare's blind admiration for Pavese provoked discussions between him and his mother. For example, on returning from one of his lessons, Gaspare said to his mother: "It seems to me that you do not care enough for the question of God." When she answered that this was possibly the result of having been too concerned with that question as a child and that, in her own way, she had resolved this problem, Gaspare remarked: "Do you know what Pavese told me? That the Catholic Church is, after all, a large home, trustworthy and secure." His mother answered: "That's true, but there are people who run away from their secure homes in search of their own freedom. It's a personal problem."

On another occasion, Gaspare, returning from his lesson with a somber face, confided to his mother: "I'm depressed because I'm sure I'll never be as intelligent as Pavese; I had too many illusions about myself." His mother said: "Very well, son, there are many ways of living, and intelligence isn't everything. I would want you to be simpler and more solid than he."

The phrase Pavese repeated with insistence to Gaspare after almost every lesson was the following: "Remember, Gaspare, that today one cannot be a good Italian if one does not kill a German." We shall later see how Gaspare Pajetta remembered Pavese's advice and what were the fates of pupil and teacher when Italy had to defend its territory and its prestige against the Germans.

Pavese often left Turin for weeks or months: he had to go to Rome to prepare the opening of Einaudi's new office in that city. He was not happy to be away from Turin, but his dedication to Einaudi had become second nature for him. In Rome, Pavese had direct rapport with those anti-Fascist intellectuals who were already contributing to the Einaudi publications: Alicata, Muscetta, Onofri, Giolitti, and others. His discussions with them, especially with Alicata, convinced him that their publishing house had to acquire a stronger political conscience. It was the same request made by Pintor in Turin. As a result, beginning that year, every Einaudi book was a manifesto of denunciation or protest.

In spite of these contacts, Pavese missed his Turin friends. He became more isolated in Rome. He spent a great deal of time reading, and each page of his diary of those months includes the name of a new writer, Italian or foreign, modern or classical. He was particularly interested in symbolism, ethnography, astrology, and prehistory. In order to combat the melancholy that assailed him in that large, unfamiliar city, he wrote his Turin friends, especially Einaudi, ironic letters, as in the period of his exile.

In a letter dated April 14, 1942, addressed to Giulio Einaudi, Pavese protested the delay in payment of his salary. He accused Einaudi of exercising a "system of complete exploitation." The closing of the letter deserves to be quoted, because it illustrates how Pavese expressed the threat to leave his job and have a good time: "We have a life to live, bicycles to ride, sidewalks to walk on, and sunsets to enjoy. In short, distinguished Publisher, Nature beckons us and we must follow."

On March 4, 1943, Pavese was unexpectedly drafted in the army, although earlier he had been exonerated from military service for being the son of a widow. His destination was Rivoli, with the 30th Infantry Regiment named "Assietta." However, as a result of his asthma, he was immediately sent to a hospital for observation and then given six months convalescence.

He returned to Rome from where, on July 19, 1943, he notified Einaudi that their Roman office had to be closed because of the continuous bombing of the city by the Allies. The most interesting part of the letter consists of small pen drawings made in the margins of each page. They begin with a man descending with a parachute, while a machine gun fires at him; then there are airplanes dropping bombs, a train that leaves behind a trail of smoke, cannons, a burnt house, a man hanged on a tree, and finally a man lying on the ground holding a revolver pointed at his temple.

14

The War in the Hills

In the first days of September 1943, when Pavese returned to Turin from Rome, the political and military situation was ruinous. After the fall of the Fascist regime, the war continued, with Italy still on the side of the Germans while incessant bombing destroyed the Italian cities.

If Pavese had been able to return to Turin and to see Cinanni, Ginzburg, Pintor, Mila, Geymonat, and Sturani again, his friends would probably have convinced him to join them in the Partisan movement; but the building on via Lamarmora had been bombed and his sister Maria and her family were safe only because she had decided to seek refuge at her sister-in-law's house in Serralunga, a small village in Monferrato. The building which housed the Einaudi office was also bombed and burned. Pavese's friends had taken to the mountains to organize the Resistance War. Cinanni had anxiously waited Cesare's return, but he too had left to take his place among the Partisans in the mountains.

Therefore, Pavese found himself alone at a most crucial moment; he could only decide to join his sister in Serralunga. The shootings, the arms, and the blood terrorized him. He remained isolated, separated from the rest of the world.

The diary of those years does not contain any reference to the political events or to the war which was going on in the hills. Pavese withdrew to his books and created a world of symbols, perhaps hoping to find an alibi or a justification for not being with his friends who were risking their lives. In February 1944, he wrote in the diary about his earlier years in Turin:

> The place where you are really yourself is that avenue in Turin, elegant yet unpretentious, broad, calm, and discreet, where it is always spring or summer and where your poetry was made. The material came from many sources, but it took shape there. This avenue with its little café was your room, your window on the world.

There is neither regret nor remorse, as if his having immersed himself in the silence of the country represented the continuation of a habit which would bring him peace. But it was an artificial peace, as revealed, after a few lines, by this cry: "The fact is that you lost your taste for seeing, feeling, accepting, and now you are eating your heart out."

On March 3, 1944, after receiving the tragic news that Leone Ginzburg had died as a consequence of tortures suffered at the prison of Regina Coeli in Rome, Pavese seemed to find merely words of evasion from grief:

> I heard the news on March 1st. Do others exist for us? I wish they did not, so I would not suffer. I am living in a sort of fog, thinking of him all the time, but vaguely. It ends with one getting used to this state, always postponing *real grief* until tomorrow; so one forgets and has *not* suffered.

When seized by anguish, Pavese tried to escape by taking long walks in the woods. While searching for mythical comforts, he was again troubled by religious doubts. He often arrived at the sanctuary of Crea, which he entered to meditate. At times he had the illusion of having found a faith, a refuge in God. He talked with priests, read the Bible, and on January 9, 1945 he noted in the diary:

> A strange, rich year. It began and ended with God, with assiduous meditations on the primitive and the savage, and it has seen some notable creative work. It could be the most important year you have ever lived. If you persevere with God, it certainly will be. (It must not be forgotten that *God* also means a technical cataclysm-symbolism prepared by years of approaches.)

But he could not persevere and soon he himself denounced his own superstition. A faith might have saved him, but a faith, no matter which, was impossible for him. The only event which stirred him during those years was seeing again in Casale, for a few days, Fernanda Pivano, who had been given a teaching position in that city.

From those months of seclusion originated his theory of the primitive: "Nature returns to a primitive state when something forbidden occurs: blood or sex." However, even when he attempted to root his thoughts and emotions in Herodotus or Vico, he was not only unable to find a definitive moral or arrive at a philosophy, but he also acted like a blind man in search of an inaccessible absolute.

Turning his back on his noblest obligations, he indulged in thoughts that served only to discredit every effort which might lead him back to reality. In the exaltation of myth, he sought to convince himself that all is memory and that "the past determines the future." "No one changes," he wrote in his defense, "everyone is his own prisoner." His desire to establish a simple and direct rapport with the world and his constant inability to do so could not find any other justification but in myth.

The strength to survive isolation came from his work. That was the period when he completed the collection of short stories *Festival Night* and elaborated the themes for his future novels: *The House on the Hill*, *The Comrade*, and *Dialogues with Leucò*.

In the diary, the imminence of the Partisans' victory was reflected only in the joy of the rebirth of nature. On March 15, 1945 he wrote: "The first breaking forth of tiny leaves is an outburst of little green flames. New buds appear among the dry branches." And on April 18, "The petals of the apple and pear trees are flying in the wind and the ground is strewn with them. They look like butterflies."

But a few months later, in two poems published in the volume titled *Death Will Come and It Will Have Your Eyes*, he would confess that he had understood the intensity of the human tragedy that had taken place around him:

> You don't know the hills
> where the blood was shed.

We all fled,
we all abandoned
our rifles and our names. A woman
watched us flee.
Only one of us stopped,
raising a closed fist,
saw the empty sky,
bowed his head and died
under a wall, in silence.
Now he is a tatter of blood
and a name. A woman
waits for us in the hills.

And then we cowards
who loved the whispering
evening, the homes,
the paths along the river,
the lights, red and dirty,
of those places, the grief
sweetened and mute—
we pulled our hands away
from the live chain
and kept silent, but the heart
shook us with blood,
and it was sweetness no longer,
no longer we abandoned ourselves
to the path on the river—
now free, we knew
of being alone and alive.

In the short novel *The House on the Hill*, published in 1949, Pavese reveals that neither the isolation nor his dialogue with myths could make him forget the drama of the civil war. The book *Before the Cock Crows*, including *The Political Prisoner* and *The House on the Hill*, would combine in an organic story the two most dramatic and influential moments in Pavese's life. His most painful experiences are relived in this story, filtered through a classical meditation and wisdom. If the diary of those years expresses one side of Pavese, these two novels reveal the other Pavese, the one who still believed in the possibility of living in contact with other men.

Corrado of *The House on the Hill* is perhaps the character in which Pavese has placed most of himself. It is of no importance that Professor Corrado spent the years of the Partisan War in the hills surrounding Turin, while Pavese lived in the hills near Casale, in Serralunga. The facts are the same, it is the same war. From the beginning of the novel, Pavese talks about the war as he used to when he was speaking to his anti-Fascist friends in Turin:

> I must say—as I begin this story of a long illusion—that war cannot be blamed for what happened to me . . . All the war did was remove my last scruple about keeping to myself, about consuming my years and my heart alone; and one fine day I realized that Belbo, the big dog, was the last sincere confidant I still had. The war had made it legitimate for one to isolate himself, to live from day to day without regretting the lost opportunities. It was as if I had been waiting for the war a long time and had been counting on it, a war so vast and unprecedented that one could easily go home to the hills, turn in for the night, and let it rage in the sky above the cities. Considering the things that were happening, the mere fact of living without complaining, almost without speaking of them, seemed a regular habit to me. That kind of mute rancor that characterized the last years of my youth found a refuge and a horizon in the war. . . .
>
> I liked to eat alone, in the darkened room, alone and forgotten, listening to the night, alert, hearing the time pass.
>
> Behind the tilled fields and the roads, behind the homes, under one's feet, the ancient indifferent heart of the earth brooded in the darkness, lived in ravines, in roots, in hidden things, in childhood fears. I began in those days to enjoy my childhood memories. One might say that beneath the rancors and the uncertainties, beneath the desire to be alone, I was discovering the boy in me in order to have a companion, a colleague, a son.

Pavese's longing for a child appears when Corrado again meets Cate, the girl he had known many years earlier in Turin, and he has the opportunity to meet her son. From that moment the suspense builds, for him and for the readers, around the suspicion that Cate's son may also be his.

When Pavese dictated this book, as well as *The Comrade*, to Maria Livia Serini who was working with him at Einaudi, he constantly asked for his collaborator's opinion. Above all, he wanted to know if the character of the son and Corrado's uncertainty about his paternity seemed appropriate and if the readers would have understood the reason for the son's presence and for that doubt. Maria Livia answered that it was not easy to understand and advised him to do away with that character, but Pavese replied: "Why, why, there are so many whys to which it is impossible to answer"; and that longing for a child of his own remained in the novel.

This theme, one of the most important in Pavese's life, dominates *The House on the Hill* along with many others: childhood, the woman who refuses to marry him, the loving girl he abandons, and suicide.

The social themes also have a relevant place in this novel. Here is an example, the description of Turin under the bombings:

A whole class of people, the lucky, the ones at the top, were going, or had gone, to their villas in the mountains or by the sea. There they lived the usual life. It was left to their servants, their doormen, the poor, to take care of their mansions in town, and, if there was a fire, to save their possessions. It was left to the porters, the soldiers, the mechanics. Then even those others began to get away at night to the woods and the inns. They slept little. Mostly they drank and discussed, ten in a hole. I felt ashamed for not being one of them, and I would have liked to meet with some of these people in the boulevards and talk.

The political awareness continues, as in the following passages:

The old woman said, "Not all of us have automobiles. Some work until night. The trolleys aren't running." Then she looked at me and lowered her voice. "The people in charge are scum," she muttered. "Dirty Black Shirts. They don't think of us. Look in whose hands they've put us."

I stayed alone with Cate. "Aren't you coming to listen to the radio?" she asked.

She took a few steps with me, then stopped. "You're not a Fascist, are you?" she said.

She was serious and laughing. I took her hand and sighed, "We all are, dear Cate. If we weren't, we would revolt, throw grenades, risk our necks. Whoever lets things go and takes it easy is already a Fascist."

From political themes Pavese passes to another of his fundamental subjects: self-criticism, the regret for not being able to participate actively in political life and to unite himself to others. The following dialogue is quite revealing:

"Are you jealous, Cate?"

"Of whom? You make me laugh. Jealous of Fonso?"

"But Fonso is a boy," I shouted. "What does he have to do with you?"

"We're all children to you," she said. "We're like your dog."

And his insistence on examining himself so cruelly persists when Cate speaks to him about her son:

"At the beginning it was rough, but I had Dino and I couldn't afford to do foolish things. I remembered what you told me once, that life is worthwhile only when you live for something or someone."

This too, I had taught her. The phrase was mine.

"If she asks for whom you are living now," I shouted to myself, "what would you answer?". . . .

"Now you suffer, and I feel sorry for you," she said gravely. "You live alone with your dog. I feel sorry for you."

I looked at her, amazed. "Am I not better, Cate? Even with you, am I not better than I was then?"

"I don't know," Cate said. "You're sort of nice in a weak way. You let things slide and don't inspire much confidence. You have nobody, you don't even get mad."

"I was angry about Dino," I said.

"You don't love anybody. . . ."

She was silent for a moment, then she added, "You're like a boy, a conceited boy. One of those boys in whose lives something has gone wrong, but they don't want anyone to know about it, to know they are suffering. That's why you're pitiful. When you talk to others, you are always resentful, malicious. You're afraid, Corrado."

Perhaps it's because of the war, the bombs."

"No, it's you," Cate said.

This is Pavese's real diary, more revealing than *This Business of Living*. In the following dialogue, Pavese delivers his most sincere human and political credo:

It was on one of those evenings that Cate's mother spoke her piece to me while we were waiting in the courtyard for the end of an air raid alarm. I had just said to Fonso, "Before the Italians can take things seriously it will take a lot of bombs."

The old lady said, ". . . For you who have your loaf of bread and can stay on the hill, the war is a pleasure. It's people like you who brought on the war." She said it quietly, without a trace of bitterness, as if I were her son. At first I didn't react. "I wish they were all like him," Cate said. I kept still. "One must survive, that's all," Fonso remarked. "We too, Mama," Cate said, "come to sleep on the hills."

The old woman was mumbling now. I wondered if she knew how justly and deeply she had reached me. The excuses the others made for me didn't count; in a sense they only made things worse.

Tono the Socialist said, "Everyone tries to save himself. We are fighting so that everyone, even the bosses, even our enemies, understands where salvation lies. That's why the Socialists oppose war."

And Fonso, "Just a minute. You don't say why the working class always has to defend itself. The bosses keep their control with war and terror. They advance by crushing us. And you have the illusion that they could understand. They've understood all too well. That's why they keep on."

Then I joined in again. "I'm not speaking of this. I'm not talking of classes. Fonso is right, of course. But we Italians are made like that: we obey only force. Then, with the excuse that it was force, we laugh it off. Nobody takes it seriously."

"Certainly not the bourgeois."

"I'm talking about all the Italians."

"Professor," Nando exclaimed, his head lowered, "do you love Italy?"

Again I had every face looking at me: Tono, the old lady, the girls, Cate. Fonso smiled.

"No," I said slowly, "not Italy. The Italians."

"Shake!" Fonso said. "We understand each other."

Although Corrado will seek safety by fleeing the war while the others go to fight, he is clearly aware that the road he has chosen is not the right one. Is this not what Pavese wanted to say in the following passage?

That morning at noon there was a sudden alarm. The hill, the valley, Turin in the distance, all was silent under the sky. I was standing in the orchard. I wondered how many hearts had stopped beating just then, how many leaves were shaking, how many dogs had flattened themselves on the ground. The ground as well, the hill and its crust must have shuddered. All at once I realized how foolish and futile my taking delight in the woods had become, that pride in the woods I didn't forget even with Dino. Under the summer sky petrified by the howling of sirens, I understood that I had always been playing like an irresponsible child.

Corrado does not join the Partisans and in order to escape from the Germans he takes refuge in a convent in Chieri, just as Pavese had done in Crea. Pavese's remorse reveals itself with greater bitterness through the characters of Fonso, Tono, Gallo, Cate, and all the others who have chosen to fight, because in them he sees his dearest friends; Mila, Ginzburg, Cinanni, Capriolo, Gaspare Pajetta, and Geymonat:

Even today I wonder why those Germans didn't wait for me at the villa, sending someone to look for me in Turin. This is the reason I am still free and up here. Why I should have been saved, not Gallo, Tono, nor Cate, I don't know. Perhaps because I'm supposed to suffer other things? Because I'm the most useless and don't deserve anything, not even punishment? Because I went into the church that time? The experience of danger makes one more cowardly every day. It makes one stupid, and I have reached a point where finding myself alive by chance, while so many better men than I are dead, does not satisfy me and is not enough. At times, after having listened to the useless radio and while looking through the window at the empty vineyards, I think that living by chance is not living. And I wonder if I have really escaped. . . .

And sometimes I think that only a boy's irresponsibility, genuine, unaffected irresponsibility could allow us to see what is going on without feeling guilty. After all, the heroes of these valleys are all boys; they have the straight and stubborn look of boys. And if it weren't for the fact that we nursed this war in our hearts—we who are no longer young, we who said: "Let it come then, if it has to come"—even war, this war, would seem a clean business. Anyway, who knows? This war burns our homes. It sows our squares and streets with executed people. It chases us like hares from refuge to refuge. It will end by forcing even us to fight, by extorting our active consent. And a day will come when nobody will be outside the war—not the cowards, nor the melancholy, nor the solitary. . . . We will all have agreed to make war. And then maybe we will have peace.

We are near the end of the novel, when Pavese takes Corrado back to the Langhe. Besides being extraordinarily beautiful, these pages are very dear to me because they recall the itinerary Pavese and I followed together in the hills of my war, when we stopped in front of my burned house and Pavese asked my father, a farmer, to tell him why the Germans wanted to shoot him. My father could only answer: "We saw so many things that it would take entire winters to relate them all." Pavese listened, pale and mute. The final pages of *The House on the Hill* are the interpretation of the kind of feelings that, as he confided in me, he had experienced that day:

It is here that the war has seized me and seizes me every day. If I walk in the woods, if at every suspicion of Fascist raiders I duck into the ravines, if I sometimes talk to passing Partisans . . . it's not that I don't see that the war is not a game, this war that has even arrived up here and seizes even our past by the throat. I don't know if Cate, Fonso, Dino, and all the others will return. Sometimes I hope so, and it scares me. But I have seen the unknown dead, the Fascist dead. It was they who woke me up. If a stranger, an enemy, becomes a thing like that when he dies, if one stops short and is afraid to walk over him, it means that, although beaten, our enemy is someone, that after blood is shed one must placate it, give this blood a voice, justify the man who shed it. Looking at some of these dead is humiliating. They are no longer other people's affairs; one doesn't seem to have happened there by chance. One has the impression that the same fate that felled these bodies holds us nailed to the spot to see them, to fill our eyes with their sight. It's not fear, not our usual cowardice. One feels humiliated because one understands—touching it with one's eyes—that we might be in their place ourselves: there would be no difference, and if we live we owe it to these dirtied corpses. That is why every war is a civil war; every fallen man resembles those who survive and asks them to explain.

It is difficult for me to say whether *The Moon and the Bonfires* contains pages so serene and human, but I am certain that Pavese was never more sincere than he was in *The House on the Hill*.

It seems to me that in this book, Pavese was able to combine his personal historical moment with the historical moment of everybody, showing that he was reconquering his share of reality.

In grasping the sense of what had occurred under his eyes amid his hills, he gave substance to that literature of the Resistance which, beyond the political commitment, aimed at rediscovering man and at motivating him to build a new society. Vittorini, Jovine, and Quasimodo wrote with the same goal in mind.

A few days after the liberation of Italy, Pavese decided to return to Turin, but only after Einaudi had called him to come and reorganize the publishing house. In the wave of joy overwhelming everybody and everything, he felt even more isolated. As he had not been able to directly participate in the struggle for liberation, he could not share the happiness around him.

He grew more depressed on learning that Carando, a friend and a fellow professor of literature at the lyceum, had been shot, together with his brother, near Savigliano; that his student Gaspare Pajetta who, although still a young boy, had joined the Partisans, and fallen in combat, and that his mother, who had run to look for him, had found him lying dead. Capriolo had been hanged by the Fascists in Turin and Pintor had met with a heroic death.

Cinanni, Mila, Sturani, Antonicelli, Guaita, Geymonat, and Bobbio were still in Partisan uniform. A feeling of anguish and deep remorse made Pavese even more distant and silent. In those first days he could not find the courage to go and greet his friends who had survived and, after the seclusion in the hills, he attempted to impose on himself a new seclusion in the freed city.

It was with Cinanni that Pavese was finally able to speak about his anguish. Cinanni had moved to Milan and Pavese visited him there, bringing him a copy of *Work Wearies* in the new edition, with this dedication: "To Cinanni, no longer my student, but my teacher."

A few days after his trip to Milan, Pavese and I met for the first time. I was working for *L'Unità* in Turin. One evening Pavese arrived at my office accompanied by an American lieutenant and Fernanda Pivano. When I realized that it was Pavese, whom I knew and admired through his books, I expressed my joy in meeting him personally. He shook my hand without saying anything, but there was pleasure in his eyes. Fernanda and the officer left soon, while Pavese chose to remain with me.

My office was small, on the ground floor on via Valdocco. The smoke from our pipes soon filled it. We spoke about our villages, and Cesare stayed with me until the office closed. All the members of the editorial staff wanted to meet him, and Raf Vallone, editor of the literary page, tried unsuccessfully to interest him in a discussion on poetry.

At 3:30 in the morning we left the newspaper and set out together in the fresh air of that May morning. He accompanied me home from where I had walked him to his home; then he wanted to return with me to my neighborhood in Piazza Benefica. To my affectionate protests he offered his insomnia as justification.

After that meeting he often came back to the newspaper. In the early afternoon we used to go to the Turin hills. Often we sat on the grass and Pavese became very talkative, speaking on a variety of subjects. One day we stopped at a small restaurant he knew. The proprietor greeted him as an old friend and Pavese ordered a half liter of barbera. When I told him I didn't drink, he looked at me, incredulous, almost irritated, and said: "But don't you come from Vinchio, the land of barbera?" He wanted to know why I didn't drink.

"Maybe because as a child I was afraid of the drunks in my village."

"Were there many?"

"Enough."

He laughed and told me that my abstinence embarrassed him. "It is like betraying one's own birthplace," he added.

He would frequently come to eat at my home on Sundays. He arrived punctually at noon with a package of pastries which he hid behind him as if he were ashamed of his kindness. He loved to speak in Piedmontese dialect with my wife and to play with my daughter. It was an unrecognizable Pavese.

Then the two of us would go out. One evening, while accompanying me home, he expressed his intention of joining the Communist Party. I did not answer him immediately; then I told him to think about it and not to hurry his decision. He only said: "I understand," and never spoke to me about it again.

I later learned that he had joined and had done so at the party's cell "Gaspare Pajetta," named after his former student. It is certain that Pavese joined the Communist Party to fulfill his need to make himself worthy of Gaspare and of his other friends who had died. That commitment was a way of redeeming himself for his absence from the Partisan War and of being in daily contact with the people. It was one of the most important decisions of his life and he made it with his full sense of responsibility.

He dedicated himself to his political activity with the enthusiasm of a neophyte. He was present at every party meeting, happily accepting the most humble tasks and stopping for hours to talk with the workers. We easily agreed on a series of articles he would write for the literary page of *L'Unità*. To Vallone, who asked him for short stories and poems, he answered he did not know how to write them.

He only wanted to speak to the people. The first article he brought me was entitled "Return to Man." Some very important points were developed in that article, published on May 20, 1945:

> These years of anguish and blood taught us that anguish and blood are not the end of everything. One thing saves us from the horror: it is the opening up of men to other men. We are quite certain of this because never has man been less alone than in these times of fearful solitude. There were days when the look, the gesture of a stranger were enough to startle us and save us from the precipice. We knew and we know that everywhere, even in the most unaware or sinister eyes, there broods a love, an innocence it is up to us to share. Many barriers, many stupid walls have fallen these days. . . . Truly, man has revealed himself in his most living feelings and now he waits for us, whose turn it is, to understand and speak.
>
> To speak. Words are our business. We say it without any shadow of timidity or irony. Words are tender things, intractable and alive, but made for man rather than man for them. We all feel that we live in a time in which words must be brought back to the solid and bare clarity they had when man created them to serve him. Just because they are useful to man, it happens that the new words move and grab us as no other voice does, not even the most solemn in the world that dies, like a prayer or a war bulletin.

Our task is difficult but alive. It is also the only one with a sense and a hope. Those who await our words are men, poor men as we are when we forget that life is a communion. They will listen to us with faith and tenacity, ready to incarnate the words we say. To disappoint them would be to betray them, it would be to betray our past as well.

After a period of absence from Turin, during which he had gone to Santo Stefano, Pavese returned to write for *L'Unità* a series of articles entitled "Dialogues with the Comrade." The first dialogues were simply the faithful transcription of his recent conversations in Santo Stefano with Pinolo Scaglione, his carpenter friend.

The "Dialogues with the Comrade" coincided with the most intense phase of his political life. He wanted to make himself understood by the workers and to understand them. He wanted to speak and to discuss with total freedom and sincerity. Here are two quotations from the first dialogue published in the Turin edition of *L'Unità* on May 1, 1946:

I will say more, comrade. One does not have *contact* with the people, one *is* the people. In our trade there is not a moment in which one can decide to write from now on in a certain way, to speak for a certain class or for certain interests. We can do it but then we sell out, even if the group which buys us is the working class. In our trade one does not *go toward* something: one *is* something. It is useless to adopt strange expressions or to speak perhaps like peasants; what you are is in your blood, in the life you've lived, in what thirty years of existence have reduced you to. There is, instead, he who feels now, right now, the duty to write for everyone, to speak like everyone, but before, during the bad times, did not feel it—you understand me.

The more time you spend with a friend, the more you know him. So it is with books. And isn't it beautiful to understand a friend who for thirty years, for his entire life, has tried to speak with you?

In those months, Pavese had important encounters at the editorial office of *L'Unità*. Among others was the one with Italo Calvino, who established such a close friendship with Pavese that he followed him to the Einaudi Publishing House and became one of its most esteemed and faithful contributors.

15

A Cat Scratches at the Door

In 1945 and again in 1946, Pavese resided in Rome while I was in Milan as the editor of the Northern edition of *L'Unità*. We nevertheless kept in contact.

Pavese's assignment was to develop the Rome office of Einaudi and to win new readers.

At that time Pavese started the "mattinale," a type of circular through which he gave and accepted orders, expressed his opinion on books, and made ironic remarks about colleagues, returning to the biting humor that characterized those times when he felt most dissatisfied with himself. Here are sections of these circulars:

> You, Mila, instead of working hard for the *abundant* salary the publisher *generously* gives you, spend your days at home composing music. I know that through music you enter the spiritual climate most suitable to you and that you consider your work in the publishing trade as an inferior material activity. But the salary is also material and yet you collect it—even if *it is usually late,* since this is the way it is paid by our mutual *exploiter.* . . .
>
> Natalia [Ginzburg] must bring a sweet note of femininity into the rude atmosphere of Corso Re Umberto, which the other insignificant women were unable to dispel . . .
>
> You must absolutely devote yourself with greater interest to your work in the technical field. Both you and Natalia belong to the "Party of

Action"[24] and you can therefore establish with greater facility rapports with Franco Venturi and with other valuable and pleasant men who are also close to my heart. After having definitively become a card-carrying member of the Communist Party, I feel in a much better position to sustain the Einaudi Turin headquarters which I've considered my domain since its birth. Our boss intends to fight for a broad political culture. It is obvious that I am supporting him. I am aware of your preoccupations, but, as to being fired, it's like the misadventures of love: one is always dismissed when, *through clear signs,* he has proved himself dismissable. We are indispensable to the publishing house even for our already ancient typographic experience . . .

You must create for yourself a work-oriented brain. The brain cannot be a poet nor an *ariose* musical composer, even less an *absentminded* scholar, but rather a secretary. One of those *secretary-housewives* who have a hand and an eye on everything and don't forget anything, from the most important to the least significant. I recommend to you *Festival Night:* the more time passes, the more it seems a *great book* to me. Meanwhile, I'm announcing—to *make you angry*—that I have resumed writing poetry. . . .

I don't tell you that you are a pig, but a fool, yes. Likewise, I must give vent to my *resentment* (note the angelic softness of this word) against Vittorini, Balbo, and Natalia, who, while I pull the cart like a mule of the Langhe, encourage a taste for vast humanistic idleness and for the discovery of *man.*

Pavese considered the time spent in Rome a period of exile. Far from Turin, he was assailed by the old melancholic thoughts, indecisions, and taste for solitude.

The climate in Rome was then one of euphoria and post-war dissipation. Pavese, however, found serious and sincere friends. They were young people with whom he spent his evenings, discussed his work, and went for long walks. He also met writers and men involved in politics, but he lost contact with the active forces of his party, with the comrades of the factories, and with the common people. He lived in a small hotel and at night he would stay for a long time at the window to "enjoy that sky."

Then came women. One in particular was able to arouse a heated passion in Pavese. That passion drove him to an anxious search for sex and an attempt to prove his virility. Once again he was dissatisfied and returned to his silence and to self-destructive thoughts. That was the period when he attempted to write a novel in collaboration with Bianca Garufi.[25] The novel was eventually left in his drawer, unfinished. It would be published after his death with the title *A Great Fire*. Pavese himself indirectly provided the most valid criticism of this book in his "Dialogues with the Comrade":

"Yes, but why always love?" Masino repeated. "Of what importance is it to me, as a reader, that someone else has found a girl?"

"It is a serious question, Masino. You must know that a story is always made of sympathy toward people. . . . But is there a better system for warming oneself, for changing the day, for enjoying people and things as they are, than becoming interested in a girl, even if only in one's imagination? It is for this reason that when you love a girl, you want to write letters to her and everything pleases you, even the dog and the rain. For the same reason he who invents a love story, if he is not an idiot or a pervert, puts himself in the position of loving all his characters, understands them better, and enjoys describing them. There are undoubtedly books without love stories, and they are also quite beautiful, but they are books of times passed. . . .

"They are not actually novels, but they are good books. Each time he who writes is strong enough to interest himself in others, to find the world beautiful and to have the desire to say so, without feeling the need to become excited like a dog at that odor, a marvelous story is born. But only very few succeed in writing these stories. More succeeded in the past, in societies organized in a way that the sexual question had not become ideology as it is today. Those people had other things to think about."

"And don't you think a new society can recreate those ancient conditions?"

"It is certainly possible."

"Then I was right to say that love stories are not essential, that you writers exaggerate and that there are more serious things?"

"You are always right, Masino. However, it depends."

A Great Fire, in which morbid and desperate characters appear, was born in the confused and tumultuous climate of postwar Italy. Pavese wrote about burning events which had deprived him of his serenity. In order to find some peace of mind he had, also in this novel, to return to memories of his childhood:

I asked myself if there was also in me that country blood which darkened the eyes of Silvia, the open-minded and city-oriented Silvia. Yes, I had been born in the country, but my country was something fantastic and light, something dreamed about in the city which had not given me any blood. The country evoked in me memories almost beyond consciousness, beyond my urban awakening. The blood in me had begun to bubble only in the city, my first passion had been my friends, my schoolmates—I had cried and fought with them. . . . Before, I had kept quiet and waited, but since the beginning I knew that my destiny, my life, would be in the city, with new people, that I would no longer speak my dialect, that I would climb stairs and look on the boulevards from windows like those of all the Silvias I have known. Because even as a boy I always knew I would find a Silvia and cry and fight with her. Now it seemed impossible that I had ever thought about another look and another mouth, but already in the most bleeding days of that summer I realized that the women who had preceded her had only announced her. That burning and primitive discord had always existed between us, that mixture of violence and tenderness which is the reaction of the country turned city. Now when I thought I had won her embrace, that I was no longer a slave of her blood, nor anyone else's, now I rediscovered childhood memories, beyond the boulevards and the houses; fantastic and light memories, similar to those of one who dreams of a destiny or of a horizon that is not the hill or the cloud, but the blood, the woman of whom the clouds and the hills are only a sign. And the Silvia I had torn away from me and suffocated was instead, with all her daring appearance, something primitive, of blood and sex.

In the diary, women again occupy a primary position. And with women, the "absurd vice," the sense of death. On November 26, 1945 he wrote:

She will die and you will be alone as a dog. Is there a remedy? Fine. But if you can accept death for yourself, how can you refuse anyone else the right to accept it? That too is charity. You can arrive at nothingness, but not at resentment, or at hatred. Always remember that nothing is owed to you. In fact, what do you deserve? Had you any claim on life when you were born?

The next day, Pavese wrote in the diary three dates, marking the times when he was abandoned by the three women to whom he had been particularly close: the woman with the hoarse voice, another woman from Turin, and a third from Rome. On December 7 he concluded:

Already twice in the past few days you have put T., F., and B. side by side. It is almost a reflection of the mythical return. What has been, will be. There is no remission. You were thirty-seven and all the conditions were favorable. You *look* for defeat.

When Pavese returned to Turin, he did not look for his old friends. He was also less interested in going to talk to the workers at the cell of the Communist Party. He spent less time in his room, more at the Einaudi office, and when he went for a walk he did it alone, perhaps brooding over his disappointments in Rome. On February 24, 1946 he wrote in the diary: "Again alone. You make your house in an office, in a cinema, keeping your jaws clenched."

He received letters from Rome, and now that he was far from that city he seemed to find comfort in being remembered by those whom he had met there, like the writer Sibilla Aleramo. Her letter, dated August 10, 1946, is proof of the affection Pavese could draw from people who were able to recognize his true character under the shy and sullen surface:

Dear Pavese,

I was truly saddened to hear that you had left Rome. You had mentioned it to me, but only as a possibility. Hearing of your departure made me realize more clearly how happy I have been to have met you. I thought: he is a friend, a thing so rare that I imagined I would never find one again. Now, can our friendship continue from one city to another? I write very few letters, and I don't know whether you've ever written any or if you must still begin. In any case, send me one in reply to this, O.K.? Tell me how you are, if you are used to the new environment, if you can "isolate yourself" there as in Rome. Are you also finding time to write?

I have been here a few days in a small ransacked villa lent to me by a girlfriend for the whole summer. I try to rest, but that's an art

I don't know. I feel I would succeed in resting if I succeeded in working. Instead I accomplish nothing, neither good nor bad.

I read a little. While here I've finished *Festival Night*. I especially like the pages on myth, the state of grace, and adolescence. I repeat to myself: it's a shame that he had to leave and we can no longer speak about it.

Have you finished reading my *Diary*? It was a lively reward for me to know that you were interested in it. However, I wanted to give you other books of mine, my poems, etc. I receive the Piedmont edition of *L'Unità*, and I envy your finding the right "tone" for your talks to the comrades. I had thought of something similar, but, as I told you, for the moment I am incapable of doing anything.

Goodbye,

With affection,
SIBILLA ALERAMO

After his first meeting with this woman writer, Pavese wrote in his diary on May 23, 1946:

I have met a truly exceptional type: Sibilla Aleramo. I felt immediately at ease with her. I understand her fully. I am better off than she is, not only because I am younger, but in an absolute sense. I know what form is, she does not. Yet she was the flower of Turin, 1900-10. She moves me like a memory. In her I see Thovez, Cena, Gozzano, Amalia, and Gobetti. She is Nietzsche, Ibsen, lyric poetry. There are all the hesitations and the difficulties of my adolescence. How long ago! There is the confusion of art and life, which is adolescence, D'Annunzianism, error; now all vanquished and in the past.

At the moment of the political crisis, when the patriotic front created during the Resistance was broken and there were the first defections of intellectuals from the Communist Party, Pavese reacted with vigor and clarity. In 1946 he wrote in his diary words he would repeat almost verbatim in a statement submitted to the leaders of the Italian Communist Party:

Those intellectuals who have broken away from the Communist Party over the question of freedom ought to ask themselves what they would do with this freedom they're so concerned about. Then they would see that—leaving aside the laziness, the hidden interests of everyone (comfortable life, vague thinking, elegant sadism)—there is not a single instance to which their own answer would be any different from the collective one of the Communist Party.

At the beginning of 1947 Pavese met a young student, Maria Livia Serini, whom he hired to work with him at Einaudi. In the next two years, Pavese would dictate his novels to her, during the lunch break or in the evening, in order not to take time away from his office hours. They almost always left the office together, strolling along the streets of Turin, and nearly every night they dined at their friend Simoni's Trattoria del Popolo. When Pavese made extra money, usually through his contributions to newspapers and magazines, he would invite Maria Livia to the restaurant Duja-Dor and would order a Barolo wine. After dinner they would go into the hills or along the banks of the Dora, or Pavese would lead Maria Livia through the cafés where, in the preceding years, he had written many of his short stories and poems.

That was a time when Pavese was serene and happy. He enjoyed being and working with Maria Livia. He dictated the pages of *The Comrade* to her, and when they took a rest, he read her the completed chapters of *Dialogues with Leucò* which for many evenings became the subject of their conversations.

Dialogues with Leucò is the book Pavese said he loved the most, and he considered it his most important work. It was the only one of his books for which he went each day to the circulation department to check its sales. When he received good news, he clearly showed his joy, but when they gave him bad news, he almost took it as a personal affront.

Dailogues with Leucò was conceived—as Pavese himself tells us in his diary—near the Sanctuary of Crea, during the long months of his voluntary and tormented reclusion in Serralunga. There he relived in his memory the places of his childhood and the events of his life as mythic places and events.

In that solitude, rendered darker and more primitive by the distant shooting and the echo of the bombings, Pavese also recalled the time when, reading Frazer's *The Golden Bough*, he discovered "the ancestral and the infantile." Hadn't he already developed a faun-like cult in the sanguinary and incestuous representation of the "He-goat God" of *Work Wearies*? And didn't the obsessions of *The Harvesters* unconsciously reflect these same mythic impulses?

When Pavese wrote *Dialogues with Leucò*, the mythological background was already available to him. Beginning with his own myths, he searched for those of all mankind and returned to the time when myths were his only reality. Later Pavese would express his conviction on the validity of myths and he would want to assure his readers that he always took mythology very seriously. In 1946 he had written in his diary:

> We are convinced that a great revelation can come only from stubborn insistence on the same difficulty. We have nothing in common with the drifters, the experimenters, and the adventurers. We know that the surest, quickest way to be amazed is to keep staring impassively at the same object. The moment will come when it will seem—miraculously—as though we have never seen it before.

The two years Pavese spent in Serralunga, during which he kept exploring his solitude and comtemplating nature, gave him the illusion that a mythic world could replace a real one. However, that illusion was soon discounted in *Dialogues with Leucò* because from the depth of those mythic and mystic meditations the human problem rose with greater force than ever before.

In returning to primordial times, Pavese searched mainly for an explanation of human tragedy, and he would persist in this search throughout his life, studying ethnography and psychoanalysis; he immersed himself many times in the reading of Freud. All these experiences seemed only to reinforce his conviction that man is constrained to a destiny of hopeless misery and desperation.

The publication of a number of letters addressed to Professor Giuseppe Cocchiara of the University of Palermo will help us understand Pavese's passion for all that concerns folklore, especially ethnology. Pavese dedicated a great deal of work to these studies and he sacrificed a part of his proceeds as a writer in order to organize a special series on ethnology at Einaudi. His correspondence with Cocchiara began in 1947 and lasted until Pavese's death.

December 13, 1947

Dear Cocchiara,

. . . I wish to thank you for your fine words regarding *Leucò*.

In the meantime, I have read, little by little, *Popular Traditions* (thank you for the dedication), and I find it a rich and important book, an indispensable guide for these studies, and a history not only for a specialization in folklore, but for the entire Italian historiographic culture of the last century. The various moments are excellently reflected and illuminated. . . .

I would like to discuss at greater length subjects of common interest—ethnological titles and theories, possibilities of exhumations, etc.; I always hope to be able to take a trip to the South and meet you, but I never seem to make it.

For now, accept my most cordial greetings.

Yours,
PAVESE

Turin, July 7, 1948

Dear Cocchiara,

I have received the four volumes but not the initial translation of Frazer that you promised me.

The best of the four, editorially and humanistically, is without a doubt *Sex and Repression* by Malinowski. We will at once write to Kegan Paul for the translation rights and a copy in English, then we can think about doing the translation.

Frazer's *Psyche* seems very old-fashioned to me. It has a didactic tone I do not like much. I hope for something better for his *Man, God,* etc. The other work by Malinowski and the one by Rivers seem too specialized . . . Actually I haven't read them yet.

Thank you again for all that you sent. You shall have it back as soon as possible. I very much hope that the Frazer will be suitable and that you can translate it.

In a few days, you'll be plunging into the festivities.[26] I envy you and I excuse myself for not being able to attend. When one is under the yoke of a publishing house, one is no longer his own master.

Cordially yours,
PAVESE

Turin, July 29

Dear Cocchiara,

I read the four books (one Rivers, two Malinowskis, and one Frazer) confirming my opinion that the only feasible one is Malinowski's *Sex* for which we have requested the rights.

I read your translation of *Man, God and Immortality*. . . . The Italian version is beautiful and readable. However, the curious structure of the text—the anthological and serial tone—makes one think more of an amiable lecture than of a doctrine. It is rather a repertory of almost common (= classical) things than a book of research. I remain of the opinion that as to Frazer it would be better to translate, in two volumes, *The Golden Bough*. I've never been able to verify who published it (in Rome?); it is a preliminary step to avoid a possible violation of copyrights. . . .

Cordial greetings,
PAVESE

Turin, November 8

Dear Cocchiara,

. . . I too very much enjoyed our conversations in Turin and I would be happy to be with you often, and also take advantage of your knowledge of the studies we both love. Who knows, perhaps some day the govenment may arrange to confine me in Sicily, since it already had the good idea to send me in exile to Calabria in 1936 . . .

It was expected that Pettazzoni would be working at UTET. I have finally received news from De Martino[27] . . . he has agreed to resume his collaboration. However, he laments that we do not let him write introductions. I gave him carte blanche, or almost. His position is that of advisor, more or less director of the series (except for our editorial *placet*) and you would do well to write to him about Frazer, also because, being in Rome, he is within easy reach of the De Bosis. He lives in Piazza Caterina Sforza No. 6, Stair H, Apartment 12. There is nothing new from Macmillan, except that we must, instead, negotiate with Watts, which we have already done. We are now waiting for an answer.

I have given Lang (*Making of Religion*) for translation to a poor devil in Milan. This is a good occasion for you scholars to write a first-rate introduction. Get together with De Martino.

I'm waiting for the books and I thank you. My best wishes to your wife and friends.

Yours,
PAVESE

Turin, January 11, 1949

. . . We are still negotiating for the Cassirer. I've been waiting for the three books you told me about, but so far they haven't arrived.

I have bad news regarding De Martino. He wrote me saying that he's in the hospital with a pulmonary lesion. It's a great shame, because his work is his whole life. Perhaps he will feel freer now, perhaps not. We must just wait. Write him something kind.

Propp's book on the fairytale is ready and should be reaching you soon. I'm not sending it for you to correct, but so that you can judge it and write an introduction.

We're also sending you, just for amusement, Einaudi's catalog for '48.

Thanks again.

Yours,
PAVESE

No news concerning the Frazer. The matter is now in the hands of the International Literary Agency. Hasn't Zanichelli reprinted *The Golden Bough?*

Turin, January 26

Dear Cocchiara,

I've received the three texts and the two small books.

Of the three, the Leeuw is obviously a gem. We wrote immediately to Holland for copyrights: we're trying to find the original and to have it translated directly. If this is not possible, we will try to translate it from the French.

The other two are less easy. The Hambly seems too heavy, and the Séchan too "French," too cute, too much like a "ballet-of-girls-in-chemise-in-the-meadows." I shall examine them better. . . .

Good news! We've gotten our hands on Cassirer's *The Myth of the State.* It seems that it would please. It should end up in a new series devoted to political and economic matters. However, it will take a long time to secure the copyrights. . . .

Many greetings and best wishes.

PAVESE

January 27

Dear Cocchiara,

I'm taking advantage of your kindness. I'm sending you *The White Goddess* by Robert Graves, the strange author of *I, Claudius,* etc. This, as you will see, is a book of staggering and very risky erudition. Would you glance through it as soon as possible and consider if it is worth publishing?

Frazer is practically ours.

Cordially,
PAVESE

Turin, February 14

Dear Cocchiara,

Frazer is ours. You can begin at once to write the preface (not more than five or six pages, I would say) and start the revision. I've not yet spoken to Einaudi about it, but I think that if your corrections are mostly orthographic and such, he will offer you about 20,000 lire, but if they are more complex, 30,000. Do you mind leaving this matter open until I can show him the copy of the old edition filled with your comments? . . .

Cordially,
PAVESE

Pavese with Constance Dowling during the winter of 1949–1950

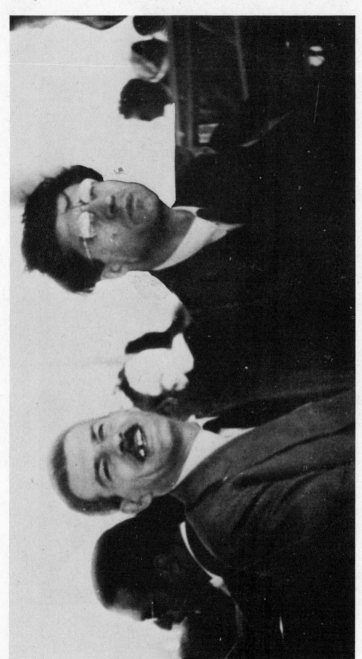

Pavese with Elio Vittorini (1950)

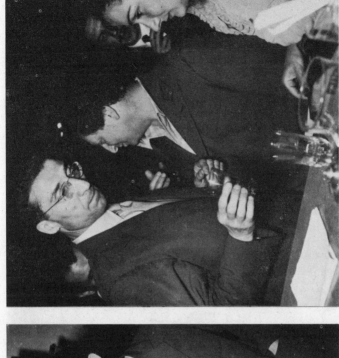

Pavese with Carlo Levi and Doris Dowling (Constance's sister) at the Strega ceremony

Pavese receiving the Strega Prize check from Maria Bellonci (1950)

The bookshelves in Pavese's room on via Lamarmora

The Hotel Roma in Turin where Pavese killed himself

Davide Lajolo (left) with Pinolo Scaglione, "Nuto"

March 11

Dear Cocchiara,

A few words. Congratulations on your success in the
examination. It is always a pleasure to hear such news. I am also
happy that De Martino has turned up. I have already written him
that you are working on Frazer. . . .

We've bought the rights to *The White Goddess*. Now I'm
beginning to regret it. As soon as I receive it back from you, I'll
begin to think of who in hell can translate it. I wouldn't want to
be tempted to do it myself. The year before last I yielded to the
temptation of these old loves for translating, then I stopped halfway
for lack of time. We shall see.

I shall remember Sergio Lupi. It's a shame we have already
chosen someone to translate Frobenius (*Kulturgeschichte
Afrikas*). . . .

Affectionate greetings and see you soon.

Yours,
PAVESE

Turin, March 22

Dear Cocchiara,

. . . Have I already written you that we are negotiating for the
Kelsen rights? You already know about Van Leeuw. Do you know
Pierre Gordon (the *Image du monde dans l'antiquité*; the *Initiation
sexuelle et l'évolution religieuse*)?

Best wishes. De Martino, who is out of the hospital, wrote me
and it seems he's about to send us Hauer's *Die Religion* and
Hubert et Mauss.

Yours,
PAVESE

April 1

Dear Cocchiara,

. . . *L'Anthropologie Nègre* belongs to the publisher Dorrea and
we examined it a year ago. We did not think much of it. It is
divided into literary genres, or almost. Some of the anecdotes

reported in it are very amusing, but this work resembles too much a collection of Jewish stories or the like. It lacks every awareness of cultural cycles. Infinitely better is the massive work by Pettazzoni.

Forgive my haste.

Yours,
PAVESE

Turin, April 27

Dear Cocchiara,

I received the *Golden Bough,* fat and fragrant like a capon, scholarly prefaced and larded. On behalf of Einaudi, I send you our congratulations and a paltry check.

Now we are faced with problems: one volume only, or two? If two, one title only or the two old subtitles *Sorcerer Kings and the Dying Gods* and *The Sacrifices and the Fire Festival?* And wasn't the division into three volumes perhaps authorized by Frazer? Have you anything to say about this matter? We must hurry because I think that the English publisher has put in the clause "within the year."

Speaking of books, Saintyves is most amusing. I am not quite sure if we want to publish it. Wimberly, although scholarly, is definitely to be excluded. Today we requested the rights to Mircea Eliade's *Treatise on History of Religions.*

So long, dear Cocchiara, and stay well.

PAVESE

Turin, June 20

Dear Cocchiara,

I'm happy you like Propp. It's having some success.

I shall stay after Kagarov and see if I can find it.

As for Eliade, I'm pleased with myself for having made the right choice, but it wasn't difficult; have you seen his *Mythe de l'eternel retour (archétypes et répétition)?* I feel it is most appropriate for our storming historicism.

Finally, I'm also happy you liked my outburst against Mario Praz in the *Rassegna d'Italia,* but rather than predicting a future in ethnology for me, try to be the ethnologist and finish your *History of Folklore*. . . .

Yours,
PAVESE

Turin, November 15

Dear Cocchiara,

I've sent you the Eliade and a new book of ours, *Russian Verse,* which you will certainly like. . . .

Malinowski, for your tranquility, has been translated from English. . . .

Croce? I think he is the agit-prop for Laterza.

Caio.
PAVESE

December 12

Dear Cocchiara,

Thank you . . .

As for the preface to Malinowski, the problem was only to satisfy De Martino who was feeling ill and neglected.

Your postscript amused me, because we are about to publish *Aeschylus and Athens* and we already have the rights to *Studies in Ancient Greek Society.* The publisher is Lawrence and Wishart, well-deserving of Marxism. We are also about to publish *Illusion and Reality* by C. Caudwell. This seems to me the most serious and most humanistic group of Marxist scholars.

Best wishes and don't get kidnapped by Giuliano[28].

PAVESE

Turin, March 21, 1950

Dear Cocchiara,

. . . I'm still analyzing Mannhardt and Pitré. The *Baroness* is something magnificent and I thank you on behalf of poetry. Now I shall see if I can get a book out of it. But it is so brief! . . .

I'm sending back to you Lévy-Bruhl with which I was already familiar and which De Martino's wife is already translating for us.

The Jeanmaire is a good book (with that solid and *inspirational* erudition which made me shed tears over Picard's *Ephèse et Claros*), but I doubt we can do it, also because this series threatens to become the cancer of the publishing house and devour all the rest. We must henceforth be more particular in our selections. . . .

PAVESE

Turin, May 9

Dear Cocchiara,

My customary disappearance is a real "descent into hell": for fifteen days "I've been working on the Frazer index." Kidding aside, I've traveled, wasted time, published a book (did you receive it?), and I've forgotten my friends.

Ciao,
PAVESE

June 16

Dear Cocchiara,

I too was involved in the activities of "Einaudi week" which seemed a great buffoonery to me. However, I was able to see with my own eyes the heroism of the distributors and representatives who "sell" our inventions. Einaudi thanks you for your activities.

Why do I *work so hard*? Because I do not frequent women. Better yet, because I haven't frequented women for four years.

Ciao,
PAVESE

Frazer should be out by June.

July 14

Dear Cocchiara,

Thank you for the avalanche of kindnesses. The prize was a sad affair, as I imagine all these things always are.

I am, instead, happy that you liked my piece in *Cultura e Realtà*. . . .

With Giuliano dead, can't they make another one?

Ciao,
PAVESE

In the years he began his correspondence with Cocchiara, Pavese published *Dialogues with Leucò* and *The Comrade*. The almost simultaneous writing of these two works helps us reflect once again upon the constant twofold characteristic of Pavese's personality. On one side, the commitment to life, the wish to maintain his dignity as an activist in a party of the masses; on the other side, a decadent justification of his renunciation, even when he seeks refuge in symbols. If *The Comrade* represents Pavese's impulses toward the people, *Dialogues with Leucò* is a withdrawal into himself.

The Comrade is the story of a group of Turin anti-Fascist conspirators set against an environment of vaudeville impresarios, pleasure-seeking women, and profiteering friends of the Fascist bosses. Pavese wanted to relate the story of his younger years in Turin, with characters he had known. In the copy he gave Cinanni he wrote this dedication: "You too are in this book."

The first eleven chapters take place in Turin, the last eleven in Rome, and they correspond to Pavese's anti-Fascist experiences. *The Comrade* is again a work into which Pavese inserts a political element. After pages dedicated to joyful evenings spent by carefree youths in cafés or in dance halls in the hills, a clandestine organization slowly comes to life. The political activity gradually enters the lives of the characters, first with allusions and mysterious phrases, then more and more openly.

At the center is a girl "with class," one who knows how to love and deal with men, always remaining on a level of superiority. She is the type of woman Pavese always desired. Even with his country shyness, he had attempted to win city women, those who knew how to wear fur and act as one should in elegant homes, who were the center of men's glances and attention. As in all his novels, in *The Comrade* Pavese concentrates in one protagonist the characteristics of two or three of his friends, and his female characters similarly reflect the women he frequented. Linda, the snob who accepts the company of Pablo (Pavese) but rejects his love proposals, combines the memories of the two women, one from Turin and the other from Rome, whom Pavese loved, and here, deliberately confuses, perhaps to give vent to his anger.

After completing *The Comrade*, he began to write another novel we have already mentioned, *The House on the Hill*. These were his most productive years. He seemed satisfied. Maria Livia Serini remembers that during their long walks in the hills Pavese was as playful as a young boy. She says that he was confident, talkative, and bold.

He also demonstrated boldness in his political life. In November 1947 he sent his reply to the leaders of the Communist Party who had asked him and other intellectuals to explain why he was a Communist. In concluding, Pavese wrote:

Is it possible for someone to become a Communist out of love for freedom? It has happened to some of us. For a writer, for a "worker of fantasy" who ten times a day runs the risk of believing that books are the only things in life, it is necessary to have the constant cure of violent shocks, of people, of concrete reality. We respect our trade too much to deceive ourselves into believing that talent and creativity are enough for us.

Nothing of value can come from our pens if not as the result of a collision with things and men. He alone is free who becomes part of reality and transforms it, not one who lives in the clouds. . . .

Now, of all the realities which fill our days, the most coherent and liberating seems to us, and has seemed for some time, the struggle carried on by the Italian Communist Party. The intellectuals who are divided over the question of freedom ought to ask themselves sincerely what they intend to do with this freedom about which they are duly concerned. Then they would see that—leaving aside the idlenesses, the hidden interests of everyone—there is not a single instance in which, if they really seek the progress of man, their own answer would be any different from the collective one of the workers. We know from experience that each individual adherence to a word, to a political appeal (even abstaining is a way of taking a position) places one in a situation of thrust and parry, in a burning trench; for just this reason, we cannot delude ourselves into believing in the existence of a situation where it is possible to be at the same time progressive and conservative. Not even the anarchists believe in this. Ours is the freedom of those who work, of those who must deal with raw, tough matter.

Pavese sent this reply during the time he was dictating *The House on the Hill* to Maria Livia. Once he had delivered his manuscript to the publisher, his bitterness and afflictions returned. His asthma grew worse. Physically weakened and having completed the books which had kept him under pressure, he experienced again those feelings best expressed in his diary on June 27, 1946:

> To have written something that leaves you like a gun that has just been fired, still quivering and hot, emptied of your vital powers; to have poured out not only all you know about yourself, but also all that you suspect and imagine, the turmoil, the ghosts, the subconscious; to have done it with long weariness and tension, days of caution, fears, sudden discoveries, failures, concentrating all your life on that one point; and then to realize that all this is nothing unless it is welcomed and warmed by a human sign, a word, a presence; and to die of cold, to be speaking in the wilderness, to be alone, night and day, like a dead man.

In that period he also lost the human presence that had assisted him until then: Maria Livia was transferred to Rome. Her departure reinforced his feelings of uselessness and convinced him that all efforts to unite himself to others were futile.

What about his other friends? It was difficult to enter Pavese's heart when he withdrew into himself for reasons he had defined as "private." It was never just one reason. His taste for contrast, his "accent on suffering," and the pessimism he savored like morphine, isolated him from others as well as from the part of himself that still had the strength to react.

And his comrades? In the presence of the workers he felt his misfortunes even more. He wrote in his diary and repeated in *The Comrade* that workers, unlike intellectuals, had a class instinct, therefore they always saved themselves. An ideology could no longer help him. Pavese had joined the Communist Party for the reasons, more sentimental than ideological, we have already mentioned. He chose to join, above all, to be coherent in his anti-Fascism; however, he never cultivated in depth the study of Marxism, nor did he strive to re-examine his philosophical theories in the light of that doctrine. On January 26, 1947 he wrote in his diary:

> There are only two attitudes, the Christian's and the Stoic's. The Communist's is probably a fusion of both. He has charity, and he is like a rock. He knows that in the end all is hard as iron, yet he does good.

Pavese was neither a rock nor a man of iron will. Alone, feeling distant from every certainty, he turned again to his "absurd vice." On April 12, 1947 he wrote:

You are alone, and you know it. You were born to live under the wing of someone else, sustained and justified by someone else who would still be kind enough to let you go on with your madness and imagine yourself capable of remaking the world single-handedly. You can never find anyone who lasts long enough; hence your suffering—not out of tenderness—when your friends depart. Hence your resentment toward the one who has gone; hence your facility—not out of cordiality—for finding a new protector. You are a woman, and like a woman you are stubborn. But alone you are not enough, and you know it.

Another quotation from the diary of that month gives further evidence of Pavese's dark mood and disillusionment: "During the clandestine period everything was hope; now everything is a prospect of disaster."

By the end of 1948, Pavese could no longer tolerate solitude, even in his own city. He left Turin and hurried to Santo Stefano Belbo to see Nuto, who will always remember Pavese's desperate words: "I had to come up here to exchange a few words. If I hadn't come to you, I wouldn't have known who to speak to."

They would then go into the hills of Crevalcuore until they found a spring, where they would stop. Under Nuto's benefic influence, Pavese slowly grew calm. Nuto's wisdom did not consist only in country proverbs, but in the way he loved life, the sky, the trees, the people who passed along the road in front of his shop. Pavese listened, ashamed of his despondency, and left after only a few days, much more serene.

Life in Turin once again consumed him. He packed his suitcase and went to Rome where he stayed two or three days, then he decided to return to Turin at night. He could not bear to look at the country in daylight from the window of a train, since it always gave him the sensation of being on his way toward exile.

Once back in Turin, Pavese spent his evenings at a movie house until it closed, often seeing the same film two or three times. During the day, seated in a café, he looked at the girls who passed by. Some nights, in order to break the monotony of his solitude, he invited to his office two or three prostitutes who were left along Corso Re Umberto without clients. They drank, chatted, and he even dared, out of spite for Einaudi, to take them to the publisher's office, leaving it dirty and disordered. If Rosita, the secretary, reproached him the following morning, Pavese would shrug his shoulders and pat her hand as if to imply a tacit agreement. Once he asked Rosita to give him an objective opinion of the manuscript *The Devil in the Hills*. Rosita's answer so affected him that he transcribed it in his diary: "It is a book that neither the bourgeois nor the proletarians will like."

He had, in any case, begun to write again. After *The Devil in the Hills* he wrote *Among Women Only* and he added to them a manuscript written in 1940, *The Beautiful Summer*, under which title the three works were published in one volume.

In the *Devil in the Hills*, the landscape, even of the hills, grows misty, and polemic against certain vices and a certain lifestyle yields to justification. Pavese seems hesitant to pass judgment. During those months, types like Poli, Gabriella, and Rosalba had entered his life. He had also met actors and actresses, some of whom had come to Italy from France and the United States, and he was attracted to the Dowling sisters, two American actresses. Pavese wanted to prove, in this environment, his skill as an actor. He always liked to act, for others as well as for himself. In those months he became so immersed in a role that he no longer knew whether he was acting or being serious. He went to Cortina d'Ampezzo, a mountain resort, with Constance Dowling, stopped in elegant hotels, and drank whiskey. *The Devil in the Hills* expresses that phase of his life.

In *Among Women Only* the situation was even worse. The true protagonist of the novel is not Clelia, the woman who wants to make her work her life, nor Rosetta, but rather the "absurd vice"—a suicide whose execution Pavese had begun to visualize in every detail. The following is a particularly revealing passage of a dialogue from the novel:

"I understand killing oneself . . . everyone thinks about it . . . but one must do it well, do it so that it is something real. . . . Do it without polemics. . . . Instead, you remind me of an apprentice dressmaker who's been abandoned . . ."

Pavese would have liked to see himself reflected in Clelia, the character who works and knows how to take life with indifference, who knows how to continue to live without having any other happiness than that of managing her business. However, Pavese identified himself with Rosetta, the only one who is aware that life, as it is, is worth nothing, and who kills herself.

The tragedy occurs silently, without a shriek or a cry. Rosetta decides to leave her home in order not to upset anyone by her suicide. She rents a room in a boarding house on via Nazione and takes an overdose of sleeping pills. A cat scratching inside the locked door of her room will lead to the discovery of her death—a dress rehearsal of Pavese's own suicide. He would evoke the same theme in his poem of April 10, 1950 entitled "The Cats Will Know." With *Among Women Only*, Pavese had already decided how he would die.

16

After the Bonfires are Out,
the Moon Still Shines

At the beginning of 1950, two letters to Augusto Monti showed that the dialogue between teacher and pupil had not ceased after the lyceum years. Monti had continued to follow, step by step, his former student. Each time Pavese returned to Santo Stefano, hoping to find again the world of his childhood, he knew he would draw the disapproval of Monti. The teacher's books, as well as his teachings, had always warned Pavese to look ahead in life rather than backward in search of the happy times of his childhood.

Pavese had sent Monti all his works. In a dedication written in *Work Wearies*, after quoting Horace's verses describing his escape from the battle of Philippi and his "ill-abandoned shield," Pavese concluded with these words: "But we shall make up for it in the next book."

Monti had persisted in pointing out to Pavese the merits and shortcomings of his writings with the same severity and affection as when he was correcting his essays on Italian literature and in Latin. After the publication of *The Beautiful Summer*, his observations became bitter reproaches. The two letters Pavese sent Monti in January 1950 answering to his sharp criticism are of particular importance because they were written within a few days of one another, seven months prior to his death. Monti had accused him of being a muscleless Capaneus, committed to a hatred of the world,

and of imitating Pastonchi and D'Annunzio. Pavese reacted very
strongly. In his second letter, Monti reiterated his accusations,
intensifying them by saying that Pavese's philosophy was more that
of a superman than a human. Pavese struck back again. Here are
the letters to Monti:

January 18, 1950

Dear Monti,

When I read your comparison of me with Pastonchi, "the other
D'Annunzian," I said, "He's become a fool, that's all there is to it."
Whether a story can be considered as belonging to this or that
school, in the past or the future, is a question to be settled by
good taste and by good reading—things that are obvious.

But a judgment on "positive ethics" is another matter and must
be discussed. It seems to me that the two stories under discussion
(*The Devil in the Hills* and *Among Women Only*—I'm not talking
of *The Beautiful Summer*, a story of virginity defending itself)
divide humanity precisely into those who are useful for something
with their work, and those who by not working and not being
useful, fall prey to gangrene and rot away. What is this story of my
being hateful toward my fellow men, according to your accusation?
The Devil is a youthful hymn based on the discovery of nature and
society; to the three boys everything seems beautiful, and it is only
little by little that each in his own way comes to realize how sordid
the "futile" world is—a certain bourgeois world that does nothing
and believes in nothing; why should I draw a veil over it? The
same thing can be said of *The Women*: here there are no young
boys, no song of discovery, here a self-made, hard-working woman
comes in contact with what? With the usual futile world of those
who believe in nothing or just in nonsense—most of all because
they are slothful—and she observes this world decaying and
destroying itself. But even in this world one tries to save what is
salvageable: in reality, the suicide is a naïve victim, the most
innocent of all, and if she dies it is just because of all (except, of
course, Clelia) she is the only one capable of feeling what she lacks.

Now, I ask myself, what sense does it make that you order me
"not to mistreat" the world I've mentioned? Because I challenge you
to find a single respectable person (producer of something useful, of

some value) who, in my two stories, is not put on a pedestal—in the first, the laborers and the peasants, Oreste's family and his cousins, the maid and the gardener of Greppo; in the second, Rosetta Mola, Clelia in her entirety, Becuccio with his world, and, for what they can do, even Nene the sculptress and Febo the architect.

I have a suspicion. You are so sentimentally attached to the upper class that it annoys you to hear anything said against it; and you are so wound up with the world of workers that you demand from a book an abstract optimism of the militant kind. In that case, it's obvious we cannot understand each other. . . .

Ciao,
PAVESE

January 21, 1950

Dear Monti,

Now that you have explained to me with textual quotations what my hatred for my fellow man, my inhuman philosophy, and my superman complex are, my answer is that you have failed the test. If, in your association with me, you had had the impression that I consider my interlocutor as litter for my horses, I would have nothing to add. But the texts are texts: the lines you quote me, and many others from the same story, are part of the confession of a "sinner," the sore of his conscience, and in more than one case he tells them to others in a frenzy, almost as if looking for an alibi. It seems clear to me that this Corrado (*The House on the Hill*) denounces and punishes himself just because he has lived and is living in a certain way—and the author who draws this worm from him knows much better, he knows that life consists entirely of something else (and, as an author, he demonstrates it by inventing other characters who have no need to make the same reproach to themselves). Moreover, the parabola of the story goes from the proud solitude of the protagonist, through the example of the simple sacrifice of others and the human enormity of the events, to the compunction and humbled simplification of the end, to his compassion for the dead. The opposite of a superman. How could you accuse me of having described remorse? It would be as if, since Corrado has brutalized a girl, you would believe that my philosophy is to brutalize or deceive or exploit girls. Do the three students of *The Devil*, or Pablo of *The Comrade* appear to you as supermen, too?

The guarantee and the hope of my "future greatness" (let's be serious) are only one: to do the work assigned to me well (sometimes work consists in looking for work). He who does his work well is at ease with his conscience; he who does not, is not. And let everyone do as I do—and let all be placed in the condition of doing so. To me this philosophy does not seem to be peculiar, nor to follow Pastonchi nor D'Annunzio.

Because this is what you cannot understand. That if, in presenting myself through my characters, it happens that at times I find myself alone and bitter (the world is what it is and nobody saves you if you don't save yourself), it does not mean that I'm acting as a superman or as a misanthrope. I've better things to do. In these cases, I concentrate the world more than ever into what I'm doing through my characters (conspiracy, guitar, fashion shop, discussions, etc.), and I wait for the next day, certain that there is always a tomorrow. Is the cousin in "South Seas" a follower of D'Annunzio too?

Sentimental ties and militant optimism were a polemical retort against your attack ("I have the suspicion that . . ."). Not accepting, as I do not, your accusation that I hate the world, I had indeed to keep in mind that there are but certain abused people in my book, and they are those gentlemen . . .

Do we understand one another? If you retract the "D'Annunzian," I take back the sentimental and the militant . . .

Ciao, keep well, and remember that Einaudi does not pay without pain.

PAVESE

Pavese sent Monti a copy of *The Moon and the Bonfires* with this dedication: "Et nunc dimitte me domine."

A month after he wrote Monti the two letters quoted above, Pavese returned to the same subject in two letters addressed to Rino Del Sasso, a critic who had reviewed *The House on the Hill* for *L'Unità*:

March 1, 1950

Dear Del Sasso,

I liked your interesting and accurate review of my book because of the courtesy in the polemics and the importance of the problem it raises.

Naturally, I'm not writing you to defend the book because it is my work. I'm not making an issue of literary laurels but of commitment.

Well, it is true that at the center of the three stories (*House on the Hill, Devil, Among Women*) is a particular bourgeois situation of impasse. Your opinion on the greater or lesser clarity of moral (or even historical) condemnation with which this world is viewed, is justifiable. But the big point is that your opinion tends to exclude every tragic theme from art. You must admit that if situations of uneasiness are represented within a reality, full justice is due to these situations—that is, they must be seen in all their factuality of human reasons. For example, the three young men of *The Devil* have, as their poetic and human substance, the adolescent boldness of intellectualistic destroyers: this is the theme of the story and one cannot, therefore, criticize its "intellectualistic, paradoxical" expressions without missing the author's precise intention. The same goes for Clelia of *Women*: she is an indignant and restless bourgeoise who believes in only one value, work, and naturally, as a bourgeoise, she cannot believe in it with a socialist view, namely in a liberated way, but always with a touch of bitterness, of stoicism. These are the two most relevant themes.

As to the girl who commits suicide and as to the executed Fascists, it is different. Either we write tragedy or we do not. If we do, we must concede to the *villain* (or to the victim, depending on the case), the fullness of his suffering, the soundness of it; also we must not forget, as the *Iliad* teaches us, that war is a sad thing above all because one must kill the enemy. Usually the best fighters are precisely those who are aware of this tragic necessity, although it is sacrosanct not to let one's arm be weakened by this awareness. Not to say, once again, that the character Corrado, besides his cowardice before action, also represents the extreme problem of every action—anguish before mystery. . . .

These are the first summary ideas inspired by your article, for which I thank you. I shall be even more thankful if you can find the time to write me your opinion on these comments.

Cordially,

PAVESE

March 20, 1950

Dear Del Sasso,

Thank you for your letter. If I accepted all its premises, you would be right and would also have written for me the literary manifesto of the future. But I disagree with some of your premises, or at least with their formulation.

I believe that:

a) There is no morality that can be superior to another without understanding and recognizing that other.

b) For the artist, all the intellectual systems somehow alive in his own time are valid, are life.

c) The "morality of inquiry" is no more conventional than that of the philistine. It's merely harder to confute.

d) Tragedy does not necessarily require a confrontation of good and bad. It is possible to write a tragedy always smiling in the person of a protagonist, and showing all of a sudden a slight flaw in his human well-being. This is what happens to the three young men and to the already famous Clelia. They represent a judgment on a certain phase of middle-class society simply because, although the flower of this social group (youthful brashness, active stoicism), they are, after all, unhappy, if only for (apparent) trifles. But note that all their experience and inner life are, in my opinion, positive, and constitute a value.

This is the substance of my thoughts on reading your letter, which is worthy and exhaustive, but fatally biased, especially in the part concerning Corrado. In short, I wanted to portray a hesitant and solitary man who, because of or in spite of his cowardice, discovers some values or at least senses that there are new values (sense of death, humility, understanding of others, etc.). If you say that I didn't succeed, you may be right, indeed you are right; if you say that it is *not* necessary to introduce these themes, then I can only shrug my shoulders. The world is big and there's room for everyone. If in my aesthetics there is the risk (I know it well) of

writing a diabolical work, in yours there is the risk of writing
Giannettino or *Cuore*.[29] I don't say that's what you aim at, but it
happens, it really does happen. Art must discover new human
values, not new institutions. Instead, in many current progressive
books I find new institutions, while the truths of the imagination
and of the heart are concoctions from the past. All things
considered, is it worth the trouble? Let's then translate the old,
educational stories into a progressive language, and let's no longer
think of new ones.

This is all. We proceed *per ignes*, it's clear. But no one ever
promised us that this road would be easy—part of its fascination is
just this, that it is *not* easy, that it must be trodden with dedication
and without any certainty of success. But that's the way it is.

Dear Del Sasso,

Ciao,
PAVESE

It is important to stress that these letters were written after Pavese
had already finished *The Moon and the Bonfires*. In only three
months, at the end of 1949, he wrote his most complete work, closed
in his room on via Lamarmora. A dramatic and gentle novel, a
magical evocation of his childhood amid the hills of Santo Stefano,
but also a novel of the Resistance, already seen by him as a lost
opportunity.

In this novel there is a strong, solid figure who does not know
discouragement. It is Nuto, the only character who is content,
logical, and sure of himself.

It was in collaboration with Nuto's counterpart, Pinolo Scaglione,
that Pavese constructed the plot of *The Moon and the Bonfires*. In
fact, during the summer of 1949, Scaglione received many letters
from Pavese wanting to know this or that detail of facts which had
taken place in the village, and of events concerning past and present
families. In his last letter, Pavese asked why, even in the years of his
own childhood, many families still asked the Town Council for a
foundling—a "bastard"—to raise. Then, not satisfied with the news
his friend sent him, Pavese returned many times to Santo Stefano.
They spent almost every night seated at a small table under a bower

of wisteria, next to the carpentry shop of the Scaglione brothers, along the main road. During the day they roamed amid the vineyards and the woods, on the ridge of the hills. Pinolo talked and Pavese listened.

The center of the novel would be precisely the Santo Stefano valley, where Nuto worked at the family carpentry shop. In the novel, the location would change name and would become the Salto hill. The surrounding hills of Moncucco, Crevalcuore, and Gaminella would serve as the background. The farmhouses that emerge from the greenery and the large villa that can be seen above Canelli are the places where the protagonists would live.

One day, while speaking of the destiny of the Santo Stefano families, Scaglione touched a sensitive cord for Pavese. "Even illnesses," he said, "are transmitted from fathers to sons." "That's why," Pavese remarked with preoccupation, "it feels like a drummer is beating here in the middle of my head. My father died of brain cancer and he was already ill when I was born."

Nuto immediately saw Pavese's apprehension. He attempted to modify what he had said and told Pavese that his father's illness was not hereditary; however, after that conversation Cesare stopped at each spring they found and wet his head where he felt the beat of the drummer.

After five or six days, Pavese returned to Turin. While getting on the train, he told Nuto: "I definitely want to write this novel on Santo Stefano. I've had it inside me for such a long time. If I succeed, I'll send you the manuscript to read and you can make your observations, telling me what I should and what I should not publish." And Nuto: "You have plenty of time to write the book. Now you are tired and you must rest. Come back here soon, the country is enjoyable even in autumn." "No, no," answered Pavese. "I must write it immediately, I'm in a hurry."

During his last trips to Santo Stefano, Pavese, contrary to his habit, wanted to meet all his relatives who still lived in the village. In order not to inconvenience them, he continued to lodge at the Posta Inn which he would call the Angelo Inn in *The Moon and the Bonfires*. At night, alone in his hotel room, he smoked medicinal cigars to calm the asthma attacks which had become more and more frequent.

Of all the relatives he met in Santo Stefano, Cesare grew particularly fond of his cousin Federica, a student in her last year of school who was the daughter of the cousin he admired so much and about whom he wrote "South Seas," the first poem of *Work Wearies*. He kept a steady correspondence with Federica, showing an interest in her studies and trying to find a position for her as an assistant in a Fiat summer camp for children. He also expressed to her the emotions he experienced in being so warmly welcomed in Santo Stefano:

Turin, December 6, 1949

Dear Federica,

I have been in Santo Stefano, but I was abducted. It is a town where one cannot do what one wants. Headmaster, Police Chief, former Mayor, etc., everyone wants to spend an afternoon, a morning, or an evening with me.

I feel like Rita Hayworth.

I assure you I would gladly have come to Valdevilla. You're right in saying I like altitudes.

They told me that you didn't go to the sea after all. It will be difficult for me to get away all through winter.

Ciao,
CESARE

Two other letters, written in June 1950, are also related to Santo Stefano:

Dear Federica,

How are all of you? It's useless to tell you that my memories of Santo Stefano are very beautiful and that I still feel moved when I think of your cordiality.

If you come to Turin you know where to find me. At home or at the office. I am always at the office.

Ciao,
CESARE

Dear Federica,

I received the request of your protégés and, not being sure of their address, I am sending my reply to you. Tell Mr. Alberto Poli to go right ahead and send us his novel. The problem is that I do not judge novels. My area involves—can you imagine—the history of religions and the Anglo-Saxon world. In any case, if, in sending the manuscript to the publisher, Mr. Poli mentions my name, it will serve as a recommendation with the reader of his novel.

I haven't written you because I have been to Rome, traveling, cavorting, and I'm half dead.

I never sent you the congratulations that the news of your being in love deserved—if it's true, I'm happy about it, I place my hands on your head, and I'm sure you will achieve what you want. I think you resemble your father a great deal (the only Pavese who, until now, has amounted to something and who has been *a man*). You are and will be a strong and good *woman*—somewhat like those foreign women your father met around the world and of whose worth I'm well aware.

I can't say right now when I'll come to Santo Stefano. I have much to do and much to think about.

Goodbye and I wish you every happiness.

Yours,
CESARE

In a letter to Pinolo Scaglione, also written in 1950, Pavese thanks him for the additional information he had sent him with regard to *The Moon and the Bonfires*:

January 9, 1950

Dear Pinolo,

I had to go to Rome for a short visit and today I am back at the pen. I received your "scientific" letter and thank you very much for the precise information which I shall utilize as much as I can.

Not being able to come in person, I've sent a small panettone for the holidays. "Take and eat . . ." I hope it has arrived. I also hope everyone is well and I intend to come one of these days to breathe the air of the Belbo.

Ciao,
CESARE

In writing *The Moon and the Bonfires*, Pavese's heart, as one can see, was full of memories of Santo Stefano. It is the novel of his return. A return to the village, not only from the city where he was taken as a young boy, but from all the journeys of his imagination, from the anguish of youth and maturity, from clandestine political life, exile, bewitched loves, symbols and philosophies; a return to rediscover the warmth of his childhood, the old faces, the hills, the woods, and the vineyards.

Together with Nuto, Pavese again brings to life in *The Moon and the Bonfires* the most important characters of his other works. Thus Pale, the boy of *Festival Night* with his teeth green from the grass he chews, reappears through Cinto, the lame bastard; likewise the girls "with class" from the city and the sea become the summer vacationers, furtively dissolute, of Canelli; and, above all, one recognizes the Partisans of *The House on the Hill* and the peasants of *The Harvesters*. But all return ripened from long experience. The questions left unanswered in *The Harvesters* find their explanations in *The Moon and the Bonfires*. Also analyzed in this novel are the reasons why the greed of the landowners makes the peasants poor and evil. Until one arrives at Nuto's comment: "The world is evil, one must make it better."

In this novel the landowners too must pay for their faults. Their wealth has been squandered from father to son. A dismal destiny awaits them like a nemesis, as punishment of their entire class. But in *The Moon and the Bonfires* there is also a place for redeeming goodness: the gentleman in financial straits does not sell his country house in order not to harm his sharecropper; the emigrant who returned to his village saves and provides for the lame foundling. Pavese seems finally to be in agreement with Nuto's statement that it is necessary and possible to improve the world.

The social issue posed in *The Comrade* and the human aspect of the Resistance presented in *The House on the Hill* return in this final novel. The enemy has been defeated, the civil war has ended with the liberation of Italy. Pavese's solitude and his "absurd vice" would also appear to be finally overcome. But it is only an illusion.

As the novel develops, the joy of the first encounters and the happy childhood memories are replaced by the bitterness of lost illusions and by the desperate awareness of maturity. Pavese confesses these feelings in a passage from *The Moon and the Bonfires*:

I'd have given anything to be able to see the world again with Cinto's eyes, to start out again at Gaminella like him, with that same father, even with that leg—now that I knew so many things and could take care of myself. It wasn't pity I felt for him; at times I envied him. It was as if I knew the dreams he had at night and the things that crossed his mind while he limped around the square. I hadn't walked that way, I wasn't lame, but how often I'd seen the noisy carts go by, with women and boys seated on them, going to the feast, to the fair, going to the merry-go-rounds at Castiglione, at Cossano, at Campetto, everywhere, while I stayed with Giulia and Angiolina under the hazels, under the fig tree, on the parapet of the bridge, on those long summer evenings, looking at the sky and the vineyards that were always the same. And then at night you could hear them coming back along the road, singing, laughing, calling out to each other across the Belbo. Those were the evenings when a light or a bonfire on the distant hills made me scream and roll on the ground because I was poor, because I was a boy, because I was nothing. I almost enjoyed it when a thunderstorm, one of those summer deluges, came and spoiled everything for them. As I think of it now, I long for those days and wish I were back in them.

By now, not even that return can save Pavese. Again there is tragedy; social justice will not be realized, the wounds cannot heal. And in *The Moon and the Bonfires* we find Valino's house burned down, we find desperation, and once again, suicide. The last woman of the novel, torn between treason and loyalty, is shot and offered to the flames as a human sacrifice. The bright horizons of the hills are also lost in the ashes, in the "bed of a bonfire."

The Moon and the Bonfire reopens and concludes forever the eternal dialogue between the real and the symbolic worlds, between loyalty and treason, between Pavese's commitment to living as a man and the despairing conviction of his incapability to do so, between love and desertion, politics and myth, childhood and maturity, the hills and the sea, the city and the country, the moon and the bonfires.

With this novel Pavese has written his most sincere autobiography. Having returned to the origin of his solitary life, he can rediscover himself in no other person than a bastard. Between Nuto, the strong and confident man, and Cinto, the lame peasant boy, Pavese chooses to see himself reflected in the latter. Nuto remains the man whom he regards with admiration, the man he would have liked to be. Nuto also knows how to act in politics because he understands the essence of things. He is, above all, the boy who knew how to grow up, continuing to be faithful to his land, to his village, without letting himself be led astray by illusions. He has not let himself be deceived by the mirage of adventures and evasions, has not emigrated to America, but stayed in Santo Stefano, loyal to himself and to his people, an anti-Fascist and a Communist, satisfied with a life that would serve the public interest.

Except for Nuto, all *The Moon and the Bonfires* seems to be pervaded by a sense of disillusion. The Resistance is seen from afar, like a marvelous legend; politics has fallen again to the level of intrigue, and religion is debased by politicking priests who seem nostalgic for Fascism and do not show any compassion for the poor.

The Moon and the Bonfires was published in the first months of 1950. Pavese sent a copy with a dedication to Pinolo Scaglione, as he had done with his previous works. In the copy of *August Holiday* Pavese wrote: "To Pinolo, who knows the places. Cesare": in *The Comrade*: "To Pinolo, we agree. Cesare"; in *Before the Cock Crows*: "With affection and gratitude. Cesare." In *The Moon and the Bonfires* the dedication carries a presage of the end: "To Pinolo this book—perhaps the last I will ever write—where I speak of him—asking forgiveness for the 'inventions,' from Cesare." Pinolo failed to understand the portent of this dedication until after his friend's suicide.

On May 30, 1950, in a letter to Aldo Camerino, a literary critic, Pavese wrote:

> In effect, *The Moon and the Bonfires* is the book I have carried
> in me the longest and which I most enjoyed writing. So much so that
> I think I shall do nothing else for a long time—perhaps forever.
> One ought not tempt the gods too much.

After this book Pavese seemed exhausted: more tormented and disillusioned than he had ever felt after any of his creative works. On July 26, 1950 he wrote to Mrs. Calzecchi Onesti who was translating the *Iliad* for Einaudi:

> Don't talk about my literary successes. These things make one feel ashamed for the flow of gossip they unearth, as well as for the disclosure of the stench existing in our professional environment. Once I would have liked the fact that you find me a tormented writer; now I like it less. Now I would like to have peace, and that's all.

He was not the same Pavese who a few months earlier had expressed his long-term literary ambition in what was almost interpreted as a challenge to his friend Vittorini. In fact, on December 29, 1949 he had written in his diary: "Has Vittorini's fame in America made you jealous? No. I am in no hurry. I shall beat him in the long run."

A month later, at the end of January 1950, Pavese accepted the invitation of some young friends, writers and critics, to contribute to a new journal, *Cultura e Realtà*. The articles he wrote are worth mentioning because, on their account as well, Pavese suffered from the incomprehension and criticism of many political and cultural sectors.

His first article attempts to determine the influence of myth, considering Vico's theories. It stresses that the word "myth" does not signify "to speak in a mystical or aesthetic language," but instead it indicates "convinced poetics and a complex historical discourse based on and justified by the myth itself." In this article Pavese also says:

> But to possess means to destroy. . . . The myth that becomes poetry loses its religious halo. When it also becomes theoretical knowledge ("human philosophy"), the process ends. . . .
> Then the artist's real suffering begins, when one of his myths has already become a visible creation, and he, having completed his work, can no longer believe in his myth. Not knowing how to resign himself to the loss of that good, that authentic faith which kept him living, he tries

to recapture that faith, insists, and becomes disgusted with it. Thus possession ends, like all possessions, unless the resourceful human constitution of the artist is such as to make him neglect or even ignore the purely contemplative aim of his work and induce him to turn to a practical aim (pedagogic, cultural, or experimental) so that his interest in the work can survive its realization.

In the second article, Pavese took a position in the polemic between Ernesto De Martino, the author of *Mondo Magico*, and Franco Fortini. The first maintained that "in the course of rationalizing the entire life of a people and of giving a scientific structure to it, as Socialism proposes, the cultural elements that would be particularly studied, understood, and asserted are those most primitive, indifferentiated, magical, prescientific, etc." The latter, instead, regretted that a Marxist scholar like De Martino could "advocate a return to archaic and primitive things," forgetting "the political damages caused by a recent irrational and basically folkloric culture."

Pavese sided with De Martino, welcoming "happily the Socialist interest in the magical and mythic mentality." He reassured Fortini "that the danger he had indicated did not exist" because "it is clear that folklore and the mythic mentality are of interest to the political man—who is 'scientifically oriented'—as events, as phenomena to be quickly reduced to clear rationality and to historical law."

His theories on myth and his defense of De Martino were also misinterpreted in some circles of the Communist Party. Pavese was saddened by this; however, he did not react. On February 15, 1950 he noted in his diary: "'Pavese is not a good comrade' . . . Tales of intrigue everywhere. Shady plots in the talk of those nearest to your heart."

Those nearest to his heart, who were then involved in many political battles, lacked the time to explain Marxism to him, or simply to show their affection. On the other hand, Pavese seemed to have withdrawn from his comrades when he no longer felt able to maintain any human contact, and when, becoming more decided about taking his life, he could no longer respect the party's discipline condemning suicide. At this point his diary seems to become a sort of medical chart. Pavese talks of his "sense of physical decay," of his "agitation," "palpitation," and "insomnia." However, he was reluctant to speak to anyone about his physical or mental state, even to his physician friend, Dr. Rubino.

The "drummer" he had mentioned to Nuto beat harder and harder in his head, and the memory of his father's death obsessed him. For a few weeks, Constance, the American woman, returned to him: a brief moment of happiness. Constance was intelligent and inspiring. But she too abandoned him; she too went to another man. So it happened with all the women Pavese loved. After Constance left, he noted in his diary on April 26: "It is a fact that there is in her not only herself, but all *my* past life."

The "absurd vice" had begun to torment him again when the relationship with Constance was nearing its end and he, through that last failure in love, was experiencing a sense of general failure. It is appropriate to recall the words Pavese wrote in his diary on March 25: "One does not kill oneself for love of *a* woman. One kills oneself because love—any love—reveals us in our nakedness, misery, vulnerability, nothingness."

In the diary he recorded the steps toward his final act with a rapid and poignant style. May 8: "The cadence of suffering has begun. Every evening, at dusk, my heart constricts until night comes." May 10: "The act—the act—must not be revenge. It must be a calm and weary renunciation, a closing of accounts, a private, rhythmic deed." May 16: "Now even the morning is filled with pain." May 27: "I contemplate my impotence, I feel it in my bones, and I am caught in a political responsibility that is crushing me. There is only one answer: suicide."

Among Pavese's papers, I found a large yellow envelope on which was the same date as the last lines quoted above. The envelope contained all his membership cards of the Communist Party.

Toward the middle of June, 1950 he received the news that he had won the Strega Prize for his novel *The Beautiful Summer*. When he arrived in Rome for the ceremony, he appeared to everyone a different man. He was even wearing an elegant new suit. He smiled when the award was presented to him. Doris Dowling, Constance's sister, was at his side.

A few weeks later his Milanese friends invited him to a dinner at Bagutta. They wanted to celebrate his victory of the Strega; in many there was the curiosity to see how Pavese, the most withdrawn writer of Italy, had succeeded in becoming a man of the world. When he arrived in Milan, he came to my office in Piazza Cavour. I bantered with him amiably about his new suit and offered him the gift I had bought him: an impressively shaped pipe of authentic English make. He barely smiled, thanked me, putting a hand on my shoulder, and hurried to tell me that he would not go to the dinner at Bagutta: "I don't have the strength. Take me to your home, instead. If your wife doesn't have anything prepared, it won't matter. Why eat? I have some tobacco. I'll try your pipe."

"What are you saying? Vergani has already prepared a speech. You can't offend those who truly care for you: Ferrata, Tofanelli, Sereni, Aldrovandi, and many others. They're all waiting for you. And there will be women. You've become a Don Juan."

"The women are not waiting for me," he answered sadly.

"Nevertheless there's one who I'm sure is waiting for you. She will tell you herself by phone." I dialed the number. A woman's voice answered. I introduced them and Pavese whispered a forced "thank you."

He finally agreed to go to Bagutta and we sat at the same table. He spoke very little. The blonde girl I had introduced to him over the telephone was doing all the talking, mainly about his books. For a while he seemed re-animated. With his eyes fixed on a bottle of mineral water, he listened to Vergani's warm speech. "Vergani is always so good," he whispered to me. We went out into the clear, summer night of Milan. "Do you see?" he asked, pointing to the sky. "The moon is still shining."

The next day Pavese left to spend some time at the sea. "At the end of August I shall come to Vinchio," he said to me on his departure, "then on foot, remember that well, on foot, we shall go to Santo Stefano to visit Nuto. I shall bring some special tobacco."

But the sea aggravated his condition. He was to remain at the beach until the end of August, but after only a few days, without telling anyone, he went to Santo Stefano. He wanted to speak once again to Nuto. Pavese repeated to him the words he had used on a previous visit: "If I don't come here to you, I can't speak to anybody."

The country seemed to calm him. He did not confide his torment to Nuto, nor the absurd plan he had in mind. He spoke, as always, about books, politics, and trees. Nuto was working to finish a vat. Pavese interrupted him: "Why don't you call the vats by their real Piedmontese name, the 'Arbe'?"

Under the wisteria arbor, Pavese confided in Nuto for the last time: "You know, tomorrow I'm going to Rome. Constance's sister will give me the answer. She expects her telephone call from America. If the answer is positive, I will marry Constance."

"Think about it again, Cesare," Nuto replied with concern. "A foreign woman, and strange as you say, is not for you. With so many beautiful simple girls who are around here, the idea of marrying an American girl . . . You'll soon regret it." And Pavese: "It doesn't matter; I know it will last at most two years. Two more years to live."

The following day he left for Rome. It was his last trip. After two days he returned to Turin. The news he hoped for had not come. It was the final blow, and it reminded him of his recurrent failure. "I didn't marry you," the woman with the hoarse voice had told him many years earlier, "because you're good at writing poetry, but you're not good for a woman." He was convinced that everything was useless, that he had nothing more to write, that he was not suited for politics, that he was of no good to women, to his friends, nor to himself.

On July 14, 1950 he wrote in his diary:

Stoicism is suicide. After all, people are dying in war again. If ever there is a peaceful, happy world, what will it think of these things? Perhaps what we think about cannibals, Aztec sacrifices, and witch hunts.

Again a desperate attempt at human contact: one evening he decided to go, alone, to hear an orchestra at the Gai dance hall. He met a girl who was also alone: she was young and pretty. He looked at her and she smiled; they left together. After that encounter, he wrote in his diary of August 16: "Why die? I have never been as alive as now, never so *adolescent*." And on the 17th: "Suicides are timid murderers. Masochism instead of sadism." But on the same day: "This is the account of the year that is not finished, that I will not finish."

On August 17 he also wrote his last letter to his sister, who was in Serralunga. It was a sad letter which ended with this polemical ring for the very religious Maria:

> . . . if God has given me great gifts, He has, however, given
> cancer to many, and others were created idiots by Him. . . . One
> does not see where this great goodness is. . . . Here are 5000 lire
> for the pastor of Castellazzo, so that he can continue to preach
> little stories—let's hope that at least he believes them.
> I wish you all well. I'm well, like a fish in ice.
>
> CESARE

His sister hurried back to Turin. She found him frighteningly thin, his eyes hollow and red. "What are you doing?" she asked. "Aren't you eating?" As usual, no response.

For two days he burned many letters and other writings, documents, and photographs in a brazier he placed in the center of his room. At night, he left all the lights on, but in the morning, when his sister called him for coffee, he no longer complained of insomnia, nor of asthma. He had become strangely patient, even kind.

He no longer wrote in his diary, which was left open on his desk where for the first time, there was only one book, *Dialogues with Leucò*. He often telephoned the girl he had met at the Gai dance hall.

On the morning of Saturday, August 26, he asked his sister to prepare the small suitcase he usually took on brief trips. Maria was not surprised: almost every Saturday, in fact, Cesare left to spend his Sundays away from Turin with the Ruatas or the Rubinos. That day he went to the editorial office of *L'Unità* and asked Paolo Spriano if there was a photograph of him in the newspaper's archives. Spriano showed him several. "This one is fine," said Pavese, pointing to the one in which his face appeared the saddest. Then, smiling, he left.

In the early afternoon, after having placed *Dialogues with Leucò* in his suitcase, he left the house on via Lamarmora waving goodbye. As usual he took the tram to Porta Nuova, but instead of walking toward the train station, he headed in the opposite direction and stopped at the Hotel Roma.

He asked for a room with a telephone. They gave him one on the third floor. He went up to his room and started making telephone calls: to three or four women. He invited them to dinner. He insisted especially with Fernanda Pivano but she, who would have gladly accepted, could not go because her husband was ill.

The following evening, Sunday, August 27, at 8:30, an employee of the hotel, worried about that guest who had not been seen the entire day, knocked at the door and finally decided to force it open. When the door gave way, a cat slipped into the room.

Pavese was dead. He was dressed and stretched out on the bed. He had only removed his shoes.

On the nightstand there were sixteen empty packets of the sleeping pills he had taken. Nearby was his copy of *Dialogues with Leucò* opened to the first page where he had written these words: "I forgive everyone and ask forgiveness of everyone. O.K.? Not too much gossip, please."

The last sentence of his diary, dated August 18, still refers to Pavese the writer: "All this is sickening. Not words. An act. I shall write no more."

Conclusion

Having arrived at the conclusion, and realizing how difficult it has been to reconstruct the life of Cesare Pavese, I'm at least certain that I have tried to give him that warmth which none of us, his friends, were able to show him during his life.

Only now, after having known him better, are we in a position to understand this line from "Dialogues with the Comrade": "Day after day, I convince myself of this: everyone seeks the writer, everyone wants to speak with him, everyone wants to be able to say tomorrow: 'I know how you're made' and use him, but no one lends him one day of total sympathy from man to man."

My book is also an act of reparation. Could we have done more when he lived among us? Could we have understood him better, we who participated in the tragedy of the same generation? Perhaps not, unhappy and tormented as we were until we were about thirty, like no other generation that Italian history can remember.

The Fascists ended up seeing the downfall of their regime after it had caused the devastation of Italy, and some of them paid bitterly. The anti-Fascists were forced to spend their best years in a state of insecurity and persecution. The bourgeois felt their world was decaying.

Without a solid faith, nothing remained for the most desperate of that generation but a renunciation of life; for the most resigned, a refusal to fight; for the neutral, a compromise with life.

Pavese represents a highly complex case of a man who lived, in his inner life and in his works, the tragedy of his generation. A life anything but simple: first the instability of those who were not Fascists, then arrest, prison, confinement, long years of special surveillance, war, fears, escape, remorse.

We have seen the writer develop in this desolate climate. He was aware, perhaps too aware, since his lyceum years, that he had to "be of worth at the pen" in order not to yield to the "absurd vice" of suicide.

Pavese succeeded in being "of worth at the pen." But that was not enough to give him the strength to live. Neither the literary awards nor the glory could provide that. He said it in *The House on the Hill*: "Being someone is something else altogether. You can't even imagine it. You need luck, courage, will power. Most of all, courage. The courage to stand alone as if others didn't exist and to think only of what you're doing. Not to worry if people ignore you. You have to wait for years, you have to die. Then after you're dead, if you're lucky, you become somebody."

Ten years later, Pavese had become somebody in Italy and in the world. Today, Americans read his works and understand contemporary Italy through them: a just reward for Pavese's efforts in making American culture known in his country.

I am not sure that this book confirms what has been said of Pavese, namely that he was the best Italian writer of his time. Nor am I sure if I have been able to interpret the most important of his myths: the myth of America as a search for freedom, the myth of Communism and of the Resistance as an escape from solitude, and the myth of politics as an effort for social commitment.

I believe I have succeeded in showing that this mythic dimension never signified an aristocratic detachment, but rather a confidence in the masses, a belief that a dialogue with them was possible even in the realm of myths and symbols. And Pavese constantly attempted to transcend both classic tradition and romantic rebellion, academicism and futurism, to reconcile his impulses toward the world with his self-withdrawal.

He found an equilibrium only when he succeeded in lyrically affirming the unity between his strong subjectivity and his dialogue with the outside world; he failed when he aspired to put the absolute in contact with man in hopes of finding in myth a justification for his inhibitions.

He ended up discrediting in advance all his efforts to estabish a simple and direct rapport with the world. He became his own prisoner, and having completed the great dialogues between the city and the country, the hills and the sea, a fantasized childhood and the real world, between politics and solitude, and between the moon and the bonfires, he decided to accomplish the supreme act, less as an escape from men than a more complete re-entry into himself.

What I have tried above all to do, is convince Pavese's readers to avoid the fundamental error of judging him from the self-portrait in his diary; in it he oscillates between vanity and fear. The public Pavese is no less real than the private Pavese, his anguished yet courageous search to bind himself to the world of men is not less important than his surrender.

I rest with the consciousness of having been faithful to his teachings and of having written, with sincerity, his biography.

Notes

1 Santo Stefano Belbo, in the Piedmont region of Italy, was Pavese's birthplace.
2 Vesime is a village near Santo Stefano Belbo.
3 This war was waged by an Italian underground against the Nazis and the Fascists from September 1943 to April 1945.
4 The Langhe are the hills in the area where Pavese was born.
5 Antonio Gramsci (1891–1937) was a philosopher and literary critic, one of the founders of the Italian Communist Party, who was imprisoned for many years by the Fascists.
6 Vittorio Alfieri (1749–1803), a major Italian poet and playwright.
7 Piero Gobetti (1901–1926), a philosopher and political activist from Turin, forced into exile by the Fascists.
8 Massimo D'Azeglio (1798–1866), author and statesman.
9 An author and music critic.
10 Pietro Bembo (1470–1547), a poet and theoretician of the Renaissance.
11 Ugo Foscolo (1778–1827), a poet and precursor of Italian Romanticism.
12 Vincenzo Monti (1754–1828), a neo-classic poet.
13 Pietro Metastasio (1698–1782), a poet and librettist.
14 "Luty" is the real or fictitious name of a girl to whom Pavese dedicated some of his first poems.
15 A literary magazine to which Pavese had sent some poems.
16 "Andare verso il popolo," a Fascist demagogic slogan.
17 "Grappa" is a brandy typical of Northern Italy, distilled from the pomace of a wine press.
18 Giovanna was Maria's maid, who was very fond of Pavese.

19 "Bacarozzo," which literally means "little insect," might allude to Sturani's slight build, and perhaps to his interest in entomology.

20 The police officer who searched Pavese's home before his arrest.

21 Probably *Mistaken Ambitions*; published in 1935.

22 An embargo against Italy maintained by countries opposing the Abyssinian War.

23 "Astratti furori," a phrase used at the very beginning of *In Sicily*.

24 "Partito d'Azione," a liberal political party active for a few years after World War II.

25 Bianca Garufi was one of Pavese's co-workers at Einaudi, and, like Pavese, was anti-Fascist. Their association, both personal and in connection with their experimental novel, remains unclear.

26 Festivities on the centennial of Sicily's 1848 successful insurrection against the Bourbons.

27 De Martino was a famous ethnologist who, like Cocchiara, specialized in Southern Italy.

28 Giuliano was a Sicilian bandit.

29 *Giannettino* is a book for children by Carlo Lorenzini (Collodi), the author of *Pinocchio*. *Cuore*, written by Edmondo De Amicis, is another children's book. These works, both published in 1886, deal with traditional moral issues.

Works by Cesare Pavese
(*Referred to with English and Italian titles, and date of first publication*)

POETRY

Work Wearies (*Lavorare stanca*), 1936
Death Will Come and It Will Have Your Eyes (*Verrà la morte e avrà i tuoi occhi*), 1951

NOVELS AND SHORT STORIES

The Harvesters (*Paesi tuoi*), 1941
The Beach (*La spiaggia*), 1942
August Holiday (*Feria d'agosto*), short stories, 1945
The Comrade (*Il compagno*), 1947
Dialogues with Leucò (*Dialoghi con Leucò*), 1947
The Political Prisoner (*Il carcere*), published in the volume *Before the Cock Crows* (*Prima che il gallo canti*), 1948
The House on the Hill (*La casa in collina*), published in the volume *Before the Cock Crows* (*Prima che il gallo canti*), 1948
The Beautiful Summer (*La bella estate*), published in the volume by the same title and with two other novels, 1949
The Devil in the Hills (*Il diavolo sulle colline*), published in the volume *The Beautiful Summer*, 1949
Among Women Only (*Tra donne sole*), published in the volume *The Beautiful Summer*, 1949
The Moon and the Bonfires (*La luna e i falò*), 1950
Festival Night (*Notte di festa*), short stories, 1953
A Great Fire (*Fuoco grande*), in collaboration with Bianca Garufi, 1959

DIARY AND LETTERS

This Business of Living (*Il mestiere di vivere*), (diary 1935–50), 1952
Letters (*Lettere 1924–1950*), 1960

E S S A Y S

American Literature and Other Essays (*La letteratura americana e altri saggi*), (essays and articles 1930–1950), 1951

T R A N S L A T I O N S

Sinclair Lewis, *Our Mr. Wrenn* (*Il nostro signor Wrenn*), 1931

Herman Melville, *Moby-Dick* (*Moby-Dick*), 1932

Sherwood Anderson, *Dark Laughter* (*Riso nero*), 1932

James Joyce, *Portrait of the Artist as a Young Man* (*Dedalus*), 1934

John Dos Passos, *42nd Parallel* (*Il 42° parallelo*), 1935

John Dos Passos, *The Big Money* (*Un mucchio di quattrini*), 1937

John Steinbeck, *Of Mice and Men* (*Uomini e topi*), 1937

Gertrude Stein, *The Autobiography of Alice B. Toklas* (*Autobiografia di Alice Toklas*), 1938

Daniel Defoe, *Moll Flanders* (*Moll Flanders*), 1938

Charles Dickens, *David Copperfield* (*David Copperfield*), 1939

Christopher Dawson, *The Making of Europe* (*La formazione dell'unità europea dal secolo V al secolo XI*), 1939

Gertrude Stein, *Three Lives* (*Tre esistenze*), 1940

Herman Melville, *Benito Cereno* (*Benito Cereno*), 1940

George Macaulay Trevelyan, *The English Revolution of 1688–89* (*La rivoluzione inglese del 1688–89*), 1941

Christopher Morley, *The Trojan Horse* (*Il cavallo di Troia*), 1941

William Faulkner, *The Hamlet* (*Il borgo*), 1942

Robert Henriques, *Captain Smith* (*Capitano Smith*), 1947

Arnold Toynbee, *A Study of History* (*Le civiltà nella storia*), done in collaboration with Charis De Bosis, 1950

Index

Some New Directions Paperbooks

For complete listing request complete catalog from
New Directions, 80 Eighth Avenue, New York 10011

† Bilingual